T0342165

Postgrowth Imaginaries:
New Ecologies and Counterhegemonic Culture
in Post-2008 Spain

Contemporary Hispanic and Lusophone Cultures

Series Editors
L. Elena Delgado, University of Illinois at Urbana-Champaign
Niamh Thornton, University of Liverpool

Series Editorial Board
Jo Labanyi, New York University
Chris Perriam, University of Manchester
Paul Julian Smith, CUNY Graduate Center

This series aims to provide a forum for new research on modern and contemporary hispanic and lusophone cultures and writing. The volumes published in Contemporary Hispanic and Lusophone Cultures reflect a wide variety of critical practices and theoretical approaches, in harmony with the intellectual, cultural and social developments that have taken place over the past few decades. All manifestations of contemporary hispanic and lusophone culture and expression are considered, including literature, cinema, popular culture, theory. The volumes in the series will participate in the wider debate on key aspects of contemporary culture.

Postgrowth Imaginaries

New Ecologies and Counterhegemonic Culture in Post-2008 Spain

LUIS I. PRÁDANOS

LIVERPOOL UNIVERSITY PRESS

First published 2018 by
Liverpool University Press
4 Cambridge Street
Liverpool
L69 7ZU

Copyright © 2018 Luis I. Prádanos

The right of Luis I. Prádanos to be identified as the author of this book
has been asserted by him in accordance with the Copyright, Designs
and Patents Act 1988.

All rights reserved. No part of this book may be reproduced,
stored in a retrieval system, or transmitted, in any form or by any means,
electronic, mechanical, photocopying, recording, or otherwise,
without the prior written permission of the publisher.

British Library Cataloguing-in-Publication data
A British Library CIP record is available

ISBN 978-1-78694-134-3 cased

Typeset in Borges by
Carnegie Book Production, Lancaster
Printed and bound by CPI Group (UK) Ltd, Croydon, CR0 4YY

A Esperanza, Daniela y Luna. Tres generaciones de mujeres
fuertes que mejoran el mundo con su energía positiva.

To all beings, present and past, that have contributed
to the vitality of the biotic community of Earth.

Contents

Part II: Urban Ecologies

Acknowledgments

This book would have not been possible without all sources of nourishment, human and nonhuman, that make my existence viable. I am especially grateful to the peoples and spirits of Abya Yala in general and Turtle Island in particular for allowing me to dwell, dream, love, think, and write on their sacred land.

Thanks to all participants in the 2014 Summer School on Socially Sustainable Degrowth, Universitat Autònoma de Barcelona, and Research & Degrowth Barcelona for all our inspiring discussions.

Special thanks go to Kata Beilin for all our fruitful collaborations and conversations on Iberian ecocriticism and environmental humanities over the last five years as well as for her generous feedback on the book manuscript. Thanks to Luis Moreno-Caballud for his thoughtful comments. The suggestions made by Kata and Luis helped me improve the quality and readability of the book. My gratitude also to Megan Saltzman and Jordi Marí for their encouraging comments on chapters 3 and 4 respectively.

Thanks to all the audiences, friends, students, and scholars who, during the last few years, critically engaged with some of the ideas developed in this book, offered feedback, and posed thoughtful questions at Miami University, Universität Zürich (ETH), Freie Universität Berlin, University of Kentucky, Universidad de Cádiz, University of California at Berkeley, University of Calabria, Balbacil (otro mundo), Harvard University, Universidade de Lisboa, and Alcalá de Henares. The multiple conversations about indigenous cosmopolitics and post-development with my friend Leonardo Figueroa Helland have always been enlightening.

My gratitude goes to Miami University in general for facilitating the development of this book through a period of research leave and, in particular, to the Department of Spanish & Portuguese for its constant support and the Luxembourg John E. Dolibois European Center for hosting me. I am especially grateful to the Humanities Center at Miami University for being a crucial part of my intellectual nourishment within the Miami community.

Thanks to all involved with ALCESXXI for being a hopeful catalyst for transformation and to Susan Larson, Palmar Álvarez Blanco, Germán

Labrador Méndez, Ellen Mayock, Steven Torres, Daniel Áres López, John Trevathan, Ben Fraser, Joseba Gabilondo, and many others for pushing our field into critical and inspiring directions. Thanks to the ASLE community (Carmen Flys Junquera, José Manuel Marrero Henríquez, Roberto Forns, Mark Anderson, Jorge Marcone, Serenella Iovino, Juan Carlos Galeano, etc.) for so many interesting conversations.

Thanks to my friend Alan Davison for editing and beautifying the language of the first draft and to Gene McGarry for his professional copy-editing of subsequent versions.

I am grateful to Chloé Johnson for being such a helpful commissioning editor and to Liverpool University Press for believing in this project.

I gratefully acknowledge permission to reprint revised or excerpted versions of the following two essays in Chapter 1: 'Degrowth and Ecological Economics in 21st Century Spain: Toward a Posthumanist Economy', from *Ethics of Life: Contemporary Iberian Debates*, edited by Kata Beilin and William Viestenz, *Hispanic Issues* 42 (Nashville: Vanderbilt University Press, 2016): 143–159, and 'Toward a Euro-Mediterranean Socioenvironmental Perspective: The Case for a Spanish Ecocriticism', from 'Mediterranean Ecocriticism', edited by Serenella Iovino, special issue, *Ecozon@: European Journal of Literature, Culture and Environment* 4, no. 2 (Autumn 2013): 30–48. Some ideas elaborated in *Postgrowth Imaginaries* will appear, in a seminal stage, in *ALCESXXI. Journal of Contemporary Spanish Literature & Film* no. 3 (2016–2017). I am deeply grateful for the generous permission to reprint the following images or texts free of charge in Chapter 3: thanks to Antonio Luque for allowing me to reproduce the lyrics of 'Vacaciones en el mar' by Sr. Chinarro in *Presidente* (Mushroom Pillow MP114, 2011); and to ECOALF for permission to reproduce the text 'manifesto tras(h)umanity' from their website. Thanks to Miguel Brieva for granting me permission to reproduce the illustration 'Somos felices porque protegemos lo nuestro', which appeared first in *Dinero: Revista de Poética Financiera e Intercambio Espiritual* (Barcelona: Random House Mondadori, 2008). Thanks to Basurama for permission to reproduce the picture of Rus Santo Domingo, Tsunami de Basurama (basurama.org CCBY-NC-SA 4.0). Thanks to José Palazón Osma for permission to reproduce the picture 'Paisajes de desolación'. Thanks to Manel Fontdevila for granting me permission to reproduce his illustration 'Llueven refugiados', which appeared in eldiario.es on November 15, 2015. Special thanks to Mónica from Basurama, Manel Fontdevila, José Palazón, and Miguel Brieva for sharing with me high-resolution versions of the images.

Finally, thanks to my parents and sisters, and to all my friends everywhere who had to listen to multiple iterations of some of the ideas included in this book during the last few years. Special thanks to Bubu and Luann for everything and to all my community in Oxford for making my daily life colorful and fun.

Introduction

This book brings together environmental cultural studies and postgrowth economics to examine counterhegemonic narratives and radical cultural shifts sparked by the global financial crisis of 2008. Furthermore, it presents a new cross-disciplinary framework for illuminating the rise of this counterhegemonic culture in Spain as well as its ecological, social, and political implications. The explanations of the crisis offered by mainstream media identify economic meltdown and lack of growth as the main causes and point to the recovery of growth as the desirable solution. Yet a number of critical voices worldwide have emphasized that in the context of a finite biosphere, constant economic growth is a biophysical impossibility and systemic social and ecological limits to growth can no longer be ignored. The problem is not a lack of growth but rather the globalization of an economic system addicted to constant growth, which destroys the ecological planetary systems that support life on Earth while failing to fulfill its social promises. According to these alternative accounts of the financial crisis, what we are really facing is a crisis of the legitimacy of the growth paradigm in general and its current neoliberal articulations in particular. The global economic crisis is thus better defined as an ongoing crisis of the growth imaginary.

Post-2008 Spain, where the crisis of growth seems to be the new normal, offers an ideal context to investigate these cultural processes, and this book demonstrates that a transition towards what I call 'postgrowth imaginaries'—the counterhegemonic cultural sensibilities that are challenging the growth paradigm in manifold ways—is well underway in the Iberian Peninsula today. Specifically, this book explores how emerging cultural sensibilities in Spain—reflected in fiction and nonfiction writing and film, television programs, photographs and graphic novels, op-eds, web pages, political manifestos, and socioecological movements—are actively detaching themselves from the dominant imaginary of economic growth and, in some cases, even articulating counterhegemonic postgrowth narratives. Additionally, my research interrogates and redefines the role of cultural studies in understanding this shift towards postgrowth imaginaries, positing that these fundamental cultural changes can be better detected and understood in the light of concepts stemming from the rapidly emerging intellectual framework provided by the environmental humanities. This emergent field recognizes, on the one hand, that the humanities provide a crucial yet underappreciated resource for dealing effectively with the human roots of the socioenvironmental crisis and, on the other, that humanist disciplines must be radically transformed if they are to effectively engage in interdisciplinary dialogue with the ecological and social sciences. By approaching the counterhegemonic cultures of the crisis through environmental criticism, this book uncovers a whole range of cultural nuances often ignored by Iberian cultural studies.

Postgrowth Imaginaries exposes the socially and ecologically harmful dominant cultural imaginary that celebrates economic growth as an object of social desire and explores how an ecologically oriented criticism could play a significant role in both understanding and promoting the ongoing emergence of more desirable economic cultures in the aftermath of the neoliberal crisis. Although it draws its examples from Iberian cultural responses to the crisis, *Postgrowth Imaginaries* inevitably grapples with pressing issues that are global in nature. Currently, humanity faces many social and ecological limits to growth. Both inequality and ecological degradation have increased rapidly in recent decades, paralleling the global spread of neoliberalism and consumerist culture. Global economic activity bears responsibility for the massive alterations of Earth's ecological systems and their disturbing consequences: environmental refugees, climate change, mass extinctions, disruption of the nutrient cycle, and so on.

To continue to maintain that the pursuit of economic growth is the main objective of societies is not only unethical, but suicidal. I claim throughout this book that in a global context where economic growth is ever more socially and ecologically costly to sustain, maintaining a dominant imaginary that is deeply ingrained in the logic of growth can be extremely counterproductive, because it funnels societies' energy and creativity towards an unachievable and destructive task. The 'cruel optimism' of sustaining our society's affective, material, and semiotic attachment to the growth paradigm is becoming increasingly unaffordable and nonviable in every way—socially, economically, and ecologically.[1] As an alternative, I argue that transitioning towards postgrowth cultural imaginaries could allow us to envision and create 'prosperity without growth' by building

---

1 See Lauren Berlant, *Cruel Optimism* (Durham, NC: Duke University Press, 2011).

desirable societies unaddicted to growth that operate within the ecological limits of the Earth.[2]

The complex interrelations among Iberian cultural practices, economic paradigms, and ecological processes are vastly undertheorized. This book intends to fill this gap and to provide an innovative and functional theoretical apparatus, articulated around the notion of postgrowth imaginaries, able to illuminate these important connections. My hope is that this intervention will contribute to a more systemic, posthumanist, and ecological understanding of culture that helps Iberian cultural studies to effectively mobilize its emancipatory political potential. I believe that, beyond Iberian/Peninsular/Spanish cultural studies, the notion of 'postgrowth imaginaries' will also prove useful to the field of cultural studies in general and will provide a valuable contribution to the transnational debates within the environmental humanities.[3] Indeed, I believe the radical cultural change which I identify in this book is by no means limited to Southern Europe but rather represents a global pattern expressed around the world in different cultural fashions based on distinct historical conjunctions. Therefore, dialogue between the cultural critique developed in *Postgrowth Imaginaries* and similar cultural processes in other regions could further illuminate the unfolding global challenge to the dominant growth paradigm and its diverse articulations of alternative economic cultures. The notion of postgrowth imaginaries could even function as a conceptual anchor for a global coalition of socioecological movements united by their radical critique of neoliberal reason, enabling them to effectively mobilize their efforts to envision and materialize desirable and sustainable economic cultures beyond growth.

In the introduction to *Aftermath: The Cultures of the Economic Crisis*, Manuel Castells, João Caraça, and Gustavo Cardoso compellingly point out that cultural dynamics and institutions shape and determine economic systems: 'As the period of triumphant global informational capitalism was linked to the hegemony of a culture of unrestricted individualism, economic liberalism, and technological optimism, any substantial socio-economic

2 See Tim Jackson, *Prosperity without Growth: Economics for a Finite Planet* (New York: Routledge, 2010).

3 I am fully aware of the debates, nuances, and contestations underpinning the terms 'Iberian', 'Spanish', and 'Peninsular studies'. Although such distinctions are not relevant for the purposes of my book, I tend to be sympathetic with most developments within Iberian studies. I believe that it has the potential to become more transformative than other more traditional approaches, but I am also concerned about some scholarship within it, which seems to oppose some oppressive ideologies only to embrace other, equally oppressive and exclusive, ones.

restructuring of global capitalism implies the formation of a new economic culture'.[4] Consequently:

> when there is a systemic crisis, there is indication of a cultural crisis, of non-sustainability of certain values as the guiding principle of human behavior ... Thus, only when and if a fundamental cultural change takes place will new forms of economic organization and institutions emerge, ensuring the sustainability of the evolution of the economic system.[5]

According to Castells, Caraça, and Cardoso, 'we may well be in such a period of historical transition'.[6] In this context, it is important to assess

> the social productivity of different cultures emerging in the aftermath of the crisis. Which cultures will ultimately come to dominate social practice may determine our collective fate: either to enter a process of social disintegration and violent conflicts, or else to witness the rise of new cultures based on the use value of life as a superior form of human organization.[7]

Nothing guarantees a desirable outcome for this transition (the transition to a less intense energy regime is biophysically inevitable, justice is not). I will argue throughout this book that our best chances lie in imagining, creating, and supporting postcapitalist and decolonial economic cultures in which social equality and ecological diversity are prioritized over any other cultural values. The debilitation of the hegemonic imaginary of economic growth is not easily visible, of course, neither when deploying the pervasive lens offered by mainstream cultural narratives and authorities—since they tend to reproduce it—nor when studying cultural production within a given academic disciplinary framework embedded in neoliberal institutions and impregnated by 'ideological forces of disconnection'.[8] Rather, *Postgrowth Imaginaries* constructs an interdisciplinary (or, even better, an indisciplinary) framework that is able to perceive the rifts that emerge from the collapsing dominant imaginary as they are reflected in cultural manifestations that are critically responding to the ongoing crisis.

---

4 Manuel Castells, João Caraça, and Gustavo Cardoso, eds., *Aftermath: The Cultures of the Economic Crisis* (Oxford: Oxford University Press, 2012), 4.

5 Castells, Caraça, and Cardoso, *Aftermath*, 13.

6 Castells, Caraça, and Cardoso, *Aftermath*, 13.

7 Castells, Caraça, and Cardoso, *Aftermath*, 13.

8 Stacy Alaimo, *Bodily Natures: Science, Environment, and the Material Self* (Bloomington, IN: Indiana University Press, 2010), 142.

I have divided the remainder of this introduction, which outlines the theoretical frameworks that inform the book, into three sections. The first is a discussion of environmental humanities and the Anthropocene (or, better, the Capitalocene), which provides the global critical context in which my work is embedded. Secondly, after defining the term 'imaginary' as used in this book, I draw on up-to-date insights from social and ecological sciences to explain why the dominant imaginary of economic growth is currently socially undesirable and ecologically unsustainable. Finally, I argue for the urgency of articulating and embracing an environmentally oriented cultural studies able to overcome the current crisis of political imagination and promote effective counterhegemonic cultures.

Environmental Humanities in the Anthropocene

The term 'Anthropocene' was coined in 2000 by Paul Crutzen and Eugene Stoermer to mark a new epoch in which human activity has unleashed a global biogeochemical force that is rapidly transforming the planet in ways that could compromise human survival.[9] Crutzen and Stoermer believe we are leaving the previous geological epoch, the Holocene, in which ecological conditions that permitted human civilization and agriculture to flourish were generally the norm. The new epoch does not guarantee a functional biosphere (from a human perspective, of course) capable of providing for human biophysical needs, given the massive ongoing anthropogenic changes. As a result of these transformations, 'about 60% of ecosystem services are already degraded and will continue to degrade further unless *significant societal changes in values* and management occur'.[10] The 2014 report of the IPCC (Intergovernmental Panel on Climate Change) suggests that, if the current trend continues, humanity may face imminent catastrophic consequences.[11]

In 2009, a team of 29 scientists coauthored a paper entitled 'A Safe Operating Space for Humanity' in which they defined:

> [Nine] planetary boundaries within which we expect that humanity can operate safely. Transgressing one or more planetary boundaries

9 Paul J. Crutzen and Eugene F. Stoermer, 'The "Anthropocene"', *Global Change Newsletter* 41 (May 2000): 17–18.

10 Will Steffen, Paul J. Crutzen, and John R. McNeill, 'The Anthropocene: Are Humans Now Overwhelming the Great Forces of Nature?', *Ambio* 36, no. 8 (2007): 620; my emphasis.

11 Intergovernmental Panel on Climate Change, *Climate Change 2014: Synthesis Report* (2014), http://ipcc.ch/report/ar5/syr.

may be deleterious or even catastrophic due to the risk of crossing thresholds that will trigger non-linear, abrupt environmental change ... We estimate that humanity has already transgressed three planetary boundaries: climate change, rate of biodiversity loss, and changes to the global nitrogen cycle.[12]

They caution that, in the absence of radical changes in the way humans relate to the planet, some of the six other boundaries are likely to be crossed very soon. To mention just two disturbing facts from a long list: the rate at which biodiversity is being lost today is hundreds of times higher than in preindustrial times, and during the second half of the twentieth century the Earth lost one-fourth of its fertile soil and one-third of its forested surface.[13] The ongoing mass extinction of species is so dire that a 2017 scientific study on vertebrate population losses and declines defines it as 'biological annihilation'.[14] It seems undeniable that, given capitalism's implication in the ongoing massive and rapid destruction of the life-support systems upon which human survival depends, the only rational plan of action 'is a radical change of course'.[15] Unfortunately, what we are witnessing in mainstream responses to the urgencies of the Anthropocene is a plethora of denials, in all shapes and sizes, that attempt to solve these problems by merely targeting their symptoms.

The combination of the ongoing globalizing dominant cultural and economic imaginary (neoliberal reason) and its associated material transformations is unsustainable; it is a biophysical impossibility that has all kinds of devastating social consequences, and thus it is crucial to understand 'how globalization and global warming are born of overlapping processes'.[16] The problem is that we in the humanities have been trained to think about humans and their cultures, economies, societies, sciences, and histories as disconnected or separate from nonhuman systems, sciences, histories, and temporal scales. But all these distinctions collapse if we accept

12 Johan Rockström et al., 'Planetary Boundaries: Exploring the Safe Operating Space for Humanity', *Ecology and Society* 14, no. 2 (2009): 1–33.

13 David Becerra Mayor, Raquel Arias Careaga, Julio Rodríguez Puértolas, and Marta Sanz Pastor, *Qué hacemos con la literatura* (Madrid: Akal, 2013), 9–10.

14 Gerardo Ceballos, Paul R. Ehrlich, and Rodolfo Dirzo, 'Biological Annihilation Via the Ongoing Sixth Mass Extinction Signaled by Vertebrate Population Losses and Declines', *Proceedings of the National Academy of Sciences of the United States of America (PNAS)*114, no. 30 (2017): 6089–6096.

15 John Bellamy Foster, Brett Clark, and Richard York, *The Ecological Rift: Capitalism's War on the Earth* (New York: Monthly Review Press, 2010), 426.

16 Dipesh Chakrabarty, 'The Climate of History: Four Theses', *Critical Inquiry* 35 (2009): 200.

the implications of the Anthropocene. Considering humans as powerful geological agents is incompatible with maintaining the distinctions between natural and human histories.[17] Ironically, while it is widely recognized that collective human agency can radically transform the Earth, it is also possible that we may lack the political, legal, and cultural capacity to bring about that transformation in a desirable and democratic fashion, as legal scholar Jedediah Purdy has argued.[18] The fundamental question remains, 'What does it mean for the humanities to address the question of the Anthropocene?'[19] The responses are both highly contested and intellectually stimulating. Fortunately, a rapidly emerging interdisciplinary field, environmental humanities, is devoting its energy to answering this very question and exploring how to 'situate humans ecologically and nonhumans ethically'.[20]

The environmental humanities is a 'useful umbrella, bringing together many subfields that have emerged over the past few decades and facilitating new conversations between them'.[21] Some of these subfields include ecocriticism, environmental history and anthropology, critical geography, environmental journalism, and environmental philosophy. Until very recently, scholars in the humanities committed to coming to terms with the agency of the nonhuman in all human matters, as well as with the cultural dimensions of the ecological crisis, were often marginalized by the mainstream academic rigidity of their traditional departments. Many of them, for the sake of survival, were unable or unwilling to disrupt their departmental culture and therefore maintained many of the self-imposed epistemological limitations inherent in their humanistic fields. In the past few years, things have begun to change. Environmental humanities is creating an encouraging academic framework that is enabling these scholars to liberate themselves from the limits and isolation of their field and to connect with other disciplines, achieve professional legitimization (through new international journals, programs, grants, institutes, and research centers), and overcome many of the harmful mannerisms ingrained in their traditional disciplinary training. At the same time, many of the traditional disciplines are being transformed and enriched by participating in the

17 Chakrabarty, 'The Climate of History', 206.

18 See Jedediah Purdy, *After Nature: A Politics for the Anthropocene* (Cambridge, MA: Harvard University Press, 2015).

19 Greg Garrard, Gary Handwerk, and Sabine Wilke, 'Imagining Anew: Challenges of Representing the Anthropocene', *Environmental Humanities* 5 (2014): 149.

20 Val Plumwood, *Environmental Culture: The Ecological Crisis of Reason* (New York: Routledge, 2002), 239.

21 Deborah Bird Rose et al., 'Thinking through the Environment, Unsettling the Humanities', *Environmental Humanities* 1 (2012): 5.

environmental humanities debate. More and more humanists are realizing that 'any question of the Humanities is a question of its web of interdependencies: animals, technology, various environmental issues, etc.'.[22]

Given that the concept of the Anthropocene and the notion of planetary boundaries emerged from ecological sciences, in particular earth system science, what kind of contribution can the humanities and social sciences make to these pressing issues? Assuredly an important one, as I hope to make clear in this book. Radical environmental social scientists offer valuable contributions in environmental sociology, urban and political ecology, ecolinguistics, and ecological economics, and this book will mobilize some concepts stemming from their work. The role of the humanities seems less obvious, but it should not be underestimated because, as Rob Nixon reminds us,

> Stories matter—they matter immeasurably. Measurement, data, metrics, and modeling are the lucrative priorities of universities these days. In the face of this pressure to quantify, it is easy for humanities scholars to lose track of what they do best, such as explaining why telling a story one way as opposed to another can have profound imaginative, ethical, and political consequences.[23]

Nixon champions the idea of socioecological interdependency and explains the dangers of analyzing the Anthropocene story of anthropogenic ecological crisis from a merely quantitative perspective, without addressing the question of the unequal distribution of resources, responsibility, and vulnerability. He points out that:

> the most influential Anthropocene intellectuals have sidestepped the question of unequal human agency, unequal human impacts, and unequal human vulnerabilities. If, by contrast, we take an environmental justice approach to Anthropocene storytelling, we can better acknowledge the way the geomorphic powers of human beings have involved unequal exposure to risk and unequal access to resources. In 2013, the world's eighty-five richest people—a group small enough to fit into a double-decker bus, in the unlikely event that

---

22 Jussi Parikka and Annika Richterich, 'A Geology of Media and a New Materialism', *Digital Culture & Society* 1 (2015): 224.

23 Rob Nixon, 'The Great Acceleration and the Great Divergence: Vulnerability in the Anthropocene', *Profession*, March 19, 2014, https://profession.commons.mla.org/2014/03/19/the-great-acceleration-and-the-great-divergence-vulnerability-in-the-anthropocene/.

they would be inclined to take a bus—had a net worth equal to that of fifty percent of the planet's population, the 3.5 billion poorest people.[24]

When dealing with 'the greatest crises of our time: the environmental crisis and the inequality crisis', we cannot successfully target one without addressing the other:

> The species-centered Anthropocene meme has arisen in the twenty-first century, a period in which most societies have experienced a deepening schism between the überrich and the ultrapoor. In terms of the history of ideas, what does it mean that the Anthropocene as a grand explanatory species story has taken hold during a plutocratic age? How can we counter the centripetal force of that dominant story with centrifugal stories that acknowledge immense disparities in human agency, impacts, and vulnerability?[25]

Here is where the humanities can play a unique role in critically understanding the discursive construction of the Anthropocene and pointing out its dangers and potentialities. Probably the best example of a critical corrective to the mainstream construction and co-option of the term can be found in the book *Anthropocene or Capitalocene?* edited by Jason W. Moore.[26] Eileen Crist's contribution provides a brilliant critique of the managerial and anthropocentric hegemonic worldviews that the term 'Anthropocene' entails.[27] The environmental humanities could pay close attention to (and enhance by dialoging with) the counter-narratives challenging hegemonic reason and exposing the fallacies of the dominant imaginary. Yet the role of environmental humanities and ecologically oriented cultural studies needs not be limited to criticism. Rather, it could become a creative force that contributes to the dissemination and promotion of postgrowth imaginaries that are socially desirable and ecologically sustainable.

In a recent essay, 'Four Problems, Four Directions for Environmental Humanities: Toward Critical Posthumanities for the Anthropocene', Astrida Neimanis, Cecilia Åsberg, and Johan Hedrén elaborate on how environmental humanities is well suited to deal with 'four problems that currently frame our relation to the environment, namely: alienation and intangibility;

---

24 Nixon, 'The Great Acceleration'.

25 Nixon, 'The Great Acceleration'.

26 Jason W. Moore, ed., *Anthropocene or Capitalocene? Nature, History, and the Crisis of Capitalism* (Oakland, CA: PM Press, 2016).

27 Eileen Crist, 'On the Poverty of Our Nomenclature', in *Anthropocene or Capitalocene? Nature, History, and the Crisis of Capitalism*, ed. Jason W. Moore (Oakland, CA: PM Press, 2016), 14–33.

the post-political situation; negative framing of environmental change; and compartmentalization of "the environment" from other spheres of concern'.[28] All of these problems are central in articulating a transformative ecocritical approach to Iberian literary and cultural studies. In this light, the environmental humanities and posthumanism should be understood not merely as aiming a humanist lens at the ecological crisis, but as turning an ecological lens on the humanities as well, for the humanities have been part of the problem of theoretically separating humans from the nonhuman and culture from nature, focusing on the former at the expense of the latter. Of course, this has potentially enormous political, material, and cultural consequences, for the focus of attention influences perception and, more importantly, determines the blind spots in our observations. Thus, a transformative environmental (post)humanism entails advancing 'a different mode of thought', one that accounts for material and nonhuman agency in relation to human political and aesthetic limits and possibilities.[29] In short, 'the decentering of the human by its imbrications in technical, medical, informatics, and economic networks is increasingly impossible to ignore', and thus 'the nature of thought itself must change if it is to be posthumanist'.[30]

It seems that Spanish cultural and literary studies are either actively avoiding this debate or, worse, unable to recognize the pervasive 'hyperobjects', such as global warming, that Timothy Morton describes as being 'massively distributed in time and space relative to humans'.[31] In any case, I hope we start paying much greater attention to the cultural narratives that are connecting social and ecological issues. Otherwise, we will remain passive spectators in the events that will radically modify our cultural imagination in the future. Therefore, I encourage Iberian cultural scholars to participate now in the environmental humanities debate and not to shy away from breaking with rigid academic practices that prevent us from focusing on vital ecocritical issues by entwining us in often pointless and politically toothless intellectual games.

28 Astrida Neimanis, Cecilia Åsberg, and Johan Hedrén, 'Four Problems, Four Directions for Environmental Humanities: Toward Critical Posthumanities for the Anthropocene', *Ethics & Environment* 20, no. 1 (2015): 69.

29 Hannes Bergthaller et al., 'Mapping Common Ground: Ecocriticism, Environmental History, and the Environmental Humanities', *Environmental Humanities* 5 (2014): 265.

30 Cary Wolfe, *What is Posthumanism?* (Minneapolis: University of Minnesota Press, 2010), xv–xvi.

31 Timothy Morton, *Hyperobjects: Philosophy and Ecology after the End of the World* (Minneapolis: University of Minnesota Press, 2013), 1.

The Dominant Imaginary of Economic Growth and Its Social and Ecological Crises

The term 'imaginary', as I will use it throughout this book, was coined by Greek-French philosopher Cornelius Castoriadis referring to what he calls 'imaginary social significations'.[32] For Castoriadis, all social realities are constructed according to pervasive dominant conceptions and postulates about humans and their relations to each other and the world. These conceptions influence every aspect of society. Imaginary social significations re-create meaning (and thus reproduce themselves) without necessarily considering complex social and ecological processes and changes that might bring about clear dysfunctionalities in their meaning-making capabilities. For example, neoliberal imaginaries operate by reducing social reality to certain social aspects (competing individuals trying to maximize their economic gains in the context of a capitalist market economy) or by attributing rationality only to certain human actors making non-emotional economic decisions (ignoring the fact that studies in neuropsychology have suggested that human intelligence is always emotional). These imaginaries have widespread material and semiotic consequences.

The currently dominant capitalist imaginary equates progress with constant economic development and growth and assumes that 'unlimited growth of production and of the productive forces is *in fact* the central objective of human existence'.[33] Castoriadis has identified what he considers to be the four most important postulates attached to this capitalist imaginary social signification: '1) the virtual "omnipotence" of technology; 2) the "asymptotic illusion" relating to scientific knowledge; 3) the "rationality" of economic mechanisms; and 4) various assumptions about humanity and society'.[34] To maintain itself, this imaginary social signification requires that no absolute limits to growth be recognized, no matter how counterintuitive that may be in the context of a finite and ecologically depleted biosphere. Nevertheless, social and ecological limitations obviously exist, and thus 'where they present themselves, have a negative value and must be transcended'.[35] For Castoriadis, then, social reality constructs itself, materially and symbolically, in the image of the

32 See Cornelius Castoriadis, *The Imaginary Institution of Society*, trans. Kathleen Blamey (Cambridge, MA: MIT Press, 1998).
33 Cornelius Castoriadis, 'Reflections on Rationality and Development', *Thesis Eleven* 10–11 (1984–1985): 24.
34 Castoriadis, 'Reflections on Rationality and Development', 29.
35 Castoriadis, 'Reflections on Rationality and Development', 25.

dominant imaginary of the time, grossly ignoring, avoiding, dispossessing, disciplining, or even criminalizing whatever or whomever does not fit within its predetermined framework. But what happens when nonhuman agency becomes more difficult to ignore and challenges, contradicts, and ultimately makes impossible what the dominant imaginary considers to be the main goal of humanity, that is, economic growth? Or what happens, for that matter, when biophysical circumstances make global growth so socially and ecologically costly, devastating, and disrupting that its association with human progress can no longer be maintained? When that occurs—and I believe that the emerging narratives of the Anthropocene and the transgression of planetary boundaries suggest that it is already happening—it will only be a matter of time before those four postulates supporting the capitalist imaginary begin to collapse.

Complementary to Castoriadis's notion of the dominant imaginary are Antonio Gramsci's theorizations on capitalist power's dependence on 'hegemony—the engineering of consent according to the dictates of a particular group. A hegemonic project builds a "common sense" that installs the particular worldview of one group as the universal horizon of an entire society'.[36] Once this dominant rationality infiltrates societal institutions (educational, political, economic), cultural values, urban planning, and lifestyles, the hegemonic common sense reproduces itself as it defines the organization of society and normalizes (masks) its ideology as ahistorical and politically neutral. Challenging the hegemonic ideology becomes more difficult as it constrains thought and action outside its self-imposed limitations. A paradigmatic example is the difficulty of criticizing capitalism in academia: anti-capitalism is perceived as a radical intellectual position while supporting capitalism, an ideology that is changing the biophysical conditions that defined the Holocene and is threatening life on Earth, is considered a moderate decision! Currently, most thinkable social problems and solutions, as well as future horizons, only exist within the pre-established parameters of the hegemonic ideology, which demand that no matter the consequences, economic growth must go on. This limits the political imagination that allows societies to reinvent themselves, even in the face of imminent civilizational collapse. Prosperity without growth cannot be imagined when the hegemonic ideology is so invested in the 'grow or perish' paradigm. But what happens when the agency of the nonhuman clearly indicates that the new rules of the game in the Anthropocene are just the opposite: degrow or perish?

36 Nick Srnicek and Alex Williams, *Inventing the Future: Postcapitalism and a World without Work* (London: Verso, 2015), 132.

The degrowth movement, largely influenced by Castoriadis's insights, is currently doing an admirable job of both exposing the ecological devastation and social corrosion brought about by the hegemonic obsession with growth and proposing new imaginaries. Degrowth, as its provocative name indicates, dares to challenge the dominant imaginary on its own terms by showing the multifarious negative consequences of the growth paradigm. Degrowth theorists, putting together Castoriadis's notion of the social imaginary and the 'anti-imperialist anthropologies in relation to mentalities', insist on the need for a 'decolonization of the imaginary'.[37] Serge Latouche, one of the main promoters of this movement, asks the key question: How do we exit the dominant imaginary?[38] Latouche elaborates on the ways in which capitalist hegemony has colonized our mentality and considers that what is needed is nothing less than a cultural revolution that includes, following Castoriadis's lead, profound changes in our psychosocial organization—a new, emancipatory, imaginary. In other words, we are dealing with an epistemological crisis in which our modes of knowing and thinking are not only failing to help us function in the world, but also reducing the conditions necessary for the possibility of achieving a good life for most, or even our chances for survival in the future. Translating our epistemological habits into economic, quantitative, and mechanical metrics and analytical mathematical abstractions prevents us from grasping (or considering in our calculations) the relational, systemic, qualitative, and bodily properties of the world, a failure that in turn produces and aggravates economic, ecological, social, and ethical crises.[39]

The dominant growth imaginary is so pervasive that most people believe, despite all evidence to the contrary, that economic growth is the solution for almost all of society's ills.[40] This 'neoliberal fantasy' is reflected and ingrained in the dominant cultural imaginary as it is re-created, reproduced, and perpetuated over and over in media representations, institutional discourses, and daily speeches. It is the job of the environmental humanities to highlight what causes this collective inability to imagine a sustainable

37 Serge Latouche, 'Decolonization of Imaginary', in *Degrowth: A Vocabulary for a New Era*, ed. Giacomo D'Alisa, Federico Demaria, and Giorgos Kallis (New York: Routledge, 2015), 119.

38 Serge Latouche, *La apuesta por el decrecimiento. ¿Cómo salir del imaginario dominante?*, trans. Patricia Astorga (Barcelona: Icaria, 2006), 143.

39 See Jordi Pigem, *La nueva realidad. Del economicismo a la conciencia cuántica* (Barcelona: Kairós, 2013).

40 Some of the ideas elaborated in this section first appeared in, and are paraphrased from my article 'An Economy Focused Solely on Growth Is Environmentally and Socially Unsustainable' (*The Conversation*, April 7, 2015).

future without economic growth in the Anthropocene. As social ecologists have long insisted, the problem arises from a logic that legitimizes structural social injustice and exploits both humanity and the nonhuman as mere economic resources to fuel constant economic growth in the context of a limited biosphere. By isolating human labor and depleting ecosystems, this capitalist rationality tends to destroy the source of all wealth, as Karl Marx taught us, and as today's radical ecological post-Marxist theorists are reminding us in diverse fashions (ecosocialists, ecofeminists, political ecologists). Presently, the global socioeconomic metabolism cannot grow much more, given the current ecological and energy situation, but needs instead to decrease significantly in order to become minimally sustainable: 'humanity needs to radically transform the global economy, reducing its size by at least one third—based on the conservative ecological footprint indicator, which finds that humanity is currently using the ecological capacity of 1.5 Earths'.[41] It has been foreseen since the 1960s that the model of economic growth, which neoliberalism would later embrace and globalize as an unquestioned faith, was doomed to run up against the biophysical limitations of the Earth. Titles such as *Limits to Growth* in the early '70s and *The Growth Illusion: How Economic Growth Enriched the Few, Impoverished the Many, and Endangered the Planet* in the early '90s have been beating the drum for decades.[42] Actually, John Stuart Mill already claimed in 1848 that a future economic tendency towards a stationary state would be both inevitable and desirable.[43]

Today it should be clear that there are many links between our society's addiction to economic growth, the disturbing ecological crisis, the rapid rise of social inequality, and the current decline in the quality of democracy. Spain is a valuable paradigm for exploring these interwoven issues playing out after 2008. Too often these issues tend to be explored as disconnected topics and misinterpreted or manipulated to match ideological preconceptions and prejudices. The fact is that they are deeply interconnected processes. Studies in the social sciences consistently show that in rich countries, greater economic growth does very little or nothing at all to enhance social

41 Erik Assadourian, 'The Path to Degrowth in Overdeveloped Countries', in *Worldwatch Institute, State of the World 2012: Moving Toward Sustainable Prosperity*, ed. Linda Starke (Washington, DC: Island Press, 2012), 24.

42 Donella Meadows et al., *The Limits to Growth* (New York: Universe Books, 1972); Richard Douthwaite, *The Growth Illusion: How Economic Growth Enriched the Few, Impoverished the Many, and Endangered the Planet* (Bideford: Green Books; Dublin: Lilliput Press, 1992).

43 John Stuart Mill, *Principles of Political Economy* (Salt Lake City, UT: Project Gutenberg, 2009).

well-being. On the contrary, reducing income inequality is the most effective way to resolve social problems such as violence, criminality, incarceration rates, obesity, and mental illness, as well as improving children's educational performance, overall life expectancy, social trust, and social mobility.[44] Comparative studies in epidemiology have found that societies that are more equal do much better in all the aforementioned areas than ones that are more unequal, independent of their GDP.[45] The focus of a successful social policy, therefore, should be to reduce inequality, not to grow GDP for its own sake. French economist Thomas Piketty, in his recent book *Capital in the Twenty-First Century*, has assembled extensive data that show how unchecked capitalism historically tends to increase inequality and undermine democratic practices, especially when the economy is shrinking—and in a limited biosphere, the economy can never grow indefinitely.[46]

If we consider the findings from the social and ecological sciences as a whole, a consistent picture emerges: constant economic growth is a biophysical impossibility in a limited biosphere, and the faster the global economy grows, the faster the living systems of the planet collapse. In addition, under neoliberal rules, this growth increases inequality and undermines democracy, multiplying the number of social problems that erode human communities and their quality of life. In a nutshell, we have created a dysfunctional economic system that, when it works according to its self-imposed mandate of increasing the pace of production and consumption, destroys the ecological systems upon which it depends; on the other hand, when the economic system fails to maintain that pace, it becomes socially unsustainable. In a game with these rules, there is no way to win!

To break this spiral of socioecological disaster, as I will show in the following chapters focused on post-2008 Spain, a new common sense needs to emerge: a postgrowth, decolonial, ecofeminist, posthumanist, and postcapitalist imaginary. This task, while not easy, is one to which the environmental humanities is well prepared to contribute. The ecological sciences are already doing their part by recording the disturbing anthropogenic environmental transformations occurring on a global scale. Environmental social scientists are doing their part too, by pointing out that the disproportionate socioeconomic activity that is

44 Richard Wilkinson and Kate Pickett, *The Spirit Level: Why Greater Equality Makes Societies Stronger* (New York: Bloomsbury Press, 2010), 3–45.

45 Wilkinson and Pickett, *The Spirit Level*, 46–169.

46 Thomas Piketty, *Capital in the Twenty-First Century*, trans. Arthur Goldhammer (Cambridge, MA: Belknap Press, 2014).

disrupting the biogeochemical flows and cycles of the Earth system is associated with the evolution of a historically specific system of social reproduction and colonization, namely, capitalism. Now it is time for the environmental humanities to do its part and bring culture and its colorful palette into the picture. This will require a revealing investigation of the stories, narratives, and practices that support the pervasive 'neoliberal fantasies' of the dominant cultural imaginary that prevents us from thinking beyond growth (and beyond capitalism). It will also require further investigation into the ways in which neoliberalism remodels subjectivity (*à la* Foucault) and impedes the countless victims of its logic (the so-called '99 percent') from thinking and acting outside of that logic. Lauren Berlant eloquently explains that 'cruel optimism is the condition of maintaining an attachment to a significantly problematic object' or 'a relation of attachment to compromised conditions of possibility whose realization is discovered either to be impossible, sheer fantasy, or *too* possible, and toxic'.[47] Environmental humanities can provide insights into how dominant post-2008 Spanish cultural narratives of the crisis harbor— and how counterhegemonic narratives and practices challenge—a cruel optimism that embraces, desires, and celebrates economic growth even though the neoliberal promises attached to such growth are never fulfilled and the side effects are more and more socially corrosive and ecologically damaging.

As an imaginative exercise in escaping the logic of the dominant 'neoliberal fantasies' and their cruel optimism, let us assume that we all agree on some basic facts: first, that the biosphere contains and supports the living systems of the planet; second, that humans are one of the many species embedded in the biosphere and dependent upon its proper functioning; and, third, that an economic system is (or should be) a tool that humans deploy to organize their societies in a functional way. Based on these facts, the economy is a subsystem of the ecology, not the other way around. Mainstream economic models become dysfunctional because they start from the premise that societies and ecosystems must adapt to the market economy. If we begin to organize our priorities according to biophysical realities rather than market-oriented mandates, it quickly becomes clear that our dominant economic system is absurd and functionally obsolete, for it destroys the very ecosystems that are the source of its wealth. Our liberation lies in rejecting the cruel optimism promoted by neoliberal fictions and relinquishing the pursuit of economic growth. The goal of a desirable economic culture is to serve the well-being of

47 Berlant, *Cruel Optimism*, 24.

communities and ecosystems, not to accumulate capital. Of course, in order to be effective in influencing and modifying the dominant imaginaries we must trigger a collective and massive mobilization, and it must occur at a transnational scale, given that neoliberal fantasies and their cruel optimism are the current globalizing hegemonic ideology.

Once we acknowledge the biophysical and social limits of growth, the next step is to embrace ecological economics (as opposed to neoclassical and neoliberal economics) as the appropriate tool for achieving our new goals. We do not need to start from scratch, for there is already a substantial literature on the topic, and numerous activists, social movements, and researchers are advancing theories and embracing practices on degrowth, postdevelopment, postextractivism, postgrowth, prosperity without growth, steady-state economics, new economics, feminist economics, economics for the common good, and so on. These scholars and activists explore and analyze diverse policies and practices which aim to reduce superfluous consumption of energy and materials while creating more just, livable, and sustainable communities for everyone.

Unfortunately, these narratives and practices are far from being widely circulated in our daily conversations and media outlets. 'The stories we live by' are very different from the postgrowth narratives and, for the most part, are based on ideologies, metaphors, and frames that promote progress narrowly defined as economic growth and capitalist development. These stories entail 'cognitive structures which influence how people think, talk and act' and 'they are implicated in injustice and environmental destruction'.[48] Arran Stibbe argues that:

> underneath common ways of writing and speaking in industrial societies are stories about unlimited economic growth as being not just possible but the goal of society, of the accumulation of unnecessary goods as a path towards self-improvement, of progress and success defined narrowly in terms of technological innovation and profit, and of nature as something separate from humans, a mere stock of resources to be exploited.[49]

These narratives are blind to the biophysical realities of a finite biosphere and oblivious to the inextricable human dependence on ecological systems. Addressing these blind spots entails envisioning radically different cultural narratives and embracing different practices embedded in new imaginaries

48 Arran Stibbe, *Ecolinguistics: Language, Ecology, and the Stories We Live By* (New York: Routledge, 2015), 10, 5.
49 Stibbe, *Ecolinguistics*, 3.

more appropriate and functional in the current social and ecological context.

Given that global ecological and social problems are increasingly difficult to ignore, many mainstream sectors are now ready to recognize them, but in order to solve them,

> turn to technological fixes or market mechanisms of one sort or another. In this respect, there is a certain continuity of thought between those who deny the climate change problem altogether, and those who, while acknowledging the severity of the problem at one level, nevertheless deny that it requires a revolution in our social system.[50]

This new kind of denial insists on claiming that the solution to sustainability problems caused by excessive growth and superfluous consumerism can be solved by adopting a different pattern of growth. According to this argument, the solution to the unsustainability of growth lies in embracing green growth (again and again we see the inability to abandon the growth paradigm and imagine a desirable future beyond growth). The green growth paradigm claims that the economy can be dematerialized by decoupling economic growth from ecological degradation and teaching the markets to internalize environmental and social externalities. However, reality indicates that this is nothing but wishful thinking because capitalism never proceeds in this fashion; instead it constantly externalizes new costs to increase profit margins.

Under a growth-oriented regime, technology is not going to compensate for the market's environmental miscalculations. On the contrary, the use of new technology to promote growth is making the present situation much worse by increasing the speed of resource extraction and ecological depletion. Technology can only be socially and environmentally benign if it is embedded in a system that prioritizes social and ecological well-being over capital accumulation and is therefore motivated to generate what Ivan Illich calls 'convivial tools', as opposed to centralized, complex technologies for spurring growth.[51] Technology, as science and technology studies demonstrate, is not something neutral that emerges in a vacuum but a tool influencing and being influenced by the dominant economic culture in which it emerges. More sophisticated technology, under the current socioeconomic system, provides more capable and efficient means for exploiting and destroying our already overstressed planet. Under a market economy

---

50 Foster, Clark, and York, *The Ecological Rift*, 427.
51 Ivan Illich, *Tools of Conviviality* (Glasgow: Collins, 1975).

devoted to growth, the gains in efficiency facilitated by new technology are historically reinvested to spur more growth and therefore end up promoting an overall increase in resource consumption rather than reducing it (a process known as the Jevons paradox or rebound effect). Samuel Alexander compellingly explains how the frequent techno-optimism displayed by the supporters of green capitalism, sustainable development, green growth, and ecological modernization is based not on empirical evidence but their own inability to '[confront] cultural and economic fundamentals' associated with economic growth, neoliberal rationality, and consumerist lifestyles. Such techno-optimism is 'a wholly inadequate response to the crises facing humanity'.[52]

The Paris Agreement on climate change signed in December 2015 likewise subscribes to the narrative of green growth, market faith, and techno-optimism. Its celebrated ability to achieve a global consensus only underlines the fact that it is based on the hegemonic ideology. The main problem with the Paris Agreement is not that it is vastly insufficient—which it is—to turn the tide of dramatic climate change, but that it is unwilling to target the root causes of the problem. The agreement assumes, and hopes, that growth and neoliberal globalization will continue, and relies on the development of technologies that are nonexistent today. It does not question, but rather embraces, the globalization of consumerism, the continuation of massive long-distance trade, and the systemic addiction to growth. In this regard, the Paris Agreement is supported by the kind of denial mentioned above. Once more, the incapacity to imagine a future with no growth is evident.

Even if a miraculous eco-efficient version of capitalist development could be universalized (which cannot happen today, because the ecological services of several planets would be required if all regions of the planet were to develop), it would most likely not be socially desirable, for so-called sustainable development has often 'failed to identify the historical and structural roots of poverty, hunger, unsustainability and inequity. These include: centralization of state power, capitalist monopolies, colonialism, racism and patriarchy. Without diagnosing who or what is responsible, it is inevitable that any proposed solutions will not be transformative enough'.[53] Put otherwise, sustainable development can never be sustained because

---

52 Samuel Alexander, 'A Critique to Techno-Optimism: Efficiency without Sufficiency Is Lost' (Postcarbon Pathways Working Paper Series, Melbourne Sustainable Society Institute, Melbourne, 2014), 13–14.

53 Ashish Kothari, Federico Demaria, and Alberto Acosta, 'Sustainable Development Is Failing But There Are Alternatives to Capitalism', *The Guardian*, July 21, 2015.

of its insistence on defining development in terms of constant economic growth and capital accumulation.

In fact, the mainstream celebration of sustainable development in recent decades coincides with a rise in neoliberal rationality, a massive increase in social inequality, and an unprecedented acceleration of ecological destruction on a global scale. The discourse of sustainable development, suspiciously, matches very well the apolitical and technocratic sensibilities brought about by the neoliberal project and 'is a manifestation of a broader process of depoliticization of public debate in liberal democracies, whereby politics have been reduced to the search for technocratic solutions to pre-framed problems instead of a genuinely antagonistic struggle between alternative visions'.[54] In *Undoing the Demos: Neoliberalism's Stealth Revolution* (2015), Wendy Brown argues that in a process that began three decades ago, 'neoliberalism, a peculiar form of reason that configures all aspects of existence in economic terms, is quietly undoing basic elements of democracy. These elements include vocabularies, principles of justice, political cultures, habits of citizenship, practices of rule, and above all, *democratic imaginaries*'.[55] Thus, economic growth is not the panacea for all social problems. Rather, the addiction to economic growth under the dictates of neoliberal globalization may be at the root of most social and environmental problems, including, as pointed out by Brown, the erosion of democratic practices and imaginaries. Indeed, the very model of neoliberal globalization is deleterious in a double sense, semiotically and biophysically, for it is destroying both our democratic imaginaries and the possibility of our biological survival. I believe that our best chance of maintaining an inhabitable planet where we can collectively envision a good life (and democratically decide what that entails) lies in conceiving of and enacting radically different postgrowth cultural imaginaries able to open the floor to new political possibilities. This will require overcoming the cruel optimism inherent in the current crisis of political imagination fostered by our toxic epistemological, material, and affective attachment to economic growth.

---

54 Giacomo D'Alisa, Federico Demaria, and Giorgos Kallis, eds., *Degrowth: A Vocabulary for a New Era* (New York: Routledge, 2015), 9.

55 Wendy Brown, *Undoing the Demos: Neoliberalism's Stealth Revolution* (New York: Zone Books, 2015), 17; my emphasis.

Environmental Cultural Studies:
Challenging Neoliberal Fantasies to Overcome the Crisis
of Political Imagination

We could interpret the ongoing global imposition of neoliberal rationality (and its crises) as the historical moment in which the dominant imaginary of economic growth has completed a planetary 'colonization of everyday life', to use Henri Lefebvre's words.[56] It is clear that neoliberalism presents itself in different ways and intersects with diverse cultures, discourses, and political traditions. However, the pervasive epistemological colonization of neoliberalism is overarching and all-encompassing as it 'transmogrifies every human domain and endeavor, along with humans themselves, according to a specific image of the economic'.[57] Wendy Brown, building on Foucault's *Birth of Biopolitics* lectures, compellingly explains how neoliberalism remakes humans as 'self-investing human capital' and repurposes nation states as corporation-like facilitators of economic growth and global competitiveness. This gross reduction of human existence and political governance to economic metrics entails 'enormous consequences for democratic institutions, cultures, and imaginaries', including the disappearance of politics beyond neoliberal economic policy and therefore of any meaningful democratic practice.[58]

The most notorious neoliberal paradox is the repurposing of the state as a growth factory in order to 'serve and facilitate an economy it is not supposed to touch'.[59] In other words, while neoliberal thinkers claim that they demand a non-interferential state to let the supposed rational mechanisms of the market work undisturbed, in practice neoliberalism 'requires a very large state to support and protect its preconditions of being'.[60] Neoliberal policies do not shrink the state but repurpose its functions and goals in very disturbing ways; instead of protecting its citizens, the state becomes a facilitator of economic growth and market competition that disregards the associated socioecological costs generated by such economic competition. Hobbes's legitimization of the political authority of a sovereign government was intended to avoid the war of all against all that he associated with the state of nature, in which the reckless competition of self-interested individuals would make human life 'solitary, poor, nasty, brutish, and

---

56 Henri Lefebvre, *Critique of Everyday Life, Vol. 3: From Modernity to Modernism*, trans. Gregory Elliott (London: Verso, 2008).

57 Brown, *Undoing the Demos*, 10.

58 Brown, *Undoing the Demos*, 35.

59 Brown, *Undoing the Demos*, 40.

60 William E. Connolly, *The Fragility of Things: Self-Organizing Processes, Neoliberal Fantasies, and Democratic Activism* (Durham, NC: Duke University Press, 2013), 7.

short'. Discounting Hobbes's essentialist and pessimistic conception of human nature, he would probably be horrified to witness the way in which neoliberal states have become the preferred place for the fearsome, nasty, and brutish competition of all solitary individuals for survival in the now-naturalized market environment. In fact, as Mick Smith compellingly argues, the very notion of sovereign political power itself is indebted to a metaphysical division between society and nature as well as the assumption of human exceptionalism and its sovereign dominion over the natural world. Smith urges us to challenge all the current proliferations of ecological sovereignty ingrained in mainstream environmentalism because 'what we need are plural ways to imagine a world without sovereign power, without human dominion'.[61]

It is important to resist neoliberal sovereign power and its perverse biopolitics. Under such rules, the fruits of the community are privatized while the responsibility for the social or ecological mess generated by neoliberal bottom-up wealth redistribution is not recognized by the state and therefore is transferred to dispossessed individuals. William Connolly has highlighted the intensified fragility of the current order brought about by the expansion of neoliberal capitalism and its acceleration of culture-nature imbrications. This fragility is marked by the 'growing gaps and dislocations between the demands neoliberalism makes upon several human activities and nonhuman fields and the capacities of both to meet them'.[62] There are many 'neoliberal fantasies' ingrained in a discourse that promises prosperity and freedom while implementing policies that undermine the social and ecological conditions necessary for such possibilities. But the most limiting fantasy of all may be the one that has to do with innovation and creativity.[63]

Neoliberalism continually celebrates innovation, creativity, imagination, flexibility, and spontaneity while restricting the uses to which they may be put to the sole purpose of economic growth and financial engineering. As such, neoliberal ideology '*inflates the self-organizing power of markets by implicitly deflating the self-organizing powers and creativity of all other systems*'.[64] Human and nonhuman systems, whose creative powers are deflated and constrained, become subordinated to what is touted as the creativity of the markets. Under this perverse logic, any creative energy that cannot be harnessed

61 Mick Smith, *Against Ecological Sovereignty: Ethics, Biopolitics, and Saving the Natural World* (Minneapolis: University of Minnesota Press, 2011), 220.

62 Connolly, *The Fragility of Things*, 10.

63 See Luis I. Prádanos, 'Teaching Limits to Enhance Creativity: The Pedagogy of Degrowth', Academe Blog, August 10, 2017.

64 Connolly, *The Fragility of Things*, 31; emphasis original.

by the markets becomes irrelevant at best and is liable to be entirely deactivated. As a consequence, most of the creative energy in our society is channeled into the creation of different ways of stimulating economic growth (rather than, say, building healthier, happier, and more sustainable communities). All human ingenuity, creativity, and innovation is employed to feed the growing machine that, as it grows bigger, prevents creativity from flourishing and thriving outside its own economic domain. In other words, real creativity that dares to think outside of the growth paradigm is not perceived as such (unless it can be appropriated by capitalist enterprises), but rather infantilized, delegitimized, disqualified, and disciplined for being unrealistic, naive, populist, utopic, backwards, unsafe, exotic, improperly academic, and so on. The dominant cultural imaginary of economic growth and its neoliberal reason reserves for itself the role of the sole source of all cultural authority and knowledge production (a reality that has been very well studied by Luis Moreno-Caballud in relation to contemporary Spanish culture).[65]

As neoliberal logic colonizes social institutions, infiltrates the habits of everyday life, and even infects vocabularies, it becomes more and more difficult to think outside of its self-imposed epistemological limitations. The Foucauldian usage of the word *dispositif* or 'apparatus', as brilliantly elaborated by Giorgio Agamben, gets to the heart of the matter. An apparatus is 'a machine that produces subjectifications, and only as such is it also a machine of governance'.[66] Agamben observes that the neoliberal phase of capitalism is defined by 'a massive accumulation and proliferation of apparatuses ... Today there is not even a single instant in which the life of individuals is not modeled, contaminated, or controlled by some apparatus'.[67] Once these apparatuses impose the rules and norms of the neoliberal project, these norms—and the fantasies they entail—become internalized by individuals and ingrained in their reasoning and construction of meaning, determining their habits, emotions, feelings, identities, beliefs, and expectations, and framing their worldviews. This normativity is eventually perceived as existing outside of any historical context, and therefore questioning it becomes not only a political impossibility but an immoral act. This order of things tends to 'reduce the freedoms associated with ethics as such to compliance with moral norms, to following rules, and ... to an internalized

65 Luis Moreno-Caballud, *Cultures of Anyone: Studies on Cultural Democratization in the Spanish Neoliberal Crisis*, trans. Linda Grabner (Liverpool: Liverpool University Press, 2015).

66 Giorgio Agamben, *'What Is an Apparatus?' and Other Essays*, trans. David Kishik and Stefan Pedatella (Stanford, CA: Stanford University Press, 2009), 20.

67 Agamben, *'What is an Apparatus?'*, 15.

relation of dependence that confines moral feeling to a self-monitoring compliance of each individual with those ideals espoused by the ruling powers'.[68] As a result, little room is left for the emergence of proper politics and ethics beyond the sphere of the hegemonic ideology and its dominant growth imaginary.

The inadequate responses to the Anthropocene mentioned previously show how deniers—not just the climate change deniers, but the deniers of the possibility of prosperity without growth—are prevented from thinking outside of neoclassical and neoliberal economic paradigms even when human biophysical survival is at stake. Neoliberal reason restricts creativity to innovations within the competitive, individualistic, consumerist, economistic logic, and it does a good job of finding clever new ways to foster capital accumulation by deploying creativity to navigate and surpass social and ecological impediments to growth. These impediments are more visible in the commodity frontiers and are expected to proliferate as hegemonic inertia blindly tries to push forward the remaining social and ecological limits to growth: 'The social and environmental impacts of extracting resources are increasing as the quality and availability of resources decreases'.[69]

This intensification of social and ecological problems under economic globalization and its potential, unpredictable, massive consequences, as well as the governmental uncertainties involved, is what Ulrich Beck identifies as the 'risk society'.[70] When the massively and asymmetrically distributed consequences of these manufactured risks are globally visible and therefore impossible to ignore, even for the elites, the approved remedies are invariably limited to treating their symptoms, given that neoliberal experts and technocrats are trained *not* to recognize the real problem, that is, the social and ecological limits to growth. The proposed solution, for instance, to the unsustainability of universalizing individual vehicles—and their associated inefficient infrastructures and aberrant urban models—is, not surprisingly, more efficient cars and bigger highways. A different urban model that redefines mobility by focusing on human needs and ecological mandates (not on private cars and their privatization of space) is out of the question, if not unimaginable. Another example is heavily investing in pharmaceutical research instead of regulating the chemical industries

68 Smith, *Against Ecological Sovereignty*, 57.

69 Marta Conde and Mariana Walter, 'Commodity Frontiers', in *Degrowth: A Vocabulary for a New Era*, ed. Giacomo D'Alisa, Federico Demaria, and Giorgos Kallis (New York: Routledge, 2015), 73.

70 Ulrich Beck, *Risk Society: Towards a New Modernity*, trans. Mark Ritter (London: Sage, 1992).

(of which pharmaceutical industries are a part) in order to combat the proliferation of cancer. Once again, the remedy makes things worse, because giving massive amounts of public funds to polluting corporations has the perverse effect of inspiring them to lobby harder and to more effectively prevent regulatory laws from passing (regulations that could, among other things, take some carcinogens out of circulation).

The growth-oriented ideology reproduces and self-amplifies itself over and over, limiting collective imaginative processes to the task of depicting different images of itself and creating innovative ways to refashion itself. William Connolly elaborates on how, once these amplification processes 'become consolidated, it becomes a more difficult system to oppose politically. Its self-organizing and reflexive tendencies now form self-amplifying loops'.[71] That is why it seems that there is no alternative to an ideology that is destroying the life-supporting systems of the Earth. Within this epistemological framework, 'the environmental crisis involves a crisis of imagination', for it becomes almost impossible to imagine a postcarbon, postgrowth, post-capitalist, post-neoliberal, post-patriarchal, decolonial society that is desirable and viable.[72]

In order to begin the transition to a postgrowth society it is crucial to challenge the cultural authority that perpetuates the dominant imaginary responsible for disconnecting economic activity from its ecological, social, political, and cultural interdependencies. The roots of the pervasive neoliberal mindset are nourished by previously drawn hierarchical distinctions (human and nonhuman, culture and nature), or what Giorgio Agamben calls the 'anthropological machine'. Agamben identifies the sociohistorically diverse ways in which metaphysical distinctions are established between humans and the nonhuman.[73] Humanity is defined and redefined again and again in opposition to the animal other, and it is the self-proclaimed 'proper humans' who reserve for themselves the right to determine what is considered fully human and what is not. That which does not fit into the 'properly human' category constructed by the 'anthropological machine' at a given historical moment is deemed inferior and may be exploited without ethical concern or legal consequence. If, under neoliberalism, humans are reduced to 'self-investing capital' and the main goal of societies is contributing to economic growth, then individuals

71 Connolly, *Fragility of Things*, 95.

72 Lawrence Buell, *The Environmental Imagination: Thoreau, Nature Writing, and the Formation of American Culture* (Cambridge, MA: Belknap Press of Harvard University Press, 1995), 2.

73 Giorgio Agamben, *The Open: Man and Animal*, trans. Kevin Attell (Stanford, CA: Stanford University Press, 2004).

who are unable to make a profit on their human capital, or communities not feeding the economic machine, can lose their status as properly human and pass into the category of the less than human. Globally, there are a growing number of surplus populations comprised of people who have lost their traditional livelihoods due to capitalist dispossession and are not formally employed by the capitalist economy.[74] Under the dominant imaginary, these populations can be identified as less than human and easily criminalized, disciplined, and sacrificed without remorse in the name of saving world markets.

The global expansion of markets and commodity frontiers often occurs under the guise of helping underdeveloped countries to develop. To be underdeveloped means, for the United Nations, not to live poorly, but to live outside the market economy. The UN's policies for achieving development are therefore not focused on promoting socioecological well-being in their target regions, but on incorporating—that is to say, forcing—non-market-oriented communities into the market economy.[75] As long as the anthropological machine is not challenged, it will continue to construct human exceptionality and justify the exploitation and abuse of the non-properly humans excluded by that definition of humanity: those perceived as savage, primitive, uncivilized, underdeveloped, unappealing for the markets, disinvested—or 'subprime', as Germán Labrador Méndez called them in the case of Spanish cultural narratives of the crisis.[76] This process will continue to create and exacerbate social and environmental injustices if not consistently confronted. It is essential to expose the fallacies of human exceptionalism and the human/nonhuman hierarchical divides that neoliberal reason perpetuates across the globe. In order to overcome the perverse consequences of these divides, it may be helpful to think in terms of social and ecological interdependency and relational ontology and pay full attention to the agency of the nonhuman in all human matters. This will entail embracing new imaginaries based on 'a posthuman environmental ethics in which the flows, interchanges, and interrelations between human corporeality and the more-than-human world resist the ideological forces of disconnection'.[77] Paradoxically, 'It was in exactly the period in which human activity was changing the Earth's

---

74 Srnicek and Williams, *Inventing the Future*, 92–98.

75 Gustavo Esteva, Salvatore Babones, and Philipp Babcicky, *The Future of Development: A Radical Manifesto* (Bristol: Policy Press, 2013).

76 Germán Labrador Méndez, 'Las vidas *subprime*: la circulación de historias de vida como tecnología de imaginación política en la crisis española (2007–2012)', *Hispanic Review* 80, no. 4 (2012): 557–581.

77 Alaimo, *Bodily Natures*, 142.

atmosphere that the literary imagination became radically centered on the human', as Amitav Ghosh notes.[78]

In this context 'a major challenge is representational', that is, how to create narratives and stories that make visible the structural 'slow violence' perpetuated by the hegemonic powers.[79] How can we craft counterhegemonic stories in a way that effectively exposes not just the fantasies of unlimited growth ingrained in our dominant imaginary but also other narratives that can be easily co-opted by neoliberal reason to continue promoting its agenda? What kind of narratives and practices can promote an ethics and aesthetics of social and ecological interrelatedness and demonstrate human and nonhuman mutual interdependency, fragility, responsibility, and connectivity? As Bruno Latour puts it, 'The problem of all of us in philosophy, science, or literature becomes: how do we tell such a story?'[80] In the Anthropocene age of unacceptable social inequality and rapid ecological collapse we cannot afford not to embrace 'the challenges of *representing* a concept at once wholly abstract and alarmingly material in aesthetically, rhetorically, and ultimately politically efficacious ways'.[81] We need new stories to counteract the pervasive fantasies of neoliberalism and to expose its social and ecological downsides. It is urgent 'to undiscipline ourselves, free ourselves from our training, and find new narratives to tell about life, literature, and learning, narratives more attuned to the harsh realities of human frailty and less calibrated to the rhythms of late capitalism'.[82] How can we revisit stories about ourselves, our communities, and our relationship to the planet in order to collectively create alternative postgrowth stories we can live by? An environmentally oriented cultural studies has the potential to contribute significantly to this pressing task, but for cultural studies to be able to challenge the ideology of disconnection in a meaningful way, it is paramount, on the one hand, to embrace the environmental humanities and, on the other, to dissect the formation of the dominant cultural authority in order to counteract it.

Given the current dimensions of the ecological crisis, it is disturbing to witness the lack of critical engagement in peninsular cultural studies with environmental issues and with the undeniable feedback loops between

---

78 Amitav Ghosh, *The Great Derangement: Climate Change and the Unthinkable* (Chicago, IL: University of Chicago Press, 2016), 66.

79 Rob Nixon, *Slow Violence and the Environmentalism of the Poor* (Cambridge, MA: Harvard University Press, 2011), 3.

80 Bruno Latour, 'Agency at the Time of the Anthropocene', *New Literary History* 45, no. 1 (2014): 3.

81 Garrard, Handwerk, and Wilke, 'Imagining Anew', 149.

82 Jack Halberstam, 'Unlearning', *Profession* (2012): 12.

cultural modes and socioecological processes. Environmental sociologists John Bellamy Foster, Brett Clark, and Richard York would explain this lack of engagement by pointing out that 'the social sciences and the humanities ... are all characterized to varying degrees by their radical separation from nature'.[83] The humanities have always played a crucial role in the articulation of the anthropological machine and the legitimization and perpetuation of the radical distinction between the human and nonhuman that justifies the dominant economic culture. The advent of the environmental humanities is only now opening the door to let a breath of fresh air into academic contexts (activist and indigenous sciences never closed that door). Cultural studies was born precisely to challenge and revisit ingrained ideological distinctions (within the humanities) about which cultural expressions deserved study and which were to be left out of the curriculum. Since its inception, the field has understood very well that everything that is left out tends to disappear from institutionalized theoretical radars and becomes aesthetically and politically irrelevant in what Jacques Rancière calls the 'distribution of the sensible'.[84] For that reason, cultural studies is well equipped (in contrast to more traditional academic disciplines within the humanities) to challenge the dominant and alienating ideologies of disconnection by resisting the radical separation of humans and the nonhuman in cultural configurations.

I concur with Neil Badmington that we should acknowledge the 'dramatic difference that cultural studies has made to the humanities ... [but, and this is important,] a problem remains ... Although it has sought to break down a series of oppressive barriers, cultural studies has systematically reaffirmed the hierarchical border between the human and the inhuman'.[85] To correct this ingrained deficiency, Badmington goes on to suggest that cultural studies would benefit from embracing posthumanism. This suggestion is not unproblematic, because 'a genuinely *critical* posthumanism ... should resist the seductions of the humanities. If "the human" is no longer a credible category, how can the humanities remain something in which to have faith?'[86] I do not claim to possess the answer to that thought-provoking question, but I am convinced it is worthy of exploration.[87]

83 Foster, Clark, and York, *The Ecological Rift*, 31–32.
84 Jacques Rancière, *The Politics of Aesthetics: The Distribution of the Sensible*, trans. Gabriel Rockhill (London: Continuum, 2012).
85 Neil Badmington, 'Cultural Studies and the Posthumanities', in *New Cultural Studies: Adventures in Theory*, ed. Gary Hall and Clare Birchall (Edinburgh: Edinburgh University Press, 2016), 261–262.
86 Badmington, 'Cultural Studies and the Posthumanities', 264.
87 For an emerging discussion of these issues in the context of contemporary

Along these same lines, Levi Bryant points out that 'ecology is the study of relations and interaction between entities ... Societies are themselves ecologies that are embedded in the broader ecologies of the natural world'.[88] The distinction between nature and society is misleading, since societies are by no means outside of nature: 'Social relations are a type of ecological relations ... Societies are embedded in natural ecologies ... and humans are animals among animals'.[89] According to Bryant, the 'dimension of material flow through social systems is too often ignored by cultural studies ... We entirely ignore the ecology of human societies'.[90] I believe this might be remedied by an ecocritical cultural studies that incorporates ecological economics. I insist that cultural studies—as long as it does not forget its radical origins (think of Raymond Williams's cultural materialism as articulated in *Problems in Materialism and Culture*), and as long as it remains attuned to the current 'material turn' taking place in ecocriticism—is in fine shape to embrace critical posthumanism and be significantly enhanced and transformed by it.[91] For Iberian cultural studies in particular, I believe the current moment is propitious to embrace an ecologically oriented approach, given that an increasing, but still insufficient, number of Iberian cultural scholars began moving along these lines in the last couple of years.[92] Significantly, Jo Labanyi, coauthor of the seminal book that established the field of Spanish cultural studies in 1995, has recently encouraged Spanish cultural scholars to 'study materiality, with reference not just to bodily processes, but also to the material world outside', and to engage with the agency of things in all cultural practices.[93] Labanyi's essay 'Doing Things: Emotion, Affect, and Materiality' implies a call to overcome the ideologies of disconnection that so often infiltrate cultural studies.

Iberian culture see *A Polemical Companion to 'Ethics of Life: Contemporary Iberian Debates'*, *Hispanic Issues On Line* 7 (University of Minnesota, 2016). The co-op conclusion is especially relevant.

88 Levy Bryant, 'Black', in *Prismatic Ecology: Ecotheory beyond Green*, ed. Jeffrey Jerome Cohen (Minneapolis: University of Minnesota Press, 2013), 294.

89 Bryant, 'Black', 294.

90 Bryant, 'Black', 299.

91 Raymond Williams, *Problems in Materialism and Culture* (London: Verso, 1980).

92 See Katarzyna Beilin and William Viestenz, eds., *Ethics of Life: Contemporary Iberian Debates* (Nashville, TN: Vanderbilt University Press, 2016), and Luis I. Prádanos, 'Ecocrítica en los estudios literarios y culturales españoles contemporáneos: una tendencia emergente desesperadamente necesaria', Nuevas tendencias literarias: el autor y su crítica (2000–2015), *La nueva literatura hispánica* 20 (2016): 281–298.

93 Jo Labanyi, 'Doing Things: Emotion, Affect, and Materiality', *Journal of Spanish Cultural Studies* 11, nos. 3–4 (2010): 223–224, 227–228.

New materialisms and material ecocriticism teach us that the flow of material and energy is as important as the circulation of narratives in understanding reality, and that both signs and matter should be considered together. 'All matter, in other words, is "storied matter"'.[94] From a biosemiotic viewpoint, meaning and matter emerge together in all living organisms, and humans are no exception. Ecological economics does an admirable job of focusing on 'social metabolism', that is, 'the entire flow of materials and energy that are required to sustain all human economic activities',[95] and cultural studies is well suited to track the processes of meaning-making involved in the coevolution of material cultures and social imaginaries. This book will converge the two. The concept of social metabolism will be a key analytical tool throughout the book that expresses dimensions of socio-natural inextricable interdependency and allow us to understand economic growth not as an abstract measure of an economy, but as an increase in its material intensification. In other words, the size of the social metabolism indicates the magnitude of the material usage and depletion of a given economic/material culture. The bigger the social metabolism, the more unsustainable it is. An economic culture addicted to growth entails the reproduction of highly entropic and unsustainable social relations and material realities. I believe that material ecocriticism in particular, and the environmental humanities in general, provide an optimal framework for understanding and challenging the dominant imaginary and contributing to the creation of new and liberating postgrowth imaginaries. The study of post-2008 Spanish counterhegemonic cultures from this perspective is one of the main tasks of *Postgrowth Imaginaries*.

I have divided the remainder of this book into three sections followed by a concluding chapter. The first two sections, 'Spanish Culture and Postgrowth Economics' and 'Urban Ecologies', correspond to chapters 1 and 2. The third section, 'Waste, Disaster, Refugees, and Nonhuman Agency', includes chapters 3 and 4.

Chapter 1, 'Towards an Ecocritical Approach to the Spanish Neoliberal Crisis', introduces the main tenets of ecological economics and the degrowth movement, in order to familiarize the reader with these notions. The first part of the chapter provides an overview of the cultural and ecological situation in twenty-first-century Spain, focusing on recent cultural critical responses to the Spanish neoliberal crisis and showing how such critical interventions

94 Serenella Iovino and Serpil Oppermann, eds., *Material Ecocriticism* (Bloomington, IN: Indiana University Press, 2014), 1.

95 Helmut Haberl et al., 'A Socio-Metabolic Transition towards Sustainability? Challenges for Another Great Transformation', *Sustainable Development* 19 (2011): 3.

might be significantly enriched by paying attention to the ongoing ecocritical transnational debate. The next section studies a number of recent Iberian socioecological essays that have adopted a cross-disciplinary perspective to critique the unsustainable social and environmental degradation caused by global capitalism and its addiction to growth. The last part of the chapter makes the case for the value of advancing a degrowth-inspired ecocriticism within a Euro-Mediterranean context. Degrowth provides an alternative to mainstream Euro-American reform environmentalism. The latter is infused with a neoliberal rhetoric, rationality, and sensibility that promote technical fixes to avoid engagement in the social and political changes needed to avert ecological collapse. While degrowthers advocate radical cultural change to achieve environmental justice, reform environmentalism only supports minor modifications to the existing order, such as sustainable development, green growth, and ecological modernization.

Chapter 2, 'Urban Ecocriticism and Spanish Cultural Studies', argues that Spanish urban cultural studies would benefit from incorporating the ecological aspects of cities into its theoretical frameworks and thereby better attune itself to the cultural changes underway in the current context of socially and ecologically unsustainable urban growth machines. I integrate the study of these cultural manifestations into four distinct but non-exclusive categories, according to the way in which the socioecological metabolism of the city is conceived and depicted in relation to both the dominant imaginary of economic growth and its unsustainable energy regime. The suggested interpretative typology and the examples I provide can be enumerated and summarized as follows: (1) The Crisis of the Urban Growth Machine (the documentaries *Sobre ruedas: el sueño del automóvil* by Óscar Clemente and *Mercado de futuros* by Mercedes Álvarez, and the experimental movie *Gente en sitios* by Juan Cavestany); (2) Urban Collapse and Post-Petroleum Futures (*El peso del corazón* by Rosa Montero and *Por si se va la luz* by Lara Moreno); (3) Non-Urban Spaces and Neo-Ruralization: Escaping the Urban Growth Machine? (*Palabras mayores: un viaje por la memoria rural* by Emilio Gancedo and the web series *Libres* by Alex Rodrigo); and (4) Postgrowth Urban Imaginaries: Imagining and Performing Ecopolis (the graphic novel *Memorias de la tierra* by Miguel Brieva, several urban projects and collectives, and short narratives generated by the Transition Town movement).

Chapter 3, 'Non-Human Agency and the Political Ecology of Waste', investigates the recent proliferation of Spanish cultural manifestations that focus on discarded materials and degraded spaces. Objects and processes that the dominant imaginary strives to keep out of sight become the main center of attention. This recentering of focus has a number of aesthetic, semiotic, and political consequences that could be better tracked from a material ecocritical perspective. A material ecocritical reading helps to illuminate what I call 'the political ecology of waste' in these cultural expressions (including *Nunca fue tan hermosa la basura* by philosopher José Luis Pardo, a street mural by Boamistura in Madrid, an installation by Basurama, a song by Sr. Chinarro, a cartoon by Miguel Brieva, and the website consumehastamorir.com). I claim that by foregrounding the agency of the massive waste generated by our linear social metabolism, these cultural manifestations expose neoliberal fantasies and seriously compromise the dominant teleological narratives of progress as unlimited economic growth. This chapter also suggests that an economic system that massively wastes and pillages resources for the sake of constant growth ultimately generates vast surplus populations (disposable humans). Thus, I analyze a prizewinning photograph taken in 2014 by José Palazón featuring African immigrants trapped while scaling the fence that separates Morocco from the Spanish city of Melilla. I argue that the image brilliantly links the fluxes of material and energy, the flow of corporate media discourses, and the human bodies mobilized by economic globalization. Through this imagery, the connection between surplus populations and a wasteful economy becomes clear (other examples include a cartoon by Manel Fontdevila, the film *La jaula de oro* written and directed by Diego Quemada-Díez, and *Interferències*, an interesting and well-researched low-budget audiovisual experiment in Spanish and Catalan).

Chapter 4, 'Disaster Fiction, the Pedagogy of Catastrophe, and the Dominant Imaginary', focuses on catastrophe fiction that explores the disturbing ecological consequences of sudden disruptions caused by extreme environmental events set in motion or exacerbated by growth-oriented activity. In this scenario, rapid anthropogenic changes in the Earth's ecological systems unleash a massive catastrophe at a regional or global level. This kind of fiction has commonly been assumed to have pedagogical implications because it highlights the destructive practices that humanity should abandon and promotes an activist lifestyle. By studying some of the most popular contemporary catastrophe audiovisual narratives in Spain (TV show *El Barco* and Juan Antonio Bayona's movie *The Impossible*), I demonstrate that the pedagogical interpretation of catastrophe should be revisited for several reasons. First, many studies in psychology indicate that creating fear is not effective in mobilizing activism. Second, apocalyptic fiction tends to focus on sensationalist and spectacular effects and the heroic individuals who deal with them, while grossly ignoring the root causes of anthropogenic climate change and environmental injustice. Thus, I claim that catastrophe fiction does not necessarily constitute a good pedagogical tool for shaping an effective political ecology because it perpetuates the current post-political dominant culture rather than contesting the growth logic that exacerbates global—but asymmetrically distributed—environmental risks. Catastrophe-oriented fiction also tends to ignore or, in the worse cases, conceal the pervasive structural violence against humans and the nonhuman resulting from global neoliberal policies and growth economic dynamics (what Rob Nixon calls 'slow violence').[96] In order to encourage an effective political ecology, I argue that other kinds of counterhegemonic narrative are much more effective and resistant to co-optation by the dominant imaginary: stories and projects that envision and perform *desirable* postgrowth imaginaries.

The conclusion, 'The Global Rise of Postgrowth Imaginaries', summarizes the main findings of the book, providing a reflection on the best and worst cultural strategies for challenging the dominant imaginary and creating counterhegemonic practices and narratives. It closes with a call for greater experimentation with cultural practices that move beyond the growth paradigm, as well as a plea to cultural critics to embrace environmental humanities frameworks in order to envision the massive implications of an emerging postgrowth economic culture. *Postgrowth Imaginaries* suggests that the only desirable way to overcome the existential crisis brought on by subscribing to the growth paradigm is to conceive of a socially just and sustainable postgrowth imaginary and to create the conditions necessary for such a society to emerge. *Postgrowth Imaginaries* shows that such a transition is currently well under way in the Iberian Peninsula and, I believe, is also part of an emerging global trend that is crossing all borders. It is my hope that this book will provide useful critical tools to assist in the understanding and promotion of this global cultural transformation.

96 Nixon, *Slow Violence and the Environmentalism of the Poor*, 3.

PART I

Spanish Culture
and Postgrowth Economics

CHAPTER ONE

Towards an Ecocritical Approach to the Spanish Neoliberal Crisis

> The greatest challenge we face is a philosophical one:
> understanding that this civilization is already dead.
> —Roy Scranton[1]

1.1. Cultural Responses to the Spanish Neoliberal Crisis and the Global Ecocritical Turn

On May 15, 2011, a number of protesters assembled improvised camps in symbolic central public spaces in many Spanish cities. This was the beginning of the 15-M (also known as the *indignados*), a massive, decentralized, and nonhierarchical social movement that responded not only to the implementation of socially devastating austerity measures after the global financial crisis, but to several decades of top-down financial and political neoliberalization that has privatized the benefits of economic growth in a few hands and socialized its associated downsides to everyone else.[2] In Spain, the severity of the global financial crisis and the increase in public debt were aggravated by the real estate bubble that had spurred the rapid economic growth of the previous decade. During the decade prior to the crisis, public and private debt was encouraged by all Spanish administrations in the name of growth. After the crisis, the Spanish economy found itself borrowing more to 'rescue the banks' and to pay interest on the debts generated by the previous growth cycle which, in turn, would force the economy to grow faster in the future in order to pay more interest in an infernal spiral of growth and debt. Six years after the 15-M movement, it is

---

1 Roy Scranton, *Learning to Die in the Anthropocene: Reflections on the End of a Civilization* (San Francisco, CA: City Lights, 2015), 23.

2 For more information on the 15-M movement, see http://www.movimiento15m.org/.

time to delve into the emergent Spanish cultural sensibilities that have been gaining visibility and questioning the dominant imaginary of economic growth since that unique historical moment. These new sensibilities are forcing many Spanish literary and cultural scholars to rethink their disciplines. While some cultural critics are discussing relevant issues like multiculturalism, neoliberal biopolitics, socioeconomic degradation, digital culture, and urban processes, the most interesting critical responses reckon with all of these factors holistically and relate them to the root of the crisis: the cultural logic of a socially and environmentally unsustainable growth imaginary.

The most generative interventions targeting the relationship between the economic crisis and Spanish culture are perhaps to be found in three journals' recent special issues: 'La imaginación sostenible: culturas y crisis económica en la España actual', *Hispanic Review* 80, no. 4 (2012); 'Democracia y capitalismo: la función de la cultura', *ALCESXXI* 1 (2013); and 'Spain in Crisis: 15-M and the Culture of Indignation', *Journal of Spanish Cultural Studies* 15, no. 1–2 (2014). In the *ALCESXXI* issue, Antonio Gómez L-Quiñones points out that the two most common responses to the economic crisis by Spanish literary and cultural studies are either silence or a politically correct critique of its symptoms that overlooks the central problem: capitalism.[3] The guest editor of the *Hispanic Review*'s special issue, Luis Moreno-Caballud, draws attention to the many Spanish *procomún* projects that are currently challenging the individualistic and competitive cultural mode of the dominant market-oriented imaginary.[4] The double issue of the *Journal of Spanish Cultural Studies* edited by Bryan Cameron, implicitly correcting the tendency denounced by Gómez L-Quiñones, invites Spanish cultural scholars to investigate the cultural repoliticization of Spain in the wake of the 15-M movement and its challenge to the neoliberal mindset.

All of these contributions (and others), taken together, are opening new avenues of inquiry in the field of contemporary Spanish literary and cultural studies. None, however, engages environmental criticism, and thus a consistent ecocritical approach to Spanish cultural responses to the crisis is still lacking.[5] Almost completely ignored by Spanish cultural

---

3 Antonio Gómez L-Quiñones, 'Aviso para navegantes: la crítica del capitalismo y sus im/posibilidades (Notas para un mapa conceptual de la crisis de 2008)', *ALCES XXI* 1 (2013): 69–73; online at http://alcesxxi.org/revista1/#revista1/page/68-69.

4 Luis Moreno-Caballud, 'La imaginación sostenible: culturas y crisis económica en la España actual', *Hispanic Review* 80 (2012): 535–555.

5 This lack of ecocritical engagement also applies to the most recent critical interventions, such as *Discursos de la crisis: respuestas de la cultura Española ante nuevos desafíos*, eds. Jochen Mecke, Ralf Junker Jürgen, and Hubert Pöppel (Frankfurt:

studies, some of the most persuasive and sophisticated critiques of the economic unfeasibility, social undesirability, and biophysical impossibility of neoliberal globalization in the past decade have been articulated by the environmental humanities. Ecocriticism in particular has been instrumental in pointing out the cultural implications and nuances of the ongoing social and ecological crises brought about by global capitalism. One of the goals of this book is to mobilize these ecocritical tools in order to study important cultural aspects of the ongoing Spanish neoliberal crisis often overlooked by Spanish cultural studies. *Postgrowth Imaginaries* is a systematic attempt to put Spanish cultural studies into fruitful dialogue with the ongoing ecocritical debate and its 'international turn'.[6] Although the majority of ecocriticism produced during the 1990s was Anglo-Saxon and focused on literature, 'since 2000 ecocriticism has greatly expanded its scope' both geographically and theoretically.[7] Especially fruitful has been the convergence of ecocriticism, environmental justice, and postcolonial theory. Ursula Heise points out that

> the ecocritical perspective has always distinguished itself by its interest in how the nonhuman interacts with human culture: how ecological conditions shape cultural expression and, conversely, how culture shapes the perception and uses of natural environments; how cultural communities structure and give meaning to humans' relations with other species; and how risk scenarios, crises, and disasters amplify or reduce sociocultural differences, define community boundaries, and change cultural practices. The question of difference in ecocriticism, in other words, is never purely human. Alterity is always also defined by the nonhuman other.[8]

Serious and sustained attention to the nonhuman can help us better understand the counterhegemonic cultural production that is currently disrupting the dominant culture in Spain.[9] The fusion of animal studies and postcolonial ecocriticism championed by the critical posthumanism of

Vervuert, 2017) and the double issue of *Romance Quarterly* 64, nos. 3–4 (2017) 'Culture, Crisis, and Renewal', ed. Jorge L. Catalá-Carrasco, Manuel de la Fuente, and Pablo Valdivia.

6 Ursula K. Heise, 'Globality, Difference, and the International Turn in Ecocriticism', *PMLA* 128 (2013): 636–643.

7 Heise, 'Globality, Difference, and the International Turn in Ecocriticism', 637.

8 Heise, 'Globality, Difference, and the International Turn in Ecocriticism', 638.

9 See Katarzyna Olga Beilin, *In Search of an Alternative Biopolitics: Anti-Bullfighting, Animality, and the Environment in Contemporary Spain* (Columbus: Ohio State University Press, 2015).

Cary Wolfe shows how institutionalized speciesism can legitimate not just the exploitation of animals, but anyone considered non-properly human by the 'anthropological machine' theorized by Agamben.[10] Through this posthumanist lens we can grasp not only the 'connection between the exploitation of animals and colonial oppression', but also the link between the human/nonhuman divide historically iterated by the anthropological machine and its many justifications for social injustice and inequality.[11] It seems that a closer look at the cultural dynamics that normalize the massive exploitation of humanity and the nonhuman is today more critical than ever, for the Anthropocene must come to terms with the widest global gap between rich and poor ever seen.

1.1.1. Social and Ecological Context
A bird's-eye view of the current socioecological situation of Spain can help to explain why the ecocritical approach is so urgent. The explosive socioeconomic situation in Spain is widely acknowledged, and studies dealing with the cultural changes spurred by this situation have proliferated. One of the most comprehensive explorations of culture in the context of the Spanish neoliberal crisis, Moreno-Caballud's *Cultures of Anyone: Studies on Cultural Democratization in the Spanish Neoliberal Crisis*, begins with an enumeration of social problems:

> The Spanish state, 2008–May 2015: unemployment rates approach 25%, and 50% among young people. Eight million living in poverty, according to official figures. The second highest rate of childhood malnutrition in Europe. The highest rise in economic inequality of all states in the OECD. Some 3 million empty homes and about 184 families evicted from their homes every day.[12]

But the ecological situation of Spain and its relation to the cultural dominant imaginary that generates these social problems is only rarely brought to the forefront, when it is not ignored completely. The problem is that, as discussed earlier, ecocriticism has never been consistently embraced by Spanish literary and cultural studies. Significant underground ecological cultures are not lacking in Spain, as I will show later in this chapter, but they have remained invisible to Spanish cultural criticism and have no place in the dominant social imaginary. Fortunately, during the last couple of years a small group of scholars have turned their attention to this gap

---

10 Wolfe, *What Is Posthumanism?*
11 Heise, 'Globality, Difference, and the International Turn in Ecocriticism', 640.
12 Moreno-Caballud, *Cultures of Anyone*, 1.

and the focus of cultural criticism is gradually expanding to include the importance of sustaining the social reproduction of life and collective care for vulnerable bodies privatized or ignored by neoliberalism. The best examples are perhaps the collected volume *Ethics of Life: Contemporary Iberian Debates* edited by Kata Beilin and William Viestenz, published in late 2016, and Beilin's *In Search of an Alternative Biopolitics: Anti-Bullfighting, Animality, and the Environment in Contemporary Spain* (2015). Other important critical interventions explore similar issues without fully mobilizing the analytical tools provided by the environmental humanities. For example, Moreno-Caballud's *Cultures of Anyone*, very much influenced by feminist economic theories, demonstrates how neoclassical economics' commitment to the reproduction of impersonal capital results in an unavoidable displacement of the reproduction of life. Two recent works by Germán Labrador Méndez also highlight the bodily nature, material as well as symbolic, of the crisis by tracing the circulation of vulnerable individuals' 'subprime stories' and the circulation of meat proteins and discourses during the crisis.[13] A recent collection of essays titled *La imaginación hipotecada* opens with four exposés on capitalist economy and its ecological unsustainability.[14] Jo Labanyi and Georgina Dopico Black have recently invited Spanish cultural scholars to 'explore the entanglements of the human with the material' and the nonhuman.[15] And finally, a 2017 special issue of *Letras Hispanas* on 'Contemporary Iberian Ecocriticism and New Materialisms' includes ten essays on the topic.

The alarming fact is that Spain today is one of the most unsustainable countries on Earth, with an ecological footprint that is three and a half times larger than its territorial biocapacity.[16] In other words, the country is both rapidly depleting its own ecological wealth and exploiting the ecological space of other regions, ignoring all the while the ethical and economic implications of its actions. Moreover, Spanish energy dependency on imported fossil fuels is extremely high—one of the highest in the European Union, which already has a geopolitical problem due to its high dependency

13 Germán Labrador Méndez, 'Las vidas *subprime*'; idem, 'The Cannibal Wave: The Cultural Logics of Spain's Temporality of Crisis (Revolution, Biopolitics, Hunger and Memory)', *Journal of Spanish Cultural Studies* 15, nos. 1–2 (2014): 241–271.

14 Palmar Álvarez-Blanco and Antonio Gómez L-Quiñones, eds., *La imaginación hipotecada: aportaciones al debate sobre la precariedad del presente* (Madrid: Libros en acción, 2016).

15 Jo Labanyi, 'Doing Things: Emotion, Affect, and Materiality', 223; Georgina Dopico Black, 'The Ban and the Bull: Cultural Studies, Animal Studies, and Spain', *Journal of Spanish Cultural Studies* 11, nos. 3–4 (2010): 235–249.

16 Becerra Mayor et al., *Qué hacemos con la literatura*, 10.

on foreign energy sources. In addition, current transportation plans and strategies in Spain, according to a study conducted by Bermejo Gómez de Segura, appear delusional when measured against the global energy crisis in general and Spain's dependence on foreign energy in particular.[17]

Under capitalism, economic growth, abundant and cheap energy, and ecological depletion go hand in hand. The reality, recognized by many economists, is that economic stagnation in advanced economies—with the exception of some counterproductive bubbles—has been the norm since the 1970s; the previous impressive growth of 'The Glorious Thirty' was only possible thanks to the availability of cheap and abundant oil (and also uncommodified land). Global fossil fuel peak and other crucial materials and energy peaks are already well known to researchers. Even the techno-optimist International Energy Agency acknowledges these realities in its 2015 report, predicting a global fossil fuel peak by 2020, although the peak of conventional fossil fuel probably began in 2006.[18] In this context, the problem is not simply that the price of importing fossil fuels is expected to rise from now on, but that their supply could be limited by increasing global demand during a time of shrinking oil production—not an encouraging scenario for a net importer of fossil fuels like Spain. Without abundant energy or raw materials to capitalize on, there is no foreseeable economic growth, so lack of growth in Spain is likely to be the norm in the near future. Spain is also one of the 30 countries suffering the greatest hydric stress, ranking second in Europe.[19] Since Francoist times Spain has never properly faced this problem and has only made it worse by attacking its symptoms; the nation's strategy has been limited to constructing dams and transferring water from one region to another within a growth and consumerist model that continually increases demand while wasting water on a vast scale. Because of Spain's geographical position, climate change is already seriously affecting the country and most of its territory is expected to suffer from moderate to severe droughts in the near future, causing massive fires, crop failures, water shortages, and massive desertification, among other problems.

The future lack of fertile soil, water, and cheap fossil fuels will greatly affect agriculture in Spain. The rapid modernization of agriculture over

17 Roberto Bermejo Gómez de Segura, 'La política de transporte española ante el fin de la era de los combustibles fósiles', in *Economía ecológica: reflexiones y perspectivas*, ed. Santiago Álvarez Cantalapiedra and Óscar Carpintero (Madrid: CBA, 2009), 77–124.

18 International Energy Agency, World Energy Outlook 2016, www.iea.org.

19 Joaquim Elchacho, 'España, incluida en la lista de países con más problemas de agua del mundo', *La Vanguardia*, September 2, 2015.

the last half-century included the reduction of biodiverse crops in favor of a few intensive and extensive monocrops produced for export. Not only has this shift required the adoption of agro-industrial models that require massive fossil fuel inputs, it has also undermined food sovereignty and communitarian resilience and provoked a massive displacement of people from rural to urban areas. This agrarian transformation began under Franco and continued when Spain adopted European agrarian policies after entering the European Union. The current agro-industrial model favors large corporations that control the food supply and force small and medium-sized farms out of business. This rapid upscaling of agriculture has had staggering cultural and social consequences that have already been analyzed by Spanish literary and cultural scholars, and ecological ones, such as the massive reduction of agrarian biodiversity (we have lost 75 percent of it in the last few decades), the acceleration of soil erosion, the creation of a food system dependent on huge amounts of irrigation and fossil fuels, and persistent chemical pollution in the soil, water, and air.

Because of its proximity to Africa, Spain will also be disproportionally affected by the ongoing displacement of environmental refugees moving north. The most disturbing fact is that rather than preparing for what seems to be a disruptive socioecological future, the Spanish government is doing the opposite by dismantling existing environmental legislation in an already deficient national environmental legal framework, even as the European Union is pressuring the government to correct the situation. Instead, Spain is implementing laws that are clearly anti-ecological, undermining communitarian socioecological resilience; constructing vast, unnecessary infrastructures completely dependent on fossil fuels; and openly embracing a neoliberal urban model that exacerbates all the aforementioned problems.

Spain is, as I write, one of the European Union countries charged with the greatest number of environmental infractions. Its neoconservative administration (under the Partido Popular) has recently created legal insecurity in relation to renewable energy that incentivizes disinvestment in the sector and undermines ongoing projects. In summer 2013 the Spanish government approved an energy reform that has been loudly rejected by most environmental organizations because it does not support renewable energies but rather benefits large corporations and promotes the continuation of Spanish energy dependency on imported fossil fuels, creating obstacles to energy self-production. The perversity and ridiculousness of this law and its outcomes have also been criticized by international media outlets: 'Storing solar energy in a battery in Spain is more criminal than spilling radioactive waste. That's the implied message written between the lines of a recently drafted law poised for fast-track approval by the government of Spain'.[20] In 2015, Spain increased its reliance on coal for the generation of electricity by 23 percent and reduced its use of renewable energy.[21] Given the energy situation in Spain and the current state of peak oil and climate change acceleration, these reforms seem to condemn Spaniards to an unsustainable economic, social, and environmental future. Another environmentally retrograde action taken by the government was to discontinue the funding of the Observatorio de la Sostenibilidad en España (OSE), the main institution overseeing the study of Spanish sustainability. As a result, the OSE closed in May 2013 (although it reopened in December 2014). Furthermore, '90 percent of European agricultural GMOs are produced in Spain'.[22]

During the liberalization of the Spanish economy (from roughly 1950 to the present), the social metabolism of Spain (the flow of materials and energy mobilized by its economic activity) has changed dramatically, from one based on renewable sources mostly within the limits of its own territorial biocapacity to the unsustainable one described above. Óscar Carpintero completed an exhaustive study on the metabolism of the Spanish economy during the second half of the twentieth century and concluded that Spain rapidly increased its material and energy intensities, importing much more than it exports and rapidly degrading the ecological services of ecosystems within its territory.[23] The Spanish economy is not dematerializing at all—that is, it is not reducing the amount of energy and materials required to grow the economy, as predicted by the environmental Kuznets curve. The Kuznets model suggests that the ecological footprint of postindustrial countries will not continue to grow unchecked but will decrease after reaching a peak. But the Kuznets model does not take into account the impact of postindustrial economies on the ecological spaces of other regions. Advanced economies do not dematerialize, rather they externalize somewhere else the vast environmental degradation resulting from their consumerist lifestyles.

20 Aisha Abdelhamid, 'In Spain, Solar Energy Storage Is Worse than Nuclear Spillage', *PlanetSavet*, June 18, 2015, http://planetsave.com/2015/06/18/in-spain-solar-energy-storage-is-worse-than-nuclear-spillage/.

21 Red Eléctrica de España, 'Estadística diaria del sistema eléctrico español peninsular', December 30, 2015, http://www.ree.es/es/balance-diario/peninsula/2015/12/30.

22 Katarzyna Beilin and William Viestenz, eds., *Ethics of Life: Contemporary Iberian Debates* (Nashville, TN: Vanderbilt University Press, 2016), xvi.

23 Óscar Carpintero, *El metabolismo de la economía española: recursos naturales y huella ecológica (1955–2000)* (Lanzarote: Fundación César Manrique, 2005).

To understand all the cultural changes in Spain in the last few decades it is necessary to relate them to the material and symbolic changes brought about by these ongoing socioecological transformations. In the context of the Anthropocene, these ecological issues will not only shape future cultural sensibilities in Spain, but they will also condition material, social, and political possibilities within Spanish territory. Ignoring these dangerous trends may seriously undermine the potentialities of our political imagination.

The widely praised Spanish modernization (equated with economic growth, cultural consumerism, and the proliferation of tourist infrastructures and monocrops) is responsible for a massive ecological degradation that will compromise the well-being of Spaniards for centuries. However, this growth was not something that average Spaniards either chose to pursue or truly benefited from. GDP growth under neoliberal policies tends to result in higher rates of criminality and health problems, increased inequality, social erosion and fragmentation, environmental degradation, and, in some cases, a loss of purchasing power by the majority of the local population. Indeed, such was the case in Spain during the years of rapid growth that preceded and exacerbated the financial crisis. Corporate mass media and the majority of the people uncritically celebrated this phenomenon, known internationally as the 'Spanish economic miracle'. However, during those years (1995–2005), the average Spanish salary lost 4 percent of its purchasing power and the environment was depleted on an unprecedented scale.[24] Capitalist accumulation did not recede during the ongoing financial crisis, it accelerated. According to *eldiario.es*, 'El número de multimillonarios en España aumenta un 44% desde 2011' [Since 2011 the number of multimillionaires in Spain increased by 44 percent].[25] Thus, capital accumulation can continue without economic growth through dispossession and redistribution from labor to capital. But this capitalism without growth becomes more socially and politically unstable.[26] This explains the rise of far-right populisms and aggressive nationalisms in Europe.

Capitalist economic expansion is always a story of dispossession, ecological deterioration, social corrosion, and the extermination of cultural and biological diversity somewhere. It is essential that cultural critics

24 Ignacio Escolar, 'La generación estafada', in *Reacciona*, ed. Rosa María Artal (Madrid: Santillana, 2011), 117.

25 *Eldiario.es*, 'El número de multimillonarios en España aumenta un 44% desde 2011', September 10, 2016, http://www.eldiario.es/economia/numero-multi millonarios-Espana-aumenta_0_557144596.html.

26 Giorgos Kallis, *In Defense of Degrowth: Opinions and Minifestos*, ed. Aaron Vansintjan (Brussels: Uneven Earth Press, 2017), 87–88.

develop the habit of systemically tracking these links in order to make sense of the cultural processes behind them. The problem is that in Spain before the crisis, the downsides of economic growth were not readily visible in corporate media, nor were they fully detected by the academic radars of cultural scholars (often pointed at cultural *objects* rather than systemic *relations* and processes), especially when the dominant cultural imaginary confused growth with progress and elevated both to teleological mandates to achieve a manifest national destiny. Now, in post-2008 Spain, the downsides of neoliberal excesses are more obvious than ever before. The tricky part is to avoid the temptation to think that, before 2008, things were somehow different and that Spaniards should thus channel all their political energy towards demanding a return to the so-called 'welfare state' without changing the rules of the game. Feminist economist Amaia Pérez Orozco compellingly recommends staying away from this counterproductive temptation, not only because the welfare state was a historical and localized exception within the capitalist system, but because the conflict between life reproduction and capital accumulation inherent in capitalism is also present in the welfare state, and hence that system of social reproduction is dependent on the same disastrous growth imaginary.[27] In other words, Pérez Orozco rightly points out that the welfare state cannot be universalized (indeed, if all regions of the planet had the ecological footprint of Spain, we would need the ecological resources of several planets) and in fact may not be socially desirable after all, since it never properly dealt with the contradictions of capitalism and its addiction to growth and inequality and the illegitimate origins of wealth accumulated by the so-called '1 percent' (especially in the aftermath of the civil war and the Franco regime). The politics of the welfare state were not really politics as such, since it never questioned or debated its unsustainable model of growth or the socioecological consequences of that model. The great appeal of the welfare state was that it managed to create a fragile illusion of collective (but asymmetrically distributed) prosperity and well-being by hiding or disguising its downsides within its national borders (under a paternalistically subsidized and depoliticized social system dependent on growth), while externalizing to peripheral regions the worst social and ecological impacts of constant economic growth.

It seems to me that in order to overcome all these accumulating socioecological problems, a radical political culture in Spain and beyond must demand nothing less than a postgrowth society that finally comes

27 Amaia Pérez Orozco, *Subversión feminista de la economía: aportes para un debate sobre el conflicto capital-vida* (Madrid: Traficantes de sueños, 2014), 264.

to terms with the iterative historical wrongdoings of the anthropological machine. This entails articulating a revolutionary political ecology that demands a just society with a sustainable metabolism. These two goals— social justice and sustainability—go hand in hand and can only be achieved in conjunction. To create the conditions propitious to such a radical political culture, it is paramount to envision new imaginaries in which humans are not reduced to individual economic actors, societies are not conceived as factories for economic growth, and the natural environment is not artificially separated from—and instrumentalized by—human socioeconomic systems that reduce everything to a resource to be exploited by the growth machine.

1.1.2. Culture of Transition and Culture of Crisis: Historical Iterations of the Growth Imaginary in Spain

Where did the present cultural imaginary come from? The dominant cultural reading of the Spanish transition to democracy, which Guillem Martínez refers to and criticizes as the Culture of Transition (Cultura de la Transición, CT), has functioned as a baseline to ingrain and naturalize the imaginary of economic growth in Spain.[28] The CT is, more than anything else, the hegemonic culture of growth. Isidro López clearly explains this in his essay '*Consensonomics*: la ideología económica en la CT'.[29] The CT is nothing but the Spanish version of the cultural hegemony of global capitalism. As such, CT implies the wholehearted acceptance of the cultural values and worldviews of a specific group, neoliberal capitalists, and the organization of Spanish society according to those values. The CT rendered invisible the historical construction of the hegemonic values and normalizes the institutionalized order of things created by them. The term 'Culture of Transition' is an invaluable critical addition because, in naming it, we invoke what the hegemony hides: its engineered nature. When we talk about CT, we are able to conceptualize the cultural, intellectual, and symbolic mesh formed by the dominant imaginary that infiltrated every aspect of Spanish reality.

Although the CT was an invisible semiotic regime for many cultural scholars before it was discursively articulated, it has long been the agent of massive socioecological consequences that restrict and direct the limits of the possible, the doable, and the thinkable. Fortunately, since 2011, the

---

28 Guillem Martínez, 'El concepto CT', in *CT o la Cultura de la Transición: crítica a 35 años de cultura española*, ed. Guillem Martínez (Barcelona: Mondadori, 2012), 13–23.

29 Isidro López, '*Consensonomics*: la ideología económica en la CT', in *CT o la Cultura de la Transición: crítica a 35 años de cultura española*, ed. Guillem Martínez (Barcelona: Mondadori, 2012), 77–88.

growing challenge to the CT has revisited and exposed the myths of the grand narrative of the Spanish transition as a long-desired and exemplary path to the country's normalization, modernization, and Europeanization (supposedly consensual and desired by most Spaniards) after the end of the dictatorship. This cultural narrative ignores the connections and continuities between the elites favored by Franco's regime and the economic and financial actors who benefited from the subsequent Spanish neoliberalization that resulted in the financial crisis. It has been proven that this dominant reading of the transition imposed itself over other narratives constructed to make sense of the Spanish transition (obviating the imposed continuity with Franco's economic regime, the extermination of rural cultures, and the forced cultural depolitization orchestrated by elites committed to a global project of neoliberalization), and how it rendered invisible other cultural sensibilities of the time that did not match the preferred cultural narrative. These 'disnarrated'[30] cultural modes are heterogeneous and have been identified by several cultural scholars. The most comprehensive and interesting example is arguably Germán Labrador Méndez's recent book *Culpables por la literatura. Imaginación política y contracultura en la transición española (1968–1986)*.[31] Graham and Labanyi's reclamation of the many potential modernities and Moreno-Caballud's 'arrested modernities' are other, less elaborated, examples.[32]

It seems to me that something similar was happening after 2008 in what we could call the 'Culture of Crisis' in Spain. The supposedly consensual grand narrative of the Culture of Crisis was that we all desire and need to get back to the rapid economic growth that made Spain the modern European country it was always destined to be (and elevated it to become the eighth-largest economic power in the world!). This hegemonic reading of the crisis ignores and silences other cultural narratives that are actively challenging the hegemonic Culture of Crisis, especially following the 15-M movement. I intend to push this exploration further by demonstrating the political ecology inherent in these countercultural responses, which is critical to understanding their subversive and transformative potential. The convergence of challenges to the dominant reading of both the Spanish democratic transition (and therefore the institutional system that arises from it) and of the crisis of 2008 contributes to the erosion of the growth

30 Gerald Prince, 'The Disnarrated', *Style* 22 (1988): 1–8.

31 Germán Labrador Méndez, *Culpables por la literatura. Imaginación política y contracultura en la transición española (1968–1986)* (Madrid: Akal, 2017).

32 Helen Graham and Jo Labanyi, 'Culture and Modernity: The Case of Spain', in *Spanish Cultural Studies: An Introduction*, ed. Helen Graham and Jo Labanyi (Oxford: Oxford University Press, 1995), 8; Moreno-Caballud, *Cultures of Anyone*, 105–112.

imaginary that is inherently taken for granted by these readings (namely, that the prefabricated consensus in both cases was about the desire of growing without ever asking why and what for). For the CT, democracy means fully immersing ourselves in growth-oriented, competitive, consumerist, European neoliberalism: an optimum transition to democracy is one that facilitates economic growth. On the other hand, for the Culture of Crisis, the current malaise is attributed to the lack of growth, and thus the optimum transition to a (normalized) non-crisis scenario is one that facilitates the return of economic growth.

It is not a coincidence that the Culture of Transition has only been widely challenged at the moment of an economic meltdown; after all, it was never really intended as a political transition to democracy, but as an economic and cultural transition to a post-political growth-oriented system of social reproduction orchestrated by elites. My main concern is that the much-needed critique of the CT that has rapidly cohered over the past few years in Spain still ignores what could be its best theoretical ally in moving beyond the hegemonic imaginary: namely, the biophysical impossibility of the neoliberal project. Of the 17 essays in the collection that popularized the term CT, *CT o la Cultura de la Transición* (2012),[33] not one seriously engages with the ecological crisis. Words such as 'environment' or 'ecological sustainability' occasionally appear as afterthoughts and are never part of the main discussion. It is reasonable to hope that the counterhegemonic cultural sensibilities emerging in the past few years are the beginnings of more radical cultural transformations that will spread as the dominant imaginary of economic growth and its cultural mutations becomes more and more socially and ecologically difficult to maintain. As cultural critics, we cannot afford to ignore these game-changing processes for they have the potential to radically transform our cultural ecology in the near future.

1.1.3. Post-Development: Towards a Decolonial Spanish Cultural Approach

Unavoidable ecological limits are increasingly difficult to ignore, not only in the Iberian Peninsula, but across the globe. Thus, the alternative postgrowth imaginaries supported and envisioned by some of the cultural productions to be studied in this book should be understood as examples of an ongoing global articulation of decolonial logics and epistemologies that challenge the economic, social, legal, cultural, political, ecological, and epistemological violence fostered by the capitalist project. This diversity

33 Guillem Martínez, ed., *CT o la Cultura de la Transición: crítica a 35 años de cultura española* (Barcelona: Mondadori, 2012).

of alternative logics is part of the 'ecology of knowledges'[34] or 'plural landscape of knowledge forms'[35] that have been denigrated, subalternized, and silenced by colonial and neocolonial hegemonic powers. Global capitalism destroys not only biodiversity but epistemological diversity as well. As Michel Serres notes, in addition to the hard pollution produced by neoliberal globalization, there is also a soft, semiotic pollution that affects our minds.[36] This mental pollution is disseminated globally by corporate media, financial institutions, neoliberal think tanks, political discourses, and intellectual authorities in order to convince people around the Earth that all non-market-oriented, communitarian, and self-sustained ways of thinking and living should be discounted. Although the negative socioenvironmental consequences of this mental pollution are geopolitically asymmetrical, the effects are global, with the global South suffering the biophysical (and psychological) consequences disproportionately. As Boaventura de Sousa Santos explains, 'A vast array of conceptions, theories, arguments ... produced in the West by recognized intellectual figures, were discarded, marginalized or ignored because they did not fit the political objectives of capitalism and colonialism at the roots of Western modernity'.[37] And if well-known intellectual figures were discounted, we can only imagine how easily less-recognized individuals and communities were excluded from the meaning-making process, as Moreno-Caballud so compellingly shows regarding the recent cultural history of Spain.[38] Both the Culture of Transition and the Culture of Crisis can be understood as Spanish versions of this global historical capitalist project that suppresses cultural and cognitive diversity. This is what Walter Mignolo means when he identifies local histories everywhere as conditioned by the global designs of capitalism and colonialism.[39]

At present, postcolonial ecocriticism, according to Ursula Heise, 'tends to see local places as traversed and reshaped by transnational vectors of power'.[40] According to Santos, 'there is no global social justice without

---

34 Boaventura de Sousa Santos, 'A Non-Occidentalist West? Learned Ignorance and Ecology of Knowledge', *Theory, Culture & Society* 26, nos. 7–8 (2009): 116.

35 Arturo Escobar, 'Development, Violence and the New Imperial Order', *Development* 47, no. 1 (2004): 17.

36 Michel Serres, *Malfeasance: Appropriation through Pollution?*, trans. Anne-Marie Feenberg-Dibon (Stanford, CA: Stanford University Press, 2011), 37–89.

37 Santos, 'A Non-Occidentalist West', 103.

38 Moreno-Caballud, *Cultures of Anyone*.

39 Walter D. Mignolo, *Local Histories/Global Designs: Coloniality, Subaltern Knowledge, and Border Thinking* (Princeton, NJ: Princeton University Press, 2000).

40 Heise, 'Globality, Difference, and the International Turn in Ecocriticism', 639.

global cognitive justice', which is why it is so important to recognize and make visible the cultural, aesthetic, and symbolic expressions that challenge the epistemological monologic of the dominant imaginary.[41] Indeed, the 'denial of diversity is a constitutive and persistent feature of colonialism. While the political dimension of colonial intervention has been widely criticized, the burden of the colonial epistemic monoculture is accepted nowadays as a symbol of development and modernity'.[42] In other words, the obsolete and simplistic view that portrays Spain as a former colonizer with a nostalgic low self-esteem due to its loss of status as a colonial power may have prevented cultural historians from paying closer attention to the colonial dynamic playing out within Spain.[43] This is why decolonizing the dominant imaginary is the task not only of neo-colonies and ex-colonies, but of everyone affected by the semiotic pollution of capitalist logic.[44]

The recurrent discourse of a Spain that constantly needs to catch up and modernize to remain at the level of other Western powers is not very different from the process, well researched by postcolonial scholars, of epistemological (and financial) dependency that convinced ex-colonial regions to embrace the reasoning of their oppressors (Euromimesis, internal colonization, neoliberal policies, and free trade agreements), no matter how devastating it proved to be for their cultural self-esteem, food sovereignty, economic independence, social well-being, and ecological health. Spain should apply to itself some of the recent environmental postcolonial theories, such as the critique of development advanced by post-development theorists. Understanding these internal neocolonial processes might allow for a fresh reading of the Spanish historical construction of the dominant imaginary of economic growth. For example, we might interpret the Spanish cultural acceptance of Franco's *desarrollismo* and the subsequent Culture of Transition's neoliberalism not as a debated political choice that never was, but as belonging to a continuing process of internal epistemological colonization linked to the transnational project of global capitalist expansion in which alternative

41 Boaventura de Sousa Santos, ed., *Another Knowledge Is Possible: Beyond Northern Epistemologies* (London: Verso, 2008), xix.

42 Santos, *Another Knowledge Is Possible*, xxxiii.

43 Joseba Gabilondo has rightly insisted for years on the need for postcolonial theory and Iberian studies to converge.

44 Luis I. Prádanos, 'Decolonizing the North, Decolonizing the South: De-growth, Post-development, and their Cultural Representations in Spain and Latin America', in *Transatlantic Landscapes: Environmental Awareness, Literature, and the Arts*, ed. José Manuel Marrero Henríquez (Alcalá de Henares: Universidad de Alcalá, 2016), 49–70.

political cultures without a growth-oriented scheme were symbolically displaced and materially exterminated. As such, decolonizing the dominant imaginary of economic growth would be the *sine qua non* of any transformative cultural repoliticization, and therefore the appropriate task of cultural studies 'as a theoretical field still capable of articulating emancipatory projects'.[45]

The concept of post-development as articulated by some Latin American scholars and activists, such as Arturo Escobar, Gustavo Esteva, and Alberto Acosta, reminds us that the idea of development (and underdevelopment) is a Eurocentric construction promoted by neocolonial powers in order to expand their markets to procure cheap raw materials and labor. The model of economic growth that propels colonial ventures has always had huge negative ecological and social impacts on the so-called 'underdeveloped' countries as well as on the lower classes of 'developed' ones.[46] Furthermore, the globalization of that economic system is responsible for the ongoing and accelerating decline of most of the living systems of the planet. Global capitalism is, from this standpoint, an ideology founded on the mass destruction of biological and cultural diversity. 'Developed' countries are not a model to follow, since they are nothing but energy vampires with disproportionate ecological footprints that squeeze, destroy, and appropriate the ecological space of the planet. They prevent the rest of the biotic community (humanity and the nonhuman) from getting what they need to survive, while simultaneously unbalancing the cycle of nutrients in global ecological systems.[47] As Gustavo Esteva observed, development means accepting a universal definition of the good life that is both undesirable and unviable.[48] As such, radical political cultures tend to contest the prefabricated definition of the good life as a function of economic growth and promote the public discussion about what a good life for all would look like on a finite planet.

Post-development theorists are exposing the ways in which the organizations that encourage globalization promote a neoliberal agenda that only benefits a minority of the global population[49] while harming

45 Bryan Cameron, 'Spain in Crisis: 15-M and the Culture of Indignation', *Journal of Spanish Cultural Studies* 15, nos. 1–2 (2014): 1–11.

46 Arturo Escobar, *La invención del tercer mundo: construcción y deconstrucción del desarrollo* (Bogotá: Norma, 2006), 397–424.

47 Jason W. Moore, 'Environmental Crises and the Metabolic Rift in World-Historical Perspective', *Organization & Environment* 13, no. 2 (2000): 123–157.

48 Gustavo Esteva, 'Más allá del desarrollo: la buena vida', *América Latina en movimiento. La agonía de un mito: ¿cómo reformular el 'desarrollo'?* 445 (June 2009): 3.

49 Esteva, Babones, and Babcicky, *The Future of Development*, 27–48.

the regions they are 'developing'.[50] The World Bank, for instance, is one of many nondemocratic institutions that promotes globalization. Its mission statement says (ironically) that its main goal is to reduce poverty by helping 'underdeveloped countries' develop. But on most occasions, when the World Bank actively intervenes, the results are extreme environmental destruction, social degradation, precariousness, and enormous debt.[51] Interestingly enough, Southern European countries today are receiving the same neoliberal medicine—structural adjustment programs—from the troika (the European Commission, the European Central Bank, and the International Monetary Fund) that was previously prescribed for the global South in the second half of the twentieth century. In all cases, the justification is the need to grow the economy in order to pay the interest on national debt, most of which was incurred without democratic control either in the pursuit of growth or to fix some of its externalities. That is, in order to feed the voracious appetite of a shrinking global North, the global South needs to expand to include Euro-Mediterranean countries. On a finite planet, for the rich to get richer, more and more people need to be impoverished. The majority of the population of Spain, Italy, and Greece are now suffering from similar 'structural adjustments' that decades ago condemned many Latin American countries to chronic poverty, violence, and inequality. As Arturo Escobar notes, it is astonishing to observe the developers' and Eurocentric thinkers' incapacity to imagine a world without or beyond development.[52] Using a post-development perspective, it is not difficult to see in contemporary Spain many of the cultural dynamics frequently found in colonized regions (discounting, of course, Spanish-based corporations still extracting ecologically sensitive resources from Latin America or grossly exploiting labor in Asia).

Two aspects of this neocolonial dynamic pointed out by post-development scholars deserve closer attention in relation to the culture of Spain. The first is the dispossession and elimination of common rights and collective knowledge encouraged by Franco's *desarrollismo* and continued by the neoliberal project of the Culture of Transition, and the second is the imposition of a universal definition of the good life that is neither desirable nor viable. The latter is skillfully examined by Eugenia Afinoguénova in

---

50 Escobar, *La invención del tercer mundo*, 397–399.

51 Carlo Petrini, *Slow Food Nation: Why our Food Should Be Good, Clean, and Fair*, trans. Clara Furlan and Jonathan Hunt (New York: Rizzoli, 2007), 110–113.

52 Arturo Escobar, 'El "postdesarrollo" como concepto y práctica social', in *Políticas, ambiente y sociedad en tiempos de globalización*, ed. Daniel Mato (Caracas: Universidad Central de Venezuela, 2005), 30.

relation to the tourist industry emerging during Franco's regime.[53] Both of these processes—the exclusion of other logics and the universal definition of the good life—are related to the advance of the hegemonic growth imaginary and its cruel optimism, and are challenged by current alternative cultural sensibilities that are envisioning a postgrowth imaginary and fostering debates about collective rights and the good life that were absent from the CT. Of course, new imaginaries are never really new. Rather, they re-emerge in different fashions from the renewed, reinvented, and redescribed memories and practices of the modernities that were displaced and disnarrated by the dominant story of petromodernity. If we are willing to listen to their whispers—overpowered by the shouted repetition of the fantasies of endless growth—they remind us that, in Bruno Latour's words, 'we have never been modern' in the purely hegemonic sense of the dominant imaginary.[54] The human exceptionalism that resulted from the human/nonhuman and society/nature hierarchical divisions, which justifies all colonial, capitalist, individualist, patriarchal, anthropocentric, and neoliberal fantasies, is an unsustainable illusion with devastating material consequences. For the longer and more convincingly we maintain it, the more easily and dramatically it collapses, rendering more visible the systemic human dependency on the more-than-human agency that capitalism denies. As Donna Haraway so beautifully notes, 'we have never been human' in an individualistic, independent, and hubristic neoclassical economic way:

> I love the fact that human genomes can be found in only about 10 percent of all the cells that occupy the mundane space I call my body; the other 90 percent of the cells are filled with the genomes of bacteria, fungi, protists, and such, some of which play in a symphony necessary to my being alive at all ... I am vastly outnumbered by my tiny companions; better put, I become an adult human being in company with these tiny messmates. To be one is always to *become with* many.[55]

53 Eugenia Afinoguénova, 'Tourism and "Quality of Life" at the End of Franco's Dictatorship', in *Ethics of Life: Contemporary Iberian Debates*, ed. Katarzyna Beilin and William Viestenz (Nashville, TN: Vanderbilt University Press, 2016), 59–87.

54 Bruno Latour, *We Have Never Been Modern*, trans. Catherine Porter (Cambridge, MA: Harvard University Press, 1993).

55 Donna Haraway, *When Species Meet* (Minneapolis: University of Minnesota Press, 2008), 3–4.

1.2. Spanish Ecocriticism and Ecological Economics: A Great Duet

On Saturday March 5, 2011, the Spanish *Boletín Oficial del Estado* published the Law on Sustainable Economy (LES). The second article of the document provides a definition of sustainable economy:

> A los efectos de la presente Ley, se entiende por economía sostenible un patrón de crecimiento que concilie el desarrollo económico, social y ambiental en una economía productiva y competitiva, que favorezca el empleo de calidad, la igualdad de oportunidades y la cohesión social, y que garantice el respeto ambiental y el uso racional de los recursos naturales, de forma que permita satisfacer las necesidades de las generaciones presentes sin comprometer las posibilidades de las generaciones futuras para atender sus propias necesidades.

> [For the purposes of the present Law, a sustainable economy is to be understood as a pattern of growth that reconciles economic, social, and environmental development in a productive and competitive economy that favors quality employment, equal opportunity, and social cohesion, and that guarantees environmental respect and a rational use of natural resources in a way that permits the satisfaction of the needs of present generations without compromising the means of future generations to fulfill their own needs][56]

The entire document is an implicit declaration of neoliberal principles that, with some adjustments, were equally embraced by all the major traditional Spanish political parties regardless of their political colors. The document is embedded in the conceptual framework of the dominant imaginary: the economy reigns above social and ecological issues, constant economic growth is taken for granted as the goal of society, and competition and productivity are desirable and inevitable. Interestingly, the word 'ecology' does not appear in a document of 203 pages that is supposed to engage sustainable economic practices (the adjective 'ecological' occurs only five times). If this definition of sustainable economy is analyzed in light of the argument laid out in the introduction to this book, many contradictions become apparent, the most notable being that a law that understands

---

56 'Ley 2/2011, de 4 de marzo, de Economía Sostenible', Documento BOE-A-2011-4117, *Boletín Oficial del Estado*, no. 55, March 5, 2011, p. 25049, https://www.boe.es/boe/dias/2011/03/05/pdfs/BOE-A-2011-4117.pdf.

sustainable economy as a pattern of growth in the context of a competitive and productive economy is anything but sustainable. Even the scarce space devoted to ecological sustainability (and let us remember the obvious: in our biosphere, whatever is not sustained ecologically is not sustainable) targets symptoms, not the systemic roots of unsustainability, and does so by espousing the principles of ecological modernization and the 'gospel of eco-efficiency' that dominates Euro-American reformist environmentalism. Even more disappointing, the political party in power as I write (PP) has not honored any of the already shallow environmental goals and strategies included in the law because, according to them, environmental regulations are obstacles to economic growth. In this official document in particular, and for the major Spanish political parties in general, the economic system is not perceived as a subsystem within an ecological system. As such, it is delusional.

The official narrative of the Culture of Crisis in Spain assumes that the crisis is due to a lack of economic growth and therefore will be solved by doing what neoconservative technocrats (or neo-Keynesian experts, according to a more progressive part of the political spectrum) tell us to do in order to get back on the path of growth. It is a post-political perspective that transforms the political issues to be debated by the people into technical issues to be targeted exclusively by experts invariably trained in the growth paradigm. Under the Culture of Crisis, all our emotions and desires, all our symbolic, aesthetic, and political possibilities, are restricted to the growth imaginary, making it difficult to recognize that what we are really facing is the crisis of the model of growth itself.

Although the cultural authority of neoliberal experts has been sharply challenged in Spain following the 15-M movement, as shown by Luis Moreno-Caballud, the disarticulation of the growth imaginary is not often the main focus of collective demands and political activism. The critique of greedy bankers, corrupt politicians, nontransparent institutions, austerity measures, the undemocratic structure of political parties, and so on, is commonly framed without reference to the systemic addiction to economic growth in a consumerist and individualist culture. A refreshing exception is found in a recent manifesto. In July 2014, a group of 258 professionals from Spain, all recognized in their respective academic, socioecological, and cultural fields, wrote, signed, and released a manifesto titled 'Última llamada: Estamos ante una crisis ... de civilización' [Last Call: We Are Facing a Crisis ... of Civilization].[57] The document states that what we are facing is

57 'Última llamada (manifiesto): Estamos ante una crisis ... de civilización', July 2014, http://ultimallamadamanifiesto.wordpress.com/el-manifiesto/.

not so much an economic crisis, but a crisis caused by an economic model based on consumerism and economic growth:

> Estamos atrapados en la dinámica perversa de una civilización que si no crece no funciona, y si crece destruye las bases naturales que la hacen posible. Nuestra cultura, tecnólatra y mercadólatra, olvida que somos, de raíz, dependientes de los ecosistemas e interdependientes.

> [We are trapped by a perverse dynamic of a civilization that does not function if it does not grow, and destroys the natural bases that make it possible if it does grow. Our culture, which worships technology and the market, forgets that we are, at root, dependent on ecosystems and interdependent]

Given the pollution it creates and the amount of material and energy that it consumes, the globalizing consumerist society is not just socially undesirable, but a biophysical impossibility: 'La sociedad productivista y consumista no puede ser sustentada por el planeta' [The productivist and consumerist society cannot be sustained by the planet]. The 'cruel optimism' which holds that economic growth is the solution to the problems caused by our systemic addiction to economic growth yields results which are counterproductive to humans' well-being while preventing us from imagining, envisioning, and creating a just and sustainable society. 'Hoy se acumulan las noticias que indican que la vía del crecimiento es ya un genocidio a cámara lenta' [Today a great deal of news indicates that the path of economic growth is already a slow-motion genocide]. The manifesto recognizes the necessity of a widespread social transformation and a change in logic to avoid the imminent collapse of civilization. While many people and communities are already working on alternatives, significant obstacles remain, in particular 'la inercia del modo de vida capitalista y los intereses de los grupos privilegiados' [the inertia of the capitalist way of life and the interests of privileged groups]. The manifesto ends by warning of the urgent need to create a new society where humans are not slaves to their economic machinery and by stressing that, given the current ecological situation, little time remains to act. A cartoon by El Roto functions as an epilogue, showing the incompatible ends we are pursuing: a man in a suit holding a calculator states, 'La solución a la crisis es sencillísima: solo hay que consumir más para reactivar la economía, y consumir menos para no cargarnos el planeta' [The solution to the crisis is really simple: we only have to consume more in order to reactivate the economy, and to consume less so as not to destroy the planet]. The manifesto makes clear the connections between economic growth, superfluous consumerism, social injustice, and ecological degradation. It was signed by a number of people, including Pablo Iglesias, who are affiliated with Podemos, a political party that emerged out of the activist culture associated with the 15-M movement and gained traction in the last municipal and national elections. Unfortunately, the party appointed two traditional neo-Keynesian economists (Vicenç Navarro and Juan Torres) to draft its economic program as soon as it achieved some electoral success, and a postgrowth discourse is now rarely articulated in the numerous public statements made by Podemos's spokespersons. Many activists in the degrowth movement were disappointed, as they had been counting on Podemos to introduce the topic into the official political debate. Currently only Equo, a small Spanish party with representation in the European Parliament, explicitly embraces a coherent postgrowth discourse.

Even today it is difficult to find a positive reference to degrowth in a Spanish corporate media outlet, where it is frequently associated with a reduction of the GDP and not appreciated as a socioecological movement that points out the biophysical impossibility and social undesirability of our society's addiction to economic growth. Exceptions include a few sympathetic op-eds, such as a short and surprisingly accurate summary of degrowth theory in *ABC*, and two interviews with Serge Latouche published in *El País* in October 2012 and August 2013.[58] Only a few alternative and independent media outlets, such as *eldiario.es*, *Diagonal*, or *El salmón contracorriente*, have dared to promulgate this perspective. There is an overwhelming asymmetry in the pervasive media presentation of economic growth as an unquestionable social goal, and the public perception of lack of growth as an evil to be avoided at all costs. However, as I will show in this chapter, significant postgrowth cultural sensibilities in Southern European socioecological movements in general, and in recent Iberian nonfiction writings in particular, have proliferated in the past few years. These movements and writings are in tune with the developments of ecological economics.

58 Jorge Villalmanzo, 'Menos es más', *ABC.es*, August 21, 2011, http://www.abc.es/20110821/comunidad-castillaleon/abcp-menos-20110821.html; Ferran Bono, 'Es posible vivir mucho mejor con mucho menos: el ideólogo francés del decrecimiento denuncia que se tire comida a la basura', *El País*, October 30, 2012, http://sociedad.elpais.com/sociedad/2012/10/30/actualidad/1351621426_032318.html; Joseba Elola, '"Hay que trabajar menos horas para trabajar todos": Serge Latouche, el precursor de la teoría del decrecimiento, aboga por una sociedad que produzca menos y consuma menos', *El País*, August 17, 2013, http://internacional.elpais.com/internacional/2013/08/15/actualidad/1376575866_220660.html.

1.2.1. Ecological Economics

Ecological economics is a transdisciplinary field of research that aims to understand economics in its inextricable environmental contexts, recognizing that the economy is a subsystem of the biosphere. The fact is that 'all of the input to the economy comes from the environment, and all of the wastes produced by it return to the environment'.[59] For neoclassical economists, however, the economic system is viewed as independent of its biophysical implications and therefore self-sufficient. Ecological economics stems from, among other things, the contributions of Nicholas Georgescu-Roegen and his writings in bioeconomics, a new approach that incorporates advances in the physical and biological sciences into economics. Once bioeconomics makes visible the obvious, namely, the physical and biological roots of the economic process, it 'cannot ignore the limitations imposed by the laws of physics: in particular the law of entropy'.[60] Another pioneer in the formation of the ecological economic field is Kenneth E. Boulding, whose 1967 essay 'Economics of the Coming Spaceship Earth' invites economists to move beyond the mainstream unsustainable 'cowboy economy' that is designed to deplete the environment and expand indefinitely, taking for granted that there is always a new frontier to exploit, to embrace a more sober 'spaceman economy' in which we recognize the limits and fragility of the blue planet in which humans and their economic activities are embedded, and organize our economic processes accordingly.[61] Today it is not sufficient to place the material economy within its ecological context; it is also necessary to take into account the financial economy and its dependency on debt-driven growth. In 2010, Peter Victor, author of *Managing without Growth*, and Tim Jackson, author of *Prosperity without Growth*, started working on what they call 'ecological macroeconomics', 'to build a new system dynamics model of national economies encompassing the financial system, the real economy, and the material, energy and waste throughput'.[62] New economics, ecological economics, feminist economics, steady-state economics, degrowth economics, postgrowth economics,

59 Rob Dietz and Dan O'Neill, *Enough Is Enough: Building a Sustainable Economy in a World of Finite Resources* (San Francisco: Berrett-Koehler, 2013), 17.

60 Mauro Bonaiuti, 'Bioeconomics', in *Degrowth: A Vocabulary for a New Era*, ed. Giacomo D'Alisa, Federico Demaria, and Giorgos Kallis (New York: Routledge, 2015), 26.

61 Kenneth E. Boulding, 'Economics of the Coming Spaceship Earth', in *Environmental Quality in a Growing Economy*, ed. H. Jarrett (Baltimore, MD: Johns Hopkins University Press, 1966), 3–14.

62 Peter A. Victor, 'The Kenneth E. Boulding Memorial Award 2014: Ecological Economics: A Personal Journey', *Ecological Economics* 109 (2015): 98.

circular economics, rethinking economics, economics for the Anthropocene, economics for the common good, and so forth are all different articulations of a rapidly emerging critique of the dominant economic growth paradigm.

The field of ecological economics is strongly represented in Spain. José Manuel Naredo and Joan Martínez-Alier are internationally recognized figures contributing to the discipline.[63] The Institut de Ciència i Tecnologia Ambientals (Universitat Autònoma de Barcelona) and Research & Degrowth Barcelona are a European hub for ecological economic research. The Association of Ecological Economics in Spain, founded in 2006, has almost 50 members as I write. Regarding the dissemination and popularization of concepts derived from ecological economics in Spain and the connections between mainstream economics' addiction to growth and the ecological and economic crises, the contributions of Ramón Fernández Durán,[64] Óscar Carpintero,[65] Jorge Riechmann,[66] Yayo Herrero,[67] and Carlos Taibo,[68] among many others, are crucial. The numerous publications under the auspices of *Ecologistas en Acción* are also invaluable in this respect. In Spain, ecological economics and the degrowth movement seem to be partners in a convergent critique of the growth imaginary. Given that many of the people involved in the degrowth movement were also active participants in the 15-M movement, the cultural repolitization of Spain after 2011 is bringing to light some of the concerns of ecological economics which until that moment were not popular outside of small activist or research circles. Prior to that moment, assuming that Kenneth Boulding was correct in his thought-provoking, playful assertion that 'Anyone who believes that exponential growth can go on forever in a finite world is either a madman or an economist', it seems that all Spaniards embracing the dominant imaginary of the CT would fit into one of those two categories.

63 Óscar Carpintero, 'Introducción: la economía ecológica como enfoque abierto y transdisciplinar', in *Economía ecológica: reflexiones y perspectivas*, ed. Santiago Álvarez Cantalapiedra and Óscar Carpintero (Madrid: CBA, 2009), 24.

64 Ramón Fernández Durán, *El antropoceno: la expansión del capitalismo global choca con la biosfera* (Barcelona: Virus editorial, 2011); idem, *Tercera Piel: sociedad de la información y conquista del alma* (Barcelona: Virus editorial, 2010).

65 Carpintero, 'Introducción'; idem, *El metabolismo de la economía española*.

66 Jorge Riechmann, 'Para una teoría de la racionalidad ecológica', in *Economía ecológica: reflexiones y perspectivas*, ed. Santiago Álvarez Cantalapiedra and Óscar Carpintero (Madrid: CBA, 2009), 169–213; idem, *Un mundo vulnerable: ensayos sobre ecología, ética y tecnociencia* (Madrid: Catarata, 2000).

67 Yayo Herrero et al., *Cambiar las gafas para mirar el mundo: una nueva cultura de la sostenibilidad* (Madrid: Libros en acción, 2011).

68 Carlos Taibo, *El decrecimiento explicado con sencillez* (Madrid: Catarata, 2011).

1.2.2. The Proliferation of Iberian Socioecological Essays

In recent years a number of politically engaged Iberian nonfiction writers have adopted a cross-disciplinary perspective to critique the unsustainable social and environmental degradation caused by global capitalism and its energy-devouring regime. These authors—among them Jorge Riechmann, Joan Martínez-Alier, Amaia Pérez Orozco, Ramon Folch, Alicia Puleo, Antonio Turiel, Ramón Fernández Durán, Emilio Santiago Muíño, Joaquín Sempere, Óscar Carpintero, Yayo Herrero, Carles Riba Romeva, Carlos Taibo, Juan del Río, and Esther Vivas—embrace social ecology, ecological economics, and political ecology.[69] Many of these writers adopt these perspectives in order to challenge and redefine the innocuous 'reform environmentalism' that dominates the European Union's official discourse. Reform environmentalism 'holds to the mainstream assumption that the natural world be seen primarily as a resource for human beings, whether economically or culturally, but it strives to defend and conserve it against over-exploitation. For the most part reform environmentalists advocate measures within the given terms of capitalist industrial society'.[70] This ambivalent environmental discourse is highly problematic in many ways: it reduces everything to a resource to be exploited and managed by economic activity reinforcing the growth-oriented rationale; it does not question the inherent unsustainability of capitalism but advocates instead the adoption of a green capitalism; it intends to solve environmental problems without reducing the overall consumption of societies, even though cultural consumerism is a well-known factor in triggering unsustainable behavior; and its preferred strategy to alleviate poverty is sustainable development and green growth, rather than redistribution, which maintains the existing unequal and competitive system of social reproduction. This pragmatic, techno-managerial environmentalism assumes that a few technological fixes within a market economy can allow for more economic growth while protecting the environment. Their assumptions are not only factually wrong, but prevent any meaningful political questions from emerging (issues regarding the unequal distribution of wealth and power, the (un)desirability of growth and capitalism, the

69 Martínez-Alier, *El ecologismo de los pobres*; Pérez Orozco, *Subversión feminista de la economía*; Ramon Folch, *La quimera del crecimiento: la sostenibilidad en la era postindustrial* (Barcelona: RBA, 2011); Alicia H. Puleo, *Ecofeminismo: para otro mundo posible* (Madrid: Cátedra, 2011); Emilio Santiago Muíño, *Rutas sin mapa: horizontes de transición ecosocial* (Madrid: Catarata, 2016); Joaquim Sempere, *Mejor con menos: necesidades, explosión consumista y crisis ecológica* (Barcelona: Crítica, 2009); Carles Riba Romeva, *Recursos energéticos y crisis: el fin de 200 años irrepetibles* (Barcelona: Octaedro, 2012).

70 Timothy Clark, *The Cambridge Introduction to Literature and the Environment* (Cambridge: Cambridge University Press, 2011), 2.

existing exploitative relations, and the authority of experts) by presenting technical adaptation, not systemic change, as inevitable. Eco-modernists, as some of these techno-managerial reform environmentalists call themselves in their 2015 manifesto, think that using resources more efficiently without changing dominant power relations and values would take care of the environmental problems. They 'confuse efficiency/intensity with scale. Using existing resources more intensively leads to more, not less, resource use ... This is the historical pattern of capitalism, the one that eco-modernists want to see accelerated'.[71]

Because reform environmentalism operates within the framework of the dominant imaginary of economic growth, it is counterproductive and unable to solve the socioecological problems of the Anthropocene. Arran Stibbe rightly points out that, from an ecolinguistic point of view, some pervasive metaphors have negative environmental consequences and are therefore 'destructive metaphors'. One of them is the 'frequently used ECONOMIC GROWTH IS A TIDE', which is often deployed in neoliberal discourses 'in the form "a rising tide lifts all boats" to represent economic growth as a solution to the problem of poverty alleviation ... The metaphor can be seen as an attempt to distract attention away from the only way to "lift the boats" of the poor within a finite world, which is redistribution'.[72] Reform environmentalism looks for efficient ways to do more of the same. But we need to do differently, not better. The question eco-modernists should ask themselves remains: Is it really smart to refine, technologically and theoretically, a system that operates by undermining the conditions necessary for our biophysical survival? Is it smart to make a destructive system smarter, more sophisticated, and more efficient? Sustainability for eco-modernists means nothing but sustaining the status quo. For those who support reform environmentalism, the problem is the tool (technology), not the logic. As Stacy Alaimo rightly notes, 'this technological focus obscures power differentials, political differences, and cultural values'.[73] A decolonial environmental humanities would ask, to paraphrase Alaimo, What is it that sustainability seeks to sustain and for whom?[74] Advocates of degrowth raise this question, aim to repoliticize environmentalism, and argue that the point is not to do better or less within the same pathological game, but to change the rules (the logic).

71 Kallis, *In Defense of Degrowth*, 52.

72 Stibbe, *Ecolinguistics*, 73.

73 Stacy Alaimo, 'Sustainable This, Sustainable That: New Materialisms, Posthumanism, and Unknown Futures', *PMLA* 127 (2012): 560.

74 Alaimo, 'Sustainable This, Sustainable That', 562.

Generally degrowth challenges the hegemony of growth and calls for a democratically led redistributive downscaling of production and consumption in industrialised countries as a means to achieve environmental sustainability, social justice and well-being. Although integrating bioeconomics and ecological macroeconomics, degrowth is a noneconomic concept. On the one hand, degrowth is the reduction of energy and material throughput, needed in order to face the existing biophysical constraints (in terms of natural resources and ecosystem's [*sic*] assimilative capacity). On the other, degrowth is an attempt to challenge the omnipresence of market-based relations in society and the growth-based roots of the social imaginary replacing them by the idea of frugal abundance. It is also a call for deeper democracy, applied to issues which lie outside the mainstream democratic domain, like technology. Finally, degrowth implies an equitable redistribution of wealth within and across the Global North and South, as well as between present and future generations.[75]

The Iberian socioenvironmental essayists I introduce here (and others hailing from different areas of the Euro-Mediterranean region) reveal the fallacies within reform environmentalism and identify the problems ingrained in capitalist economic dynamics: epistemological reductionism and economicism, biological annihilation, cultural consumerism, environmental injustice, asymmetrical transnational power relations, lack of systemic thinking, and the disproportionate ecological footprint of some regions. These authors propose and explore socially fair and ecologically sound integral alternatives to the hegemonic cultural imaginary. By analyzing the capitalist economy in terms of material and energetic transformations that accelerate entropy and decrease both biological and epistemological diversity, these authors view cultural consumerism as a suicidal ideology and propose the reduction of our economic throughputs to allow others (both human and nonhuman) to live. By uncovering the anthropocentric, utilitarian, androcentric, neocolonial, and reductionist blind spots of global capitalism, these writings promote a posthumanist and materialist understanding of economy that takes into consideration the agency and interdependency of all forms of life. By rematerializing and posthumanizing the economy, the authors are in line with the 'material turn' that has recently occurred in ecocriticism in particular and the environmental humanities in

75 Federico Demaria, Francois Schneider, Filka Sekulova, and Joan Martinez-Alier, 'What is Degrowth? From an Activist Slogan to a Social Movement', *Environmental Values* 22, no. 2 (2013): 209.

general. They challenge the official discourses that equate economic growth with well-being and social progress, most of which are based on fictitious separations between human and nonhuman, subject and object, observer and observed system, or economy and environment.

In the next few pages, I will follow the path blazed by the Iberian socioenvironmental critics I have mentioned to unmask the unscientific assumptions behind the neoclassical economics that currently dominate both the global cultural imaginary in general and the economic debates within the European Union in particular. I will then analyze the common ground found in the alternatives they have proposed. Finally, I will highlight the connection between the ideas advanced by these authors in Spain and the emergence of a transnational debate in environmental humanities and posthumanism. In this regard, these authors should not be considered in the context of their national framework alone, but as participants in a wider critique of neoliberal globalization from a Euro-Mediterranean perspective. My study of these works of nonfiction confirms Ursula Heise's observation that 'nonfictional genres have assumed a prominence in transnational ecocriticism that they do not have in other types of comparatist research', which 'has over the last few years enabled a transdisciplinary collaboration with environmentally oriented scholars'.[76]

Overall, these Iberian authors prioritize two crucial currents in the discussion. The first is the inseparability of social and environmental problems and the interrelationship between socioenvironmental destruction, the asymmetrical global distribution of wealth and power, and the degradation of political civil society. The great acceleration of economic growth since the 1950s translates not only into a planetary environmental and energy crisis, but also a distribution crisis and, as a result, a crisis of democracy. The greatest difficulty preventing any meaningful communitarian participation in relevant political decisions arises from the ubiquity of the neoliberal economic reductionism. The second current is the ongoing globalization of an unsustainable economic system based on the biophysical impossibility of constant economic growth and, more importantly, the globally imposed anthropocentric, androcentric, reductionist, colonial, and hubristic logic behind such a system. This logic, which presents itself as the only legitimate way of knowing, exacerbates the problems it creates by trying to address them using the same instrumental and reductionist reasoning that generated them in the first place, while preventing any alternative from being envisioned and incorporated. This logic renders any creative solution unthinkable and inconceivable. As such, we are not just facing a social,

---

76 Heise, 'Globality, Difference, and the International Turn in Ecocriticism', 641.

economic, environmental, or political issue, but a more nefarious problem that encompasses all four—a vicious epistemological circle. Alicia Puleo writes that for Max Horkheimer and Theodor Adorno, 'la Ilustración se había marcado inicialmente por objetivo destruir los mitos y alimentar la imaginación con el saber pero, más tarde, la Razón instrumental se convirtió en un mito que traza nuevos límites al pensamiento' [The Enlightenment was marked by the desire to destroy myths and feed the imagination with knowledge but, later on, instrumental Reason morphed into a new myth imposing new limits on thought].[77] Today, that instrumental reason is at the service of the fundamentalism of the market economy, which excludes any solution that is not expressed in terms that champion economic growth and debt-driven financial capital accumulation.

In order to avoid the above-mentioned limitations imposed on thought, the new wave of Iberian socioecological critics employs a systemic and transdisciplinary approach to expose the blind spots in the hegemonic discourse. In that respect, they challenge the modern, arbitrary, and disciplinary epistemological divide that prevents creative thinking outside of its obdurate reasoning, and they adopt instead more appropriate, inclusive, systemic, and holistic frameworks that focus, for instance, on 'socioecology',[78] 'socionatural metabolism',[79] 'social metabolism',[80] 'ecofeminist degrowth',[81] 'ecosocial transition',[82] and 'ecological rationality'.[83] All of these frameworks point to the interdependency of social, ecological, and semiotic systems. These approaches are integrated within ecological economics and the degrowth movement to emphasize the inseparability of the human and nonhuman spheres for a proper understanding of pressing global problems. From this vantage point, the economic system is not independent of the system of the biosphere, as perceived by neoclassical economics, nor is the environment a subsystem of the economic system, as it is treated by neoliberalism and its 'greener' version, namely, environmental economics. The economic system is nothing but a subsystem embedded in, and dependent on, the system of the biosphere. By necessity, the activity of the economic system, to be sustainable, is restricted by the limits of the

77 Puleo, *Ecofeminismo*, 90.
78 Folch, *La quimera del crecimiento*, 91–92.
79 Sempere, *Mejor con menos*, 164–165.
80 Martínez-Alier, *El ecologismo de los pobres*, 350.
81 Pérez Orozco, *Subversión feminista de la economía*, 223.
82 Santiago Muíño, *Rutas sin mapa*; Fernando Prats, Yayo Herrero, and Alicia Torrego, *La gran encrucijada: sobre la crisis ecosocial y el cambio de ciclo histórico* (Madrid: Ecologistas en acción, 2016).
83 Riechmann, 'Para una teoría', 193.

biosphere and must be compatible with the ecological laws that govern its functions. The economic system cannot ignore, for example, the laws of thermodynamics.[84] Hence an economic system based on constant economic growth, planetary urbanization, and the ever-faster production and consumption of commodities is undesirable, destructive, unendurable, and unrealistic. The constant expansion of this economic activity is radically altering the global environment and transgressing planetary boundaries. This socioecological critique urges us to abandon the dominant social imaginary that separates the economic system and the environment so that we can begin to scientifically and politically analyze the flux of materials and energy mobilized and transformed by capitalist economic activity, and use that information to organize our societies in just and sustainable postgrowth ways.

In the meantime, the global expansion of the current hegemonic economic model results in irreversible ecological degradation. This economic model extracts raw materials and energy and transforms them into toxic waste and pollution at an ever-accelerating pace. The negative social consequences of this environmental degradation disproportionately affect the poorest populations. The response of disenfranchised communities to this environmental injustice has been termed 'the environmentalism of the poor'[85] to contrast it with previous, less socially oriented environmental movements that originated in the United States. If observed outside of its own unrealistic and hubristic discourse, neoliberal globalization is an ideology of death, since it globally disrupts the ecological cycle of nutrients and depends on a constant increase of human biomass usage (quantified as the human appropriation of net primary productivity) detrimental to other forms of life and alternative ways of human life. The more social metabolism and human appropriation of net primary productivity increase, the less biodiversity and cultural diversity remain on the planet. In other words, the faster capitalist societies appropriate productive landscape and seascape by expanding the ecological space impacted by their socioeconomic activities (extractivism, urbanization, agroindustry, overfishing, communication and transportation infrastructures, waste disposal and pollution, and so on), the faster other species, as well as non-market economy-oriented cultures, go extinct. Thus, when the global economy grows, the living systems of the planet shrink, and cultural diversity is diminished.

---

84 Carpintero, 'Introducción', 15; Riechmann, 'Para una teoría de la racionalidad ecológica', 190.

85 Ramachandra Guha and Joan Martínez-Alier, *Varieties of Environmentalism: Essays North and South* (London: Earthscan, 1997).

When neoclassical and neoliberal economists talk about generating wealth, they are referring to the destruction, depletion, and appropriation of the real wealth generated by ecosystems. 'La contabilidad económica es por tanto falsa, porque confunde el agotamiento de recursos y el aumento de entropía con la creación de riqueza' [The economic accounting is therefore false, because it confuses the depletion of resources and the increase in entropy with the creation of wealth].[86] Unfortunately, this globalizing economic system currently dominates the international political economy (including the World Trade Organization, the International Monetary Fund, and the World Bank) and dictates our way of life and social organization: 'Es una sociedad construida sobre la economía, y una economía construida sobre la negación tenaz de la realidad' [It is a society constructed upon the economy, and an economy constructed upon the constant denial of reality].[87] Thus, our mainstream economic system remains blind to the constraints of biophysical reality. The main tenets of this system are anachronistic and obsolete, since they were constructed from the old mechanistic scientific paradigm dominant in the nineteenth century. That paradigm conceives of the world as a machine made of different articulated parts rather than as an integrated dynamic living system; as Óscar Carpintero notes, 'La ciencia económica tradicional es pretermodinámica, preevolutiva y preecológica' [The science of traditional economics is pre-thermodynamics, pre-evolutionary, and pre-ecological].[88] Orthodox economics has ignored the scientific advances of other disciplines during the last century.[89] In sum, it offers a logic ill-equipped to deal with the global ecological crisis, which is exacerbated precisely by the globalization of its very logic.

Many of the aforementioned Iberian socioecological essayists point out that, in order to maintain the destructive system's unsustainable model, the previously described hegemonic discourse disseminates a blind faith in modern Western techno-science. Technology and science are presented as the remedy for all our present excesses and abuse. Paradoxically, while this discourse maintains an unwavering faith in science, it ignores or rejects what the vast majority of the scientific community confirms and cherry-picks some decontextualized data. Furthermore, under the current circumstances, technological and scientific research and innovation depend on, and are guided by, corporate funding. Their main motivation is profit, and not necessarily the well-being of communities and ecosystems. Most

86 Martínez-Alier, *El ecologismo de los pobres*, 350.
87 Riechmann, 'Para una teoría de la racionalidad ecológica', 190.
88 Riechmann, 'Para una teoría de la racionalidad ecológica', 191.
89 Carpintero, 'Introducción', 23.

new technologies are created under the industrial logic of faster production. They are designed to accelerate the expansion of social metabolism and to quicken the pace of the extraction of materials and the use of fossil fuel energy. These technologies tend to aggravate ecological problems by raising the level of human biomass usage to ecologically unsustainable proportions. Rather than targeting existing problems, many technological improvements create new, doubtful, necessities and a greater dependency on energy and material consumption. Such is the case of forced mobility, created by the expansion of car use and the resulting dispersed urban model.[90]

Perhaps the most important technological danger, according to many Iberian socioecological critics, is the role of new information and communication technology in making the socioecological global crisis invisible:

> La sociedad de la imagen y la información ayuda a ocultar aún más la gravísima crisis ecológica que enfrentamos, sobre todo porque incentiva el desplazamiento de la atención de la biosfera a la infosfera (ciberespacio, realidad virtual), invisibilizando todavía más el deterioro de la Primera Piel, de la Madre Naturaleza.

> [The society of image and information helps to hide even more the very serious ecological crisis we face, especially because it encourages a shift in focus from the biosphere to the infosphere (cyberspace, virtual reality), making more invisible still the deterioration of the First Skin, of Mother Nature][91]

The currently celebrated information society is another misleading cruel optimism, and many of these authors prefer to speak of it as a 'disinformation society' due to the overabundance of meaningless information.[92] In truth, while corporate mass media is disseminating and celebrating the notion of the information age, economic globalization is drastically reducing the real information of the Earth—encoded in biological genetic information and cultural diversity—due to the mass extinction of species and cultures that is taking place on a planetary scale.[93]

In the following pages, I will explore the alternatives suggested by these critiques in order to address the aforementioned issues. According to these thinkers, the two most crucial and urgent changes needed are, first of all,

90 Sempere, *Mejor con menos*, 152.
91 Fernández Durán, *El antropoceno*, 90.
92 Riechmann, *Un mundo vulnerable*, 80.
93 Fernández Durán, *El antropoceno*, 90–92.

a significant reduction of social metabolism on a global scale; and second, a radical cultural change. Because the main objective is to learn how to live well while using less material and energy, we need to rethink what it means to 'live well' by democratically redefining notions such as 'progress' and 'development'. It is important to distinguish vital needs from superfluous or artificial needs. It is urgent to find more ecological and more socially efficient ways to satisfy those needs within each specific socionatural context. Here the distinction between needs and satisfiers proposed by Chilean economist Manfred A. Max-Neef becomes relevant.[94] All humans have needs that must be satisfied in order to enjoy a life of dignity, and different societies have different strategies to satisfy such needs (satisfiers). Some satisfiers require more intensive material and energy throughput than others in order to fulfill the same need. According to Max-Neef, there are 'destructive satisfiers' that fulfill a need by compromising the conditions necessary either for fulfilling other needs or for fulfilling that same one in the future; such is the case with industrial agriculture, as Esther Vivas demonstrates.[95] So-called developed countries or advanced economies are societies with sadly inefficient satisfiers, and as a result they use a disproportionate amount of material and energy per capita to meet their human needs. In doing so, they are robbing the ecological space of other regions and preventing them from maintaining the material and energy required to meet their own needs. With neoliberal globalization imposed all over the world, more and more regions are persuaded or forced to adopt the inefficient satisfier strategies deployed by developed regions. This is a sure path to both ecological collapse and geopolitical conflict. The ultimate challenge is for developed countries to create a postgrowth social metabolism that is able to meet the vital needs of all their citizens by using satisfiers that require less material and energy. Successfully doing so would liberate the unfairly captured ecological space of other regions, so that they could decolonize and develop whatever satisfiers they consider culturally appropriate.

To be holistic and to avoid economic reductionism, the study of human needs must expand beyond superfluous material and energy consumption. It must incorporate emotional, psychological, social, spiritual, and environmental aspects. It requires a posthumanist and systemic conception of health and well-being. This is not an unproblematic task, since vague

94 Manfred A. Max-Neef, *Human Scale Development* (New York: The Apex Press, 1991).

95 Esther Vivas, 'Novedad editorial: 'El negocio de la comida', *Esther Vivas*, November 6, 2014, https://esthervivas.com/2014/11/06/novedad-editorial-el-negocio-de-la-comida/.

concepts such as 'quality of life' have been used repeatedly by numerous ideologies and groups in Spain (and elsewhere) during the second half of the twentieth century to justify unsustainable developmental projects and the environmental degradation associated with mass tourism, as pointed out by Eugenia Afinoguénova.[96] All these ideologies represent different articulations of the same modern Western anthropocentric, growth-oriented logic and none proposes a posthumanist or relational definition of 'quality of life'. Perhaps the postgrowth approach to socioenvironmental issues supported by the authors I discuss here might foster a better dialogue with indigenous conceptions of 'living well', such as the Andean, based on the interdependence and reciprocity of the biotic community (human and nonhuman), because most Euro-American humanist articulations of 'quality of life' have never seriously questioned anthropocentrism or consistently incorporated the science of ecology into their theoretical models.

According to Jorge Riechmann, cultural consumerism and economic growth must be replaced by ecological rationality.[97] This new rationality will focus on the satisfaction of human needs through a sustainable (smaller) social metabolism.[98] The main goal is not to maximize, but to optimize (to target sufficiency not efficiency).[99] In order to halt the ongoing global ecological and social degradation, the industrial and postindustrial regions of the planet must begin a socioecological transition towards a permanent reduction in their use/waste of materials and energy.[100] It is a change that will require a cultural shift in dominant values and ways of thinking, as well as the redefinition of humans' role in the biotic community. It is important to emphasize that 'todos los seres humanos son interdependientes y ecodependientes, pues el *homo economicus* competitivo e independiente es una absoluta ficción' [all human beings are interdependent and ecodependent, since the competitive and independent *homo economicus* is a total fiction].[101] This cultural shift will call for socially and ecologically sustainable degrowth based on the priority of social life and relational goods (rather than individual material accumulation and consumption); creative and communitarian leisure time; the redistribution of working time; the reduction of productive, administrative, and transportation infrastructures; the relocalization, decentralization, and simplification of economic and

96 Afinoguénova, 'Tourism and "Quality of Life" at the End of Franco's Dictatorship'.
97 Riechmann, 'Para una teoría de la racionalidad ecológica', 180.
98 Sempere, *Mejor con menos*, 228.
99 Sempere, *Mejor con menos*, 223; Riechmann, 'Para una teoría de la racionalidad ecológica', 180.
100 Martínez-Alier, *El ecologismo de los pobres*, 345.
101 Fernández Durán, *El antropoceno*, 98.

social life; and, in the individual sphere, the appreciation of voluntary simplicity and the revalorization of the ethics of care.[102]

Unfortunately, the vast majority of current political and economic leaders are moving in the opposite direction by focusing only on GDP growth rather than socioenvironmental well-being. To change this inertia, collective political action on a global scale is needed. Given that decisions regarding the size and nature of social metabolism affect all of humanity, present and future, they should be made with the participation of all.[103] The global financial crisis of 2008 demonstrated once again that global public opinion is not being taken into account, and that important decisions are made unilaterally by 'technocrats' and 'experts' trained in the growth paradigm. The current disagreement in Europe about what is the best way to grow after the global financial crisis is a good example of this obduracy. Neoliberals recommend austerity in government spending, tax cuts, and salary reductions to improve global competitiveness and to favor the exportation dynamic, while neo-Keynesians say that salaries and government spending must grow so that consumption may grow too. Neither party recognizes that, given the socioecological situation, the first option is socially and ecologically unsustainable while the second is environmentally unviable. The possibility of degrowing is never mentioned.

Even if the elites became sensitive to the biophysical restrictions, however, entrusting the rich and powerful with the task of degrowing our society and changing the cultural imaginary would be, if possible at all, very dangerous. The powerful and privileged are not well-suited to changing the cultural imaginary in a socially desirable fashion, for many reasons. First and foremost is that their self-perceptions and identities are deeply rooted in the neoliberal fantasy and its lack of an ethical center. Recent studies have found that individuals from higher social classes are more likely to exhibit unethical behavior and to justify existing inequality while rationalizing their privileges as well as the social benefits of greed.[104] That said, a desirable change of course can only happen if meaningful and collective participation in global political actions is widely pursued. Rapid cultural repoliticization is required to collectively produce activist knowledge outside of the neoliberal monopoly on meaning-making practices in order to create the necessary conditions for a desirable postgrowth society. Because the hegemonic system 'pollutes' people's minds with harmful illusions and

---

102 Taibo, *El decrecimiento explicado con sencillez*, 52–53.
103 Sempere, *Mejor con menos*, 190.
104 Paul K. Piff et al., 'Higher Social Class Predicts Increased Unethical Behavior', *Proceedings of the National Academy of Sciences* 109, no. 11 (2012): 4086–4091.

destructive metaphors—what Michel Serres calls 'soft pollution'—and masks the real problem, it is important to interrupt the dominant narrative disseminated by corporate media, publicity, and private interests.[105] We can draw on a variety of approaches, from the insights of social psychology[106] to the deconstruction of myths related to the information and communication age[107] to the foregrounding of feminist economics.[108]

Because the dominant imaginary reduces everything to a fiscal metric of material accumulation, the decolonization of education and media is crucial to enact counterhegemonic narratives and practices:

> Debemos rechazar tal simplificación de la complejidad, tal exclusión de lenguajes de valoración. Debemos aceptar, por el contrario, el pluralismo de valores inconmensurables entre sí para evitar que la ciencia económica se convierta en un instrumento del poder en la toma de decisiones.

> [We must reject such simplification of complexity, such exclusion of languages of valuation. We must embrace instead the pluralism of incommensurable values in order to prevent economic science from becoming the instrument of power in decision-making][109]

It is paramount, according to these Iberian essayists, to focus on complexity, and to incorporate the knowledge developed by the systemic paradigm of the last century, in order to understand current problems and find effective solutions.[110] For a society to participate meaningfully in politics and make collective decisions, knowledge should not be the exclusive possession of experts—since the so-called experts are biased by all the agendas of their academic disciplines and ideologies—but a human right in the public domain.[111] It is crucial to listen to, and learn from, other epistemologies and values grounded in a variety of traditions and experiences. Many indigenous and activist sciences can offer valuable insights into the optimization of communitarian living within a relatively small social metabolism. Unfortunately, many of these diverse sources of knowledge have been extinguished by the globalization of neocolonial logic and the expansion of global markets. For this reason it is difficult to enact the 'plural landscape

105　Serres, *Malfeasance*, 62.
106　Riechmann, *Un mundo vulnerable*, 69.
107　Fernández Durán, *Tercera Piel*, 63–68; Folch, *La quimera del crecimiento*, 115–120.
108　Pérez Orozco, *Subversión feminista de la economía*, 44.
109　Martínez-Alier, *El ecologismo de los pobres*, 358.
110　Riechmann, 'Para una teoría de la racionalidad ecológica', 195.
111　Folch, *La quimera del crecimiento*, 244–245.

of knowledge forms'[112] or 'ecology of knowledge'[113] necessary to generate creative alternatives to the globally imposed mono-logic, and its resulting mental and biophysical homogenization.

The Iberian essayists mentioned above are valuable contributors to the ongoing transnational debate about degrowth and ecological economics. Although Spanish mainstream politics and cultural modes have not fully embraced the concerns that these thinkers wish to disseminate, following the global financial crisis a new cultural sensibility has emerged that is more receptive to notions related to degrowth and ecological economics. Carles Riba Romeva believes that the European Union as a whole may be forced to transition to energy degrowth and progressively shrink its social metabolism:

Ahora, con las reservas de energía fósil casi agotadas y con unos recursos de la biosfera limitados en relación a su población, Europa se encuentra, a su pesar, en la punta de lanza de un cambio no tan fácil: liderar el 'decrecimiento energético'.

[Now, with the fossil energy reserves almost exhausted and with the biosphere's resources limited in relation to its population, Europe finds itself involuntarily spearheading a difficult change: to lead 'energy degrowth'][114]

At present, however, ecological rationality is only practiced in small circles and is far from the norm in Europe in general or in Spain in particular. The hegemonic discourse that confuses progress and quality of life with economic growth and the urbanization of capital is still ingrained in the mentality of many Spaniards. This is not surprising given the tenacity with which technocrats and politicians in Spain and elsewhere sold that discourse during the second half of the last century. A renovation of the field of Spanish cultural studies, along with the consolidation of more radical Iberian and transatlantic studies, could contribute to the global dissemination of these ideas at the cultural level by seriously adopting ecocritical and posthumanist approaches. The Iberian thinkers covered in this section contribute to both the ongoing global critique of capitalism and the challenge of the growth-oriented cultural hegemony of Spain.

The relevance of this socioenvironmental thought is not limited to the Iberian context. Joan Martínez-Alier—one of the international leaders in ecological economics and degrowth—has claimed in a recent article that

---

112 Escobar, 'Development, Violence and the New Imperial Order', 17.
113 Santos, 'A Non-Occidentalist West?', 116.
114 Riba Romeva, *Recursos energéticos y crisis*, 272.

the potential exists for an alliance between the 'environmental justice organizations of the global South and the small degrowth movement in Europe':

> This alliance must be based on a common stance against 'debt-fueled' economic growth and the hegemonic of economic accounting, and in favor of a pluralism of values, the acceptance and support of bottom-up feminist neo-Malthusianism, the defense of human rights and indigenous territorial rights along with the rights of nature, the recognition of the ecological debt, and the critique of ecologically unequal exchange.[115]

The ideas developed by Iberian socioecological thinkers are more compatible with postcolonial environmental justice movements than with the hegemonic reform environmentalism of the Euro-American tradition, since this 'reform environmentalism has become part of a system of global managerialism, closely related to institutions like the IMF or the World Bank'.[116] Thus their thinking can be understood as a Euro-Mediterranean contribution to the emerging transnational debate in environmental humanities. I believe that this debate should be consistently incorporated into Iberian cultural studies, where it has been almost completely absent until recently. A parallelism exists between the Iberian essayists' version of postgrowth thought developed in the previous pages and the most popular, recent, and interesting concepts advanced by the environmental humanities—such as trans-corporeality (Alaimo), vital materialism (Bennett), and slow violence (Nixon). These concepts will be recursively mobilized throughout the book.

One example is the vital materialism advanced by Jane Bennett in her book *Vibrant Matter: A Political Ecology of Things*. Heavily influenced by Latour's actor network theory and its focus on the agency of networked assemblages of human and nonhuman actors, Bennett complains that

> theories of democracy that assume a world of active subjects and passive objects begin to appear as thin descriptions at a time when the interactions between human, viral, animal, and technological bodies are becoming more and more intense. If human culture is inextricably enmeshed in vibrant, nonhuman agencies, and if human intentionality can wield agency only if accompanied by a vast entourage

115 Joan Martínez-Alier, 'Environmental Justice and Economic Degrowth: An Alliance between Two Movements', *Capitalism Nature Socialism* 23, no. 1 (2012): 66.
116 Clark, *The Cambridge Introduction to Literature and the Environment*, 120–121.

of nonhumans, then it seems that the appropriate unit of analysis for democratic theory is neither the individual human nor an exclusively human collective, but rather the (ontologically heterogeneous) 'public' coalescing around the problem.[117]

This statement resonates with the main tenets of degrowth. It makes clear that the kind of epistemology—based on the hierarchical separation of humans and the nonhuman—which currently dominates economic and political discourses and practices cannot account for the social and ecological violence that is perpetuated by neoliberal globalization. This 'slow violence' is made invisible by 'the sensation-driven technologies of our image-world'.[118] Furthermore, it is important to recognize that the same logic that exploits humans also depletes nonhumans. Thus, 'human rights are indissociable from environmental justice'.[119] In the past few years, more and more environmental humanists have concluded that social and environmental problems cannot be treated separately, or solved by using the same reductionist and anthropocentric logic that generated them. *Postgrowth Imaginaries* thus strives to converge environmental, social, and cultural studies in order to dialogue with socioecological movements (such as degrowth) and transdisciplinary fields (such as ecological economics and social ecology). I believe that—if we want to effectively promote emancipatory postgrowth imaginaries—decolonial thinking, cultural studies, and ecocriticism can no longer ignore one other.[120]

It is clear that the dominant logic, a logic based on the separation between human individuals and the nonhuman world, cannot track the connections among, for instance, economic activity, chemical pollution, and the proliferation of cancer cells in a child's body. A new epistemological framework is needed to understand these interconnections and interdependencies and to push for a coherent political ecology able to overcome and challenge the growth paradigm.

The ecological economics and political ecologies advocated by the Iberian socioecological essayists discussed here intend, precisely, to posthumanize and rematerialize the economic culture, thereby making their contributions complementary to the new epistemological paradigm advanced by posthumanism and material ecocriticism. In this context, posthumanism

---

117 Jane Bennett, *Vibrant Matter: A Political Ecology of Things* (Durham, NC: Duke University Press, 2010), 108.

118 Nixon, *Slow Violence and the Environmentalism of the Poor*, 3.

119 Nixon, *Slow Violence and the Environmentalism of the Poor*, 265.

120 Elizabeth DeLoughrey and George B. Handley, eds., *Postcolonial Ecologies: Literatures of the Environment* (New York: Oxford University Press, 2011), 339.

recognizes that 'the decentering of the human by its imbrications in technical, medical, informatics, and economic networks is increasingly impossible to ignore' and that 'the nature of thought itself must change if it is to be posthumanist'.[121] In this regard, the constant insistence on a change of logic advocated by the Iberian writers discussed here confirms that they are moving towards a posthumanist understanding of economics, which is both radical and vital for the future viability of humanity. The current context of a global crisis of political imagination and creative thinking—fueled by the semiotic and biophysical pollution disseminated by the anthropocentric growth-oriented economic paradigm—that we (the biotic community) continue to suffer could be interrupted by a greater number of radical voices and practices participating in a global critique.

1.3. Challenging Acceleration and Techno-Optimism: The Case for a Euro-Mediterranean Degrowth-Inspired Ecocriticism

The time has come to discuss the properties and possibilities of an emerging Euro-Mediterranean ecocriticism and to examine its implications for a more established transnational ecocritical theory. The Euro-Mediterranean region is positioned in a complex and undefined economic and political area in relation to the dynamics of neoliberal globalization. The region's participation in European capitalism is both central and peripheral. Beyond its ideological position, the region's geographic position is also a factor in environmental thought, for the region is particularly exposed to the many risks presented by climate change. As a result, Euro-Mediterranean-focused ecocriticism has the potential to challenge the mainstream Euro-American environmental imagination and connect it to social theories such as the postcolonial and environmental justice approaches that have proliferated in the last decade. Nevertheless, most European ecocritical theory is produced in the United Kingdom and Northern Europe. A recent and important volume titled *Ecocritical Theory: New European Approaches* reflects on the lack of any meaningful Southern European contributions.[122] This lack is not indicative of an absence of ecological concerns in that region, but rather a sign that most of the ecological activism, practices, and thought that exists in Euro-Mediterranean countries has yet to be translated into ecocritical theory and practice by cultural scholars. This section aims to assist in this translation process.

---

121 Wolfe, *What Is Posthumanism?*, xv–xvi.
122 Axel Goodbody and Kate Rigby, eds., *Ecocritical Theory: New European Approaches* (Charlottesville: University of Virginia Press, 2011).

1.3.1. Degrowth and the Slow Movement

To begin, we will focus on degrowth and the 'slow' movement, two socioecological movements that have emerged in European-Mediterranean regions during the past two decades. Both movements challenge the 'illogical logic' of constant economic growth in the context of a limited biosphere and denounce the social and ecological degradation generated by unchecked global capitalism. They also articulate a redefinition of European environmentalism by opposing the hegemonic environmental thinking of the strong Euro-American tradition—a tradition deeply ingrained in the official discourse of the European Union, such as the 'gospel of eco-efficiency'[123]— that tries to solve ecological problems using the same logic which causes and perpetuates them, resulting in growth-oriented strategies such as green capitalism, sustainable development, and ecological modernization. Rather than offering an alternative form of growth, the degrowth and slow movements call for systemic and sustainable alternatives to growth that are socially desirable and ecologically possible.

These alternatives are based on the recognition of ecological limits and the need to replace neoliberal fantasies with a system of social reproduction more attuned to human frailty and socioecological interdependency, one that promotes care, conviviality, voluntary simplicity, slowness, communitarian ethics, and the reduction of the economic metabolism. They point out the need for an epistemological change and question the tyranny of industrial time (which is designed to constantly augment the pace of production and consumption). The movements argue that in some regions we can and should live better with less, since it is more desirable, sustainable, and just. Since the financial crisis, the degrowth and slow movements have acquired a certain popularity and visibility beyond their Euro-Mediterranean context. In the last few years, a growing international interest in ecological economics and degrowth has yielded numerous publications in English dealing with such topics, including *Managing without Growth: Slower by Design, Not Disaster* (2008) by Peter Victor, *The End of Growth* (2011) by Richard Heinberg, *Prosperity without Growth: Economics for a Finite Planet* (2009) by Tim Jackson, and *Deep Economy: Economics As if the World Mattered* (2007) by Bill McKibben.[124] The growing

---

123 Martínez-Alier, *El ecologismo de los pobres*, 31.
124 Peter Victor, *Managing without Growth: Slower by Design, Not Disaster* (Cheltenham: Edward Elgar, 2008); Richard Heinberg, *The End of Growth: Adapting to Our New Economic Reality* (Gabriola Island, BC: New Society, 2011); Jackson, *Prosperity without Growth*; Bill McKibben, *Deep Economy: Economics as if the World Mattered* (New York: St. Martin's Griffin, 2007).

visibility of some independent organizations and think tanks, such as the New Economics Foundation, the Great Transition Initiative, and the Post Carbon Institute, also bears witness to the rise in interest in alternative economic cultures. This makes the advocates of degrowth and slow living visible actors in the fast-emerging global environmental justice movement critiquing the globalization of the growth imaginary.

The European Union's reaction to the 2008 financial crisis, inspired by neoliberal formulas, has proven to be not only wrong but highly counterproductive. Many critiques of that reaction have proposed neo-Keynesian strategies in order to reconstruct the signature welfare state that marked many Western European countries before its recent dismantling (especially noticeable in Southern European countries). But no mainstream discourse within the European Union challenges the model of growth and its socioenvironmental consequences on a regional or global scale. As Joan Martínez-Alier confirms, the discourse of the 'gospel of eco-efficiency' dominates social and political environmental debates in Europe. Terms such as 'sustainable development' or 'ecological modernization' are constantly parroted by economists and engineers working in the fields of environmental economics and industrial ecology.[125] Although these disciplines are finally considering the environment within their techno-managerial philosophies, they do not question the economic paradigm that has generated the ecological and social crisis.

The degrowth and slow movements are both critical reactions to the planetary expansion of the growth-oriented paradigm and its massive destruction of biological and epistemological diversity, and their approaches to these problems share many similarities. The degrowth and slow movements illuminate many of the blind spots in the current growth system by showing the material effects of global economic activity on environments, communities, and human health. In this regard, these movements attempt to rematerialize the economy by accounting for, and reducing, its 'social metabolism', and they also aim to make visible the growth-oriented economy's hidden violence (Nixon's 'slow violence'). The two movements advocate similar strategies of behavior that focus on participatory democracy, the reduction of working hours, redistribution, communitarian ethics, environmental enhancement, social justice, and conviviality, a ban on advertising, and the elimination of superfluous consumption. They reject the dominant imaginary of economic growth and cultural consumerism and emphasize the incompatibility of current neoliberal globalization with participatory democracy and socioecological

125 Martínez-Alier, *El ecologismo de los pobres*, 20–21.

well-being. They also point to the necessity of developing global ethical concerns, active social engagement, and communitarian lifestyles.

The Slow Food movement started in northern Italy as an alternative to the culture of fast food and strives to maintain traditional and regional cuisine:

> Slow Food seeks to catalyze a broad cultural shift away from the destructive effects of an industrial food system and fast life; toward the regenerative cultural, ecological, social, and economic benefits of a sustainable food system, regional food traditions, the pleasures of the table, and a slower and more harmonious rhythm of life.[126]

It encourages biodiversity through the organic cultivation of seeds and livestock characteristic of local ecosystems or bioregions, and promotes food communities that practice sustainable production, transportation, and consumption.[127] There are now Slow Food chapters in many countries, and the movement has increased steadily since its emergence in 1989. A broader 'slow movement' now encompasses multiple aspects of life: slow cities, slow travel, slow education, slow money, and so on. Slow cities, for instance, apply a slow-movement philosophy to all aspects of city life. The goal is to enhance the quality of life of residents and the biodiversity that shapes their cultural traditions by reducing noise, pollution, and stress, and by investing in community, public spaces, cooking and gardening, and healthy habits like walking and cycling.

Unlike the slow movement, which is rooted in sensual and communal experiences and the phenomenology of daily life, degrowth is a more confrontational political, economic, and social movement based on political ecology and ecological economics. At the individual level, degrowth likewise promotes convivial simplicity as a way of life, but recognizes that this is not enough to counter the systemic and structural inertia of our society's addiction to economic growth.[128] At the collective level, degrowth implies a cultural revolution.[129] It calls for a democratically led 'equitable downscaling of production and consumption that increases human well-being and enhances ecological conditions'.[130] Degrowth

---

126 Petrini, *Slow Food Nation*, back cover.

127 Carlo Petrini, *Terra Madre: Forging a New Global Network of Sustainable Food Communities* (White River Junction, VT: Chelsea Green, 2010), 27–30.

128 Latouche, *La apuesta por el decrecimiento*, 97; Sempere, *Mejor con menos*, 205.

129 Serge Latouche, *Farewell to Growth*, trans. David Macey (Cambridge: Polity, 2009), 32.

130 François Schneider, Giorgos Kallis, and Joan Matínez-Alier, 'Crisis or Opportunity? Economic Degrowth for Social Equity and Ecological Sustainability', *Journal of Cleaner Production* 18, no. 6 (2010): 511.

advocates the shifting of taxes from labor to consumption, energy, pollution, and resource use in general, and offers specific proposals for policy: citizen debt audit, work sharing, basic and maximum income, green tax reform, halting subsidies for polluting activities and supporting the solidary economy, optimizing the use of buildings, reducing advertising, establishing environmental limits, and abolishing the use of GDP as an indicator of economic progress.[131] Like the slow movement, degrowth also emphasizes the correlation between fast production and consumption, technological acceleration, and fast environmental and social degradation. Both movements argue that 'consumerism is an ideology that pillages and wastes resources, but ultimately fails to satisfy needs'.[132] Both challenge the reductionism of a global capitalist system that only considers economic growth as an indicator of human well-being, without considering other more holistic factors: in most cases, an increase in GDP actually results in a drop in quality of life and an acceleration of environmental destruction and social fragmentation.[133]

Both movements also address the socioecological effects of scientific and technological development operating under the growth-oriented paradigm. Degrowth claims that the dominant imaginary perpetuates a blind and arrogant faith in modern technology and science[134] as a future savior and the remedy, respectively, for all our present excesses and abuses.[135] Advocates of degrowth point out that this approach ignores a number of studies which deny that techno-science is a panacea, disregards the unintended and uncontrollable consequences of the dramatic modification of a complex system, and fails to deploy the common-sense principle of prevention. The Slow Food movement explores the negative social and environmental impact and the low efficiency of centralized industrial and technological food production (petro-food), which requires a huge amount of energy, erodes the soil, pollutes the water and air, reduces biodiversity, impoverishes local rural communities, creates massive migration, fosters food insecurity and price volatility, spreads disease, and is unsustainable.[136] Additionally, the Slow Food movement stresses that the profit motive explains why

---

131 Kallis, *In Defense of Degrowth*, 122, 100–102.

132 Petrini, *Terra Madre*, 43.

133 Fernando Cembranos, 'Decrecimiento e indicadores económicos. Pérdidas que hacen crecer el PIB', in *Decrecimientos: sobre lo que hay que cambiar en la vida cotidiana*, ed. Carlos Taibo (Madrid: Catarata, 2010), 169–181; Maurizio Pallante, *La decrescita felice* (Rome: GEI, 2009), 23; Latouche, *La apuesta por el decrecimiento*, 52–53.

134 Herrero et al., *Cambiar las gafas para mirar el mundo*, 97–112.

135 Latouche, *La apuesta por el decrecimiento*, 48.

136 Petrini, *Slow Food Nation*, 23–27.

abundant corporately funded research focuses on risky biotechnology while agroecology and permaculture are woefully underfunded.

In short, the degrowth and slow movements both explore alternatives that challenge the official discourse that 'more and faster is better'.[137] These movements propose that the 'logic of quantity' should be replaced by the 'logic of quality'. Both also operate according to an understanding of sustainability that differs from that promoted by the dominant imaginary. Where reform environmentalism promises that technology holds the key to achieving sustainable ecological practices, even as it transgresses planetary boundaries and accelerates extractive processes, the degrowth and slow movements eschew technological solutions and maintain that a sustainable culture is one that does not try to exceed the pace of the regenerative cycle of the ecological system in which it is embedded. It is a culture that recognizes and lives within the limits of the Earth. Lowering consumption and adopting a slower lifestyle are thus paths towards sustainability as well as overall justice, health, and happiness.

1.3.2. Questioning Acceleration and Techno-Optimism

As I have shown in a number of previous publications, in the past decade, several fiction writers have employed sophisticated narrative strategies to focus on aspects of global capitalism, challenging the neoliberal discourse by questioning society's blind faith in technological progress and economic growth and advocating instead for a change of logic and lifestyle. These narratives can be read as counterparts to the Euro-Mediterranean socioenvironmental movements discussed above, because they articulate a meaningful critique of the capitalist myths of progress, development, and economic growth by exposing the ecological and social consequences of capital accumulation. On the other hand, many fiction writers are still perpetuating the mainstream discourse of the European Union by privileging the uncritical celebration of digital culture, progress, and globalization while failing to acknowledge their relation to the culture of new capitalism and its environmental and social impacts. In other words, some recent fictional narratives reflect the concerns of the degrowth and slow movements while the majority of fiction continues to replicate the neoliberal fascination with technology, speed, and cyberspace.

Ecocritical approaches to Spanish texts are still rare but have the potential to contribute substantially to the interpretation of recent narratives dealing with current global issues. The socioenvironmental perspectives advanced

137 Maurizio Pallante, *Meno e meglio. Decrescere per progredire* (Milan: Bruno Mondadori, 2011), 6.

by the degrowth and slow movements can fruitfully be translated into ecocritical practices in order to illuminate the narrative discourses and cultural representations that challenge commonplaces and official discourses related to technological acceleration and economic growth. However, few Spanish cultural scholars are trained in environmental criticism and thus able to read cultural manifestations in ecocritical terms. For this reason, some otherwise sophisticated critics seem to celebrate and embrace the new digital environment of the information age, claiming that it is necessary to adapt to its mutations and speed while emphasizing its multiple creative possibilities. They perpetuate an unjustified technological optimism that appears to be very similar to the official Western hegemonic discourse ingrained in the European Union's environmental imaginary. These critics are oblivious to the material and biological implications, and the resulting socioenvironmental global injustice, of the techno-social changes they praise and normalize (indeed, as we will explore further in Chapter 3, digital technology is supported by a socioenvironmentally disruptive and energy-intensive material infrastructure). The more they talk about the digital environment and its network of connections, the less they mention the biological environment and its living interconnectivity. The more they promote new virtual territories and innovative artificial intelligence, the more they reinforce the mainstream consumerist dynamic that destroys cultural and biological diversity (the real collective intelligence related to real territories). They claim that we should adapt to technological speed as well as global market dynamics, which seems to be very much in line with neoliberal/transhumanist aspirations. In their techno-market-evolutionary discourse, they emphasize the Western technological implications of human/machine coevolution, but ignore or minimize the ecological violence of that process and the global social asymmetries generated by it. The postgrowth ecocritical perspective I propose in this book will reveal that the main obstacles to articulating an emancipatory political imagination able to deal effectively with the most pressing social and ecological issues arise not only from conservative denialism but also, and more disturbingly, from the aforementioned progressive techno-optimism.

Several recent novels that celebrate technology are the work of the so-called 'Nocilla' or 'Mutantes generation'. Most of these authors started publishing in the twenty-first century. Their novels share certain commonalities, such as the tremendous importance placed on new communication and information technologies, the integration of many interdisciplinary Western concepts, the use of multimedia, and a fluent dialogue with the globalizing consumerist culture and its mass-media vehicles. The key question for me is whether these authors are reflecting or perpetuating the growth-oriented, techno-optimist dominant imaginary (probably both). Among the most active members of this generation are Agustín Fernández Mallo, Manuel Vilas, and Vicente Luis Mora. Although their works have the potential to be illuminated by an ecocritical or posthumanist approach,[138] a number of critics tend to accept their valorization of consumerist globalization and Western techno-science without questioning its logic in any profound way. Some of these texts can also be interpreted as social critiques due to their cynical and ironic tone, but their ambiguity suggests that they are in fact playing the postmodern game of satirizing hegemonic discourses while perpetuating them. This is the case with Vicente Luis Mora's *Alba Cromm* (2010) and Manuel Vilas's *Aire Nuestro* (Our Air, 2009).[139] Instead of presenting some of the novels of the Mutantes themselves—which are not useful for the purposes of this book, given their ambiguity—I have chosen to examine, from an ecocritical perspective, a work of criticism that praises this generation of writers. This will allow me to expose the blind spots of critics who assess these writers positively, to the unintended advantage of the hegemonic economic and political discourse, and to demonstrate the importance of developing an ecocritical approach to correct this situation and enrich the reading of technology-infused fiction by contributing a different point of view.

A literary-critical article by Christine Henseler, one of the most visible advocates of the new generation of writers, is a good illustration of critical interpretations that fail to consider the relationship between Mutantes fiction and the dominant neoliberal discourse.[140] In 'Spanish Mutant Fictioneers: Of Mutants, Mutant Fiction and Media Mutations', Henseler asserts that these authors acknowledge a 'breakdown of traditional hierarchical structures' that perceives 'contemporary society not as a vertical, but as a horizontal web'. Their works translate technological 'spaces of communication' such as the internet and virtual reality into a 'dissolution of linear time for a more absolute presence and circularity, virtual identity, a return of a totality understood in terms of a multiple and instantaneous globality, a non-existence of locals, and a non-existence of truth concepts'. In addition, these authors 'are global

138 See Katarzyna Beilin, 'Die and Laugh in the Anthropocene: Disquieting Realism and Dark Humor in *Biutiful* and *Nocilla experience*', in *Ethics of Life: Contemporary Iberian Debates*, ed. Katarzyna Beilin and William Viestenz (Nashville, TN: Vanderbilt University Press, 2016), 89–111.

139 Vicente Luis Mora, *Alba Cromm* (Barcelona: Seix Barral, 2010); Manuel Vilas, *Aire Nuestro* (Madrid: Alfaguara, 2009).

140 Christine Henseler, '*Spanish Mutant Fictioneers*: Of Mutants, Mutant Fiction and Media Mutations', *Ciberletras* 24 (December 2010), http://www.lehman.cuny.edu/ciberletras/v24/henseler.html.

nomadic citizens with backgrounds in a host of disciplines'. They celebrate their lack of roots and the convergence of old and new media in a consumerist global culture as well as in the rise of intercultural and transcultural connections. They are both self-critical and self-promotional in their use of social digital networks and multimedia platforms. Finally, they perpetuate the idea of dematerialization in the information age.

An ecocritic responding to this characterization of the Mutantes from a degrowth perspective will notice immediately the similarities between the aforementioned statements and the neoliberal discourse related to the 'eco-modernists'. Both the novels and the critics who praise them promote the necessity of adapting technologically and mentally to the culture of the global market economy rather than to the limits of the biosphere. Paradoxically, the celebration of digital convergence and social horizontality ignores the ecological unity of the biosphere (the actual systemic convergence of all networks) and its degradation by the asymmetrical and highly hierarchical global economic powers that are exacerbated by digital financial innovations. Additionally, the dissolution of linear time associated with network technologies does not translate into the appreciation of and adjustment to ecologically regenerative, communitarian, and cyclical time—a necessary condition for sustainability. On the contrary, it embraces the fast pace of consumerism and the acceleration of market dynamics that are causing the annihilation of most living systems on the planet. Furthermore, these novels and critics are reinforcing an ideology of progress and development that is sustained by the illusion of the possibility of constant economic growth and technological innovation—concepts associated with and created by linear modes of thinking. The silenced fact is that, at the time I write, 'the server farms that allow the internet to operate and that provide cloud-based digital computing [have] surpassed the airline industry in terms of the amount of carbon dioxide released into the earth's atmosphere'.[141]

When these authors and critics talk about transcultural connections, global citizenship, and the nonexistence of locals, they are not seeing the global picture from the vantage point of non-Western epistemologies. It is well recognized in decolonial and indigenous studies that neoliberal globalization is rapidly destroying not only biodiversity, but cultural and epistemological diversity as well, since biological and cultural diversity go hand in hand. When Henseler mentions the lack of roots and global nomadism, it is obvious that she is not referring to ecocosmopolitanism[142]

---

141 Stephen Rust, Salma Monani, and Sean Cubitt, 'Introduction: Ecologies of Media', *Ecomedia Key Issues*, ed. Stephen Rust et al. (New York: Routledge, 2015), 3.
142 Heise, *Sense of Place and Sense of Planet*, 205–210.

or a transnational ethic of place,[143] but rather to the cosmopolitan elite that moves through what Marc Augé calls 'nonplaces', such as airports, gas stations, malls, taxis, and global hotel chains.[144] She avoids the fact that most people live in a real territory and that their livelihood and cultural survival depends on it. The fact that some privileged groups can have no roots comes with a huge externalized socioenvironmental cost, since such groups depend on the consumption of huge amounts of fossil fuels. Furthermore, as Rob Nixon explains, using the distinction between the nomadic and the rootless articulated by Abdelrahman Munif, nomadic cultures are not rootless, since they are inscribed in the land through movement (belonging-in-motion), 'but the deracinations of the oil age plummeted them into a rootlessness that was nomadism's opposite. Driven from their lands, increasingly urbanized, repressed and exploited by a corrupt upper class in cahoots with American oil interests, many lower-class Bedouin found themselves culturally humiliated and politically estranged'.[145] Therefore, it seems urgent to revisit (from a more critical perspective) the way in which this generation of writers and their critics use the terms 'nomadism' and 'rootlessness'.

The Mutantes authors' acclaimed interdisciplinarity and fascination with science and technology is highly ethnocentric, since their approach exclusively embraces modern Western disciplines, science, and technology. They tend to avoid any reference to the imperial, androcentric, and (neo) colonial logic behind the global expansion of modern Western epistemology (and its technology). The question of digital colonialism—how the internet reinforces social, economic, and cultural hegemony—is never seriously entertained.[146] This point becomes obvious when attention is paid to what indigenous epistemologies, ecofeminism, and decolonial thinking say about modern Western culture, science, and technology. But, apparently, decolonial thinking and ecofeminism do not register within the so-called interdisciplinarity of these writers. Some of the Mutantes writers and their critics seem more attracted to the networked and connected individualism promoted by global capitalism than to a more ecological and equitable posthumanist communitarian ethic. When they play with commercial and hyper-consumerist discourses, they appear to be more interested

143 Nixon, *Slow Violence and the Environmentalism of the Poor*, 143.
144 Marc Augé, *Non-places: An Introduction to Supermodernity*, trans. John Howe (London: Verso, 2009).
145 Nixon, *Slow Violence and the Environmentalism of the Poor*, 76.
146 See 'Digital Colonialism & the Internet as a Tool of Cultural Hegemony', http://www.knowledgecommons.in/brasil/en/whats-wrong-with-current-internet-governance/digital-colonialism-the-internet-as-a-tool-of-cultural-hegemony/.

in how this game can enable them to enhance or market their artistic expressions than in how the toxic materiality of consumerism negatively affects human and nonhuman communities around the globe (more on this in Chapter 3). Finally, as Ramón Fernández Durán points out, 'The society of image and information helps to hide even more the very serious ecological crisis we face, especially because it encourages a shift in focus from the biosphere to the infosphere (cyberspace, virtual reality), making more invisible the deterioration of the First Skin, of Mother Nature'.[147] The acclaimed information society is an illusion that hides the rapid loss of real information (genetic, biological, cultural); the more colorful and defined the virtual images become on our computer screens, the faster real information disappears due to the ecological degradation and massive extinction provoked by the urban-agro-industrial system and its ongoing digital-financial accelerations.[148]

Some of these authors and critics seem to be more conventional than they would like to acknowledge. While they claim to be subverting or questioning the official discourse, they are actually perpetuating and embroidering it. The point is that global capitalism with its digital culture allows (and sometimes encourages, for commercial reasons) the subversion and transgression of norms, but never tolerates the epistemological transformation of the growth paradigm that would reduce social metabolism and decelerate daily life. Transgressing without transforming only reinforces the hegemonic imaginary. This coincides with the critique of some tendencies in North American cultural studies advanced by Cary Wolfe, following Tilottama Rajan and Gayatri Spivak. The problem seems to be the evolution of cultural studies 'from a site of "decentering innovation" into "a symbiosis with globalization" and the New World Order, in which "its dereferencialization is what makes it dangerous to some of its original components"'.[149] In other words, Wolfe writes, 'the effect of academically mainstreamed cultural studies is ... "to simulate the preservation of civil society after the permutation of the classical public sphere" into an essentially market and consumerist logic of "representation"'.[150] I see the obsession of the Mutantes (critics and authors alike) with hybridification, evolution, adaptation, convergence, integration, and mutation not as a posthumanist understanding of social and political ecology, but rather as an unintended promotion of 'the liberal project of incorporation and "recognition" that is an expression of, not a

---

147 Fernández Durán, *El antropoceno*, 90.
148 Herrero et al., *Cambiar las gafas para mirar el mundo*, 233–261.
149 Wolfe, *What Is Posthumanism?*, 104, quoting Tilottama Rajan.
150 Wolfe, *What Is Posthumanism?*, 104, quoting Tilottama Rajan.

critique of, globalization'.[151] To Henseler's assertion that 'to read the texts of the Mutantes 2.0 demands a 2.0 Literary Critic', I add that to see the blind spots of both Mutantes 2.0 and 2.0 Literary Critics demands an ecocritical approach.[152] Perhaps the emerging field of ecological digital humanities, 'developed from the mingling of the environmental humanities and the digital humanities', will soon provide some much-needed critical tools in this regard.[153]

In conclusion, we need more narratives and practices that contribute to decolonizing the dominant imaginary and its ideology of cultural consumerism, technological acceleration, and economic growth. As this chapter suggests and the rest of the book will demonstrate, the incorporation of a postgrowth ecocriticism attentive to issues of environmental justice can make a significant difference for Iberian cultural studies. In this regard, the ecological digital humanities could help ecocritical cultural studies to understand the new media dynamics involved in neoliberal globalization and provide creative options for decolonizing it, rather than reducing all life to a colonized ecology of new media. Fortunately, the Spanish cultural repolitization during and after the 15-M movement may be doing just that, as Moreno-Caballud explains, by using the internet to enhance a collaborative creation of value that challenges the 'type of technoscientific cultural authority that tends to monopolize the production of meaning'.[154] The Spanish cultural outcome of this appropriation of neoliberal technology to challenge the dominant imaginary remains to be seen.

151 Wolfe, *What Is Posthumanism?*, 105.
152 Henseler, '*Spanish Mutant Fictioneers*'.
153 Jeffrey Jerome Cohen and Stephanie LeMenager, 'Introduction: Assembling the Ecological Digital Humanities', *PMLA* 131 (2016): 340.
154 Moreno-Caballud, *Cultures of Anyone*, 144.

PART II

Urban Ecologies

PART II

Urban Ecologies

CHAPTER TWO

Urban Ecocriticism
and Spanish Cultural Studies

> How do we stop ourselves from fulfilling our fates as suicidally
> productive drones in a carbon-addicted hive, destroying ourselves
> in some kind of psychopathic colony collapse disorder?
> —Roy Scranton[1]

2.1. Spanish Urban Ecocriticism

In 1999, Michael Bennett and David W. Teague complained about 'the historical gap between environmentalism, cultural studies, and the urban experience'.[2] These urban cultural scholars had noticed that ecocriticism paid insufficient attention to the urban environment and that there was a need for an urban ecological cultural criticism. In response, they edited a volume of essays—*The Nature of Cities: Ecocriticism and Urban Environments*—intended to 'provide the parameters for an urban ecocriticism that offers the ecological component often missing from cultural analyses of the city and the urban perspective often lacking in environmental approaches to contemporary culture'.[3] Although cultural critics' interest in urban ecocriticism today is greater than ever before, it is still relatively scarce, and there is plenty of room for further scholarly explorations of the topic. In a recent book, *Urban Ecologies*, Christopher Schliephake rightly argues that

> urban life, rather than constituting a solely human-dominated domain,
> is conditioned by the interaction with nonhuman life forms and agents—
> interactions that are themselves subject to public debate and cultural

1 Scranton, *Learning to Die*, 85–86.
2 Michael Bennett and David W. Teague, 'Urban Ecocriticism: An Introduction', in *The Nature of Cities: Ecocriticism and Urban Environments*, ed. Michael Bennett and David W. Teague (Tucson: University of Arizona Press, 1999), 10.
3 Bennett and Teague, 'Urban Ecocriticism', 9.

imagination. In other words, spatial-material processes constitute the framework of urban life, and it is on the cultural-discursive level that their inner workings and interrelations are reflected and imbued with meaning. It is in and through culture that urbanity emerges as an ecological system.[4]

Schliephake finds that cultural urban ecology proves very fruitful for 'the analysis of cultural representations of contemporary urbanity'.[5]

Of course, these cultural urban ecocritical approaches are still extremely rare in Spanish cultural studies, where frameworks born of ecocriticism or urban studies were never fluid, let alone convergent. Spanish ecocriticism is only now emerging timidly. Nevertheless, the last decade has seen an impressive growth of scholarship in Iberian literary and cultural studies that places the city at the forefront of its cultural analysis, following the pioneering works of scholars such as Susan Larson, Malcolm Compitello, and Joan Ramon Resina.[6] Special issues focusing on Hispanic cities and culture have mushroomed over the last decade in academic journals such as *Letras Peninsulares*, *Colorado Review*, *Letras Femeninas*, *Ciberletras*, and the *Arizona Journal of Hispanic Cultural Studies*. A book series devoted to Hispanic urban studies, edited by Benjamin Fraser and Susan Larson, has recently been created, and new volumes on urban cultural studies are appearing in existing series such as Contemporary Hispanic and Lusophone Cultures, published by Liverpool University Press. Nevertheless, although Iberian cultural studies has avidly incorporated urban approaches in the past few years, these approaches rarely move beyond urban geography and sociology itself to take into account how urban cultural processes interact with the socioecological intricacies of cities. While most of these contributions deal with notions of urban space and representation, hardly any of them consider how the environmental aspects of the city affect culture, and how urban culture in turn shapes the ways in which we approach and transform (materially and symbolically) that environment.[7]

---

4 Christopher Schliephake, *Urban Ecologies: City Space, Material Agency, and Environmental Politics in Contemporary Culture* (Lanham, MD: Lexington Books, 2015), xiii.

5 Schliephake, *Urban Ecologies*, xxvii.

6 See, for instance, Susan Larson, *Constructing and Resisting Modernity* (Madrid: Vervuert/Iberoamericana, 2011); Malcolm Alan Compitello and Edward Baker, *De Fortunata a la M:40: un siglo de cultura de Madrid* (Madrid: Alianza Editorial, 2003); Joan Ramon Resina, *Iberian Cities* (New York: Routledge, 2001).

7 One exception is a recent article by Matthew Feinberg and Susan Larson, 'Cultivating the Square: Trash, Recycling, and the Cultural Ecology of Post-Crisis

The very absence of a Spanish urban ecocriticism is significant because it draws our attention to the blank spaces on our theoretical radars, which in turn indicate our epistemological limitations. To fill these spaces, this chapter intends to combine the momentum of current Spanish urban cultural studies with insights from urban ecocriticism in particular and the environmental humanities in general. My movement towards a Spanish urban ecocriticism is not driven by a tortuous theoretical argument. Rather, it follows the logical path that appears if the transformative and interdisciplinary spirit of urban cultural studies is developed to its fullest extent.

Inspired by Marxist urban theorist Henry Lefebvre, in his recent book *Toward an Urban Cultural Studies* Benjamin Fraser envisions an 'urban cultural studies' that places the humanities and the social sciences in dialogue to achieve an emergent 'framework for understanding urban culture in general terms … forcing literary and cultural studies to think the city geographically and forcing geography to think the city artistically'.[8] Although this movement is certainly welcome, it is not sufficient to 'disalienate humanities scholarship' by dismantling 'the divisions across disciplines—their alienation from one another'.[9] Given that cultural production in particular and humans in general are embedded in the biophysical space of the planet and depend on the proper functioning of the systems and cycles of the biosphere, why not go a step further and include the ecological sciences in the conversation, as the environmental humanities would recommend? If we recognize that cities and their urban cultural and material processes have played a huge role in the massive biogeochemical changes that the Anthropocene has wrought—due to the fact that urban metabolisms mobilize energy, materials, and imaginaries far beyond their geographical limits—why not include these socioecological processes and the 'hyperobjects' they produce when we explore the mutually constitutive relationships 'between material conditions and cultural imaginaries'?[10] Rather than merely investing in an 'urban-centered work of interdisciplinarity scholarship',[11] we could push this interdisciplinarity momentum further and focus on a more decentered cultural urban ecology that recognizes the interconnections between cultural transformations, urban metabolisms, and ecological dynamics on a global scale. If we are willing to take interdisciplinarity seriously in the age of the

Madrid', in *Ethics of Life: Contemporary Iberian Debates*, ed. Katarzyna Beilin and William Viestenz (Nashville, TN: Vanderbilt University Press, 2016), 113–142.

8 Benjamin Fraser, *Toward an Urban Cultural Studies: Henri Lefebvre and the Humanities* (New York: Palgrave Macmillan, 2015), 2–3.

9 Fraser, *Toward an Urban Cultural Studies*, 81.

10 Fraser, *Toward an Urban Cultural Studies*, 20.

11 Fraser, *Toward an Urban Cultural Studies*, 4.

Anthropocene (which also entails the age of the planetary urbanization of capital), we must collapse not only the barriers between the humanities and the social sciences but, more importantly, those between human and natural history and all that this implies.

Neil Badmington remarks that 'while cultural studies has transformed the humanities, it has not, in my opinion, questioned one of the most troubling aspects of the humanities', namely, 'the hierarchical border between the human and the inhuman'.[12] In my opinion, for any emancipatory urban cultural criticism to make sense of the Anthropocene, it must, among other things, move to the foreground the underappreciated Marxist notion of the 'metabolic rift' while abandoning the anthropocentric impulses ingrained in cultural studies which fuel the many neoliberal fantasies of human exceptionalism and planetary managerialism. Otherwise, we risk reproducing over and over different versions of the same anthropological machine that unleashes its exploitative and rapacious rationality on everything.

The preceding remarks should not be interpreted as a critique of Fraser's innovative and suggestive elaboration of a Lefebvrian urban cultural studies. Rather, they offer an invitation to take his argument further. Why must an interdisciplinary approach to the age of the Anthropocene be limited to the humanities and social sciences? Why not champion the recalibrated Marxism of Lefebvre, rearticulated by Fraser, and elaborate upon the concept of urban alienation in relation to the more-than-human world? Why not bring together cultural studies and urban political ecology? This fusion will allow us to investigate the interconnected social and ecological alienation inherent in urban capitalist cultures and to explore how this alienation depletes both humans and the nonhuman as they interact with and mutually constitute each other. Fraser suggests (and I could not agree more) that a cultural critic's most important task should be to reconcile the various alienated spheres of specialized knowledge (and, I add, nonspecialized knowledge as well). Unfortunately, as Fraser rightly laments, criticism could easily end up doing just the opposite by reaffirming 'existing alienations that prevent an apprehension of the totality of contemporary urban life'.[13] I would argue that any approach to culture that constantly and unconsciously overlooks the ecological dimension at a moment when the ecological crisis is impossible to ignore risks perpetuating the more dangerous alienation that allows different kinds of social and ecological exploitation: namely, the human-nonhuman divide.

12 Badmington, 'Cultural Studies and the Posthumanities', 261, 262.
13 Fraser, *Toward an Urban Cultural Studies*, 86.

Like Fraser, urban geographer David Harvey pays little attention to the possibilities and potentialities of an urban political ecology in his own Lefebvre-inspired and recalibrated Marxist book, *Rebel Cities*. Harvey clearly articulates the crucial role that urbanization has played historically in the absorption of capital accumulation by dispossession through predatory urban practices.[14] He also emphasizes the need to mobilize the revolutionary anticapitalist political possibilities of the impoverished heterogeneous masses who are excluded from decisions regarding the urban model and denied access to the enjoyment of the urban commons to whose creation they have contributed. However, if we prioritize the struggle of the urban precariat, we risk overlooking the fiercer and bloodier struggle occurring on the commodity frontiers, what Naomi Klein calls 'Blockadia'.[15] Most of these struggles are not urban-centric, but they are key actors in the global socioecological revolution of which the urban precariat is only a part. Focusing excessively on the urban precariat could contribute to silencing and diminishing the important struggle of a 'new environmental precariat' led by women and indigenous peoples who are resisting the metabolic expansion of the urban-agro-industrial system.[16] The main scenario of the struggle for this environmental precariat is not always the city, but they are all nonetheless resisting the process of planetary urbanization from the operational landscapes that make the extension of such processes possible.

Neoliberal urban policy, Harvey observes, conceives the planned city in the image envisioned by financial speculators, bankers, developers, and technocrats. As such, 'capitalist urbanization perpetually tends to destroy the city as a social, political and livable commons' and, I would add, depletes the planet as a biologically and culturally diverse place through its expansive appropriation and absorption of biomass, nutrients, and energy, as well as waste production.[17] The 'urbanization of capital presupposes the capacity of capitalist class power to dominate the urban process. This implies domination ... [over populations'] lifestyles as well as their labor power, their cultural and political values as well as their mental conceptions of

14 David Harvey, *Rebel Cities: From the Right to the City to the Urban Revolution* (London: Verso, 2012), 22, 53–57.

15 'Blockadia is not a specific location on a map, but rather a roving transnational conflict zone that is cropping up with increasing frequency and intensity wherever extractive projects are attempting to dig and drill, whether for open-pit mines, or gas fracking, or tar sands oil pipelines'. Naomi Klein, *This Changes Everything: Capitalism vs the Climate* (New York: Simon & Schuster, 2014), 294–295.

16 Foster, Clark, and York, *The Ecological Rift*, 47, 440.

17 Harvey, *Rebel Cities*, 80.

the world'.[18] I concur with Harvey that, to effectively resist and contest this domination, we need to collectively enact our right to recreate the city 'in a completely different image' and not limit the struggle to reclaiming 'a right to that which already exists'.[19] I claim that to do this it is important to envision postgrowth urban imaginaries. In order to challenge the dominant imaginary and to create something beyond the epistemological limitations self-imposed by the hegemonic rationality, it is paramount to expose the roots of the dominant logic that separates human and nonhuman concerns. To keep this in mind as cultural critics, it would be helpful to mobilize the following socioecological concepts when approaching city *naturecultures*: metabolic rift and urban metabolism.[20]

2.1.1. Metabolic Rift and Urban Metabolism

The notion of a metabolic rift was popularized by Karl Marx, who pointed out the problem of the growing rift in the metabolic exchange between humans and the planet provoked by capitalist urbanization. Although Marx focused mostly on the disruption of nutrient cycles generated by the increasing urban demand for externally produced agricultural products, the notion can be extended to include the rapid transgression of planetary boundaries that we are witnessing today. Marx interpreted the increase in agricultural produce sent from the countryside to the cities as a robbery of nutrients that do not return to the soil but instead remain in the cities and cause pollution.[21] Today, given that the number of people living in urban settlements has grown exponentially and that agroindustry is the main contributor to ecological destruction—in the form of biodiversity loss, soil erosion, water depletion, and nutrients' disruption—the metabolic rift caused by the urbanization of capital is even wider. Intense ongoing transformations in both urban and rural areas are the consequence of this planetary urban process. As Neil Brenner explains, this process includes not only changes in the physical space of cities, but also the transformation of massive 'non-urban' operational geographies needed to maintain the functions of the urban agglomerations (waste sinks, agro-industrial enclosures, and extractive, logistic, and communication and transportation infrastructures, etc.). This process of 'extended urbanization', as Brenner

---

18 Harvey, *Rebel Cities*, 66.

19 Harvey, *Rebel Cities*, 138.

20 See Luis I. Prádanos, 'Exploring the Political Ecology of Iberian Studies', in *A Polemical Companion to 'Ethics of Life: Contemporary Iberian Debates'*, ed. Katarzyna Beilin and William Viestenz (Nashville, TN: Vanderbilt University Press, 2016), 49–54, https://drive.google.com/file/d/oB6nyHHBXY48bY3Q5NUVVM2JjMkU/view.

21 Foster, Clark, and York, *The Ecological Rift*, 45.

calls it, transforms all the planet—including terrestrial, subterranean, oceanic, and atmospheric space—by putting it in the service of a process of urban capitalist development in constant acceleration and intensification.[22] As such, the metabolic rift is the result of the urban growth-oriented imaginary as it materializes. This rift 'can only be healed through a new revolutionary transformation in human social and ecological relations' entailing the unification of the struggles for social justice and ecological sustainability.[23] I believe that urban cultural studies could contribute to this radical transformation by embracing urban ecocriticism and investigating the social and ecological consequences (in the urban environment and beyond) of global metabolic urban processes and their coevolving cultural imaginaries.[24]

The work of Jason W. Moore achieves a fruitful combination of world systems theory, environmental history, and a revitalized notion of metabolic rift that illuminates the relationship between capitalist expansive dynamics and the current organization of world ecology.[25] He argues that capitalism always resolves its main contradiction, its dependency on the availability of uncapitalized nature (human and nonhuman) and its tendency to rapidly deplete it, by 'endless geographical expansion and endless innovation'.[26] Expansion and innovation are processes that cannot be separated either materially or symbolically. Moore considers that the current phase of capitalism 'has reached the limits of its developmental possibilities', as shown by the 'interconnected food, energy, and financial crises of 2008'. The development of the late capitalist ecological regime was made possible by 'the two great commodity booms—both centered in oil and agriculture—of the end of this long 20th century'. The era of cheap food and cheap oil is now over.[27] In other words, globally there is no more room to easily expand the metabolic order of capitalism and its planetary urbanization of capital without collapsing the planet's ecology. It is important to remember that, in the urban-agro-industrial system, food and fossil-fuel energy are

---

22 Neil Brenner, *Teoría urbana crítica y políticas de escala*, ed. Álvaro Sevilla Buitrago (Barcelona: Icaria, 2017): 263–266.

23 Foster, Clark, and York, *The Ecological Rift*, 49.

24 Fernández Durán, *El antropoceno*, 16–23.

25 Moore, 'Environmental Crises and the Metabolic Rift in World-Historical Perspective'.

26 Jason W. Moore, 'Ecology and the Accumulation of Capital. A Brief Environmental History of Neoliberalism', paper presented at the workshop 'Food, Energy, Environment: Crisis of the Modern World-System', Fernand Braudel Center, Binghamton University, October 9–10, 2009, 22.

27 Moore, 'Ecology and the Accumulation of Capital', 26.

highly interdependent (each calorie of urban petro-food requires about ten calories of fossil fuel). If Moore is right in suggesting that we are facing an 'epochal shift in the history of capitalism that expresses the (asymptomatic) exhaustion of frontiers', the problem cannot be solved by the usual process of innovation and imperialistic expansion without transgressing more planetary boundaries and causing a socioecological collapse.[28] The only rational reaction to this situation 'is a radical change of course'.[29]

Cultural and urban ecologist Herbert Girardet clearly explains why 'modern cities'' use of resources is highly problematic. They have an essentially linear, unidirectional metabolism, with resources flowing through the urban system without much concern about their origin, or about the destination of wastes. Inputs and outputs are treated as largely unconnected'.[30] This linear metabolism interferes with the biosphere cyclical processes of reabsorption and regeneration and depletes the resources deployed by the urban system, generating massive pollution and biological annihilation. 'As they perform their function, then, cities are "entropy accelerators"—they deplete and downgrade the resources they depend on in the process of using them'.[31] But urban systems would not have to be that way if they were able to detach from the dominant growth-oriented, linear logic. They could actually enhance biospheric capabilities.[32] Although the historical relation between the evolution of capitalism and the evolution of modern industrial cities with linear metabolisms is correlative, this does not mean that the existence of cities is contingent upon the acceptance of unsustainable linear metabolisms. Under a different imaginary, new urban models can emerge. Through a feedback loop, cities with circular metabolisms could regenerate themselves and their imaginaries, as Girardet suggests. An urban circular system would minimize external inputs and generate near zero waste, and thus cities would be designed so that all spent resources are reintegrated into the metabolic process over and over again. Such cities could even become carbon sinks rather than carbon factories. According to Girardet, this transition requires trading the Petropolis model (cities whose functions depend on massive inputs of fossil fuels and many other resources) for an Ecopolis model (cities that are not only sustainable, but socially and ecologically regenerative).

28 Moore, 'Ecology and the Accumulation of Capital', 22.
29 Foster, Clark, and York, *The Ecological Rift*, 426.
30 Herbert Girardet, *Creating Regenerative Cities* (New York: Routledge, 2015), 68.
31 Girardet, *Creating Regenerative Cities*, 69.
32 Saskia Sassen, 'A Third Space: Neither Fully Urban nor Fully of the Biosphere', in *Climate Architecture and the Planetary Imaginary* (New York: Columbia Books on Architecture and the City, 2016), 172–179.

This transition will not be easy, for the current rules of the 'carbon-capital complex' encourage the perpetuation of a Petropolis that is constantly competing with other cities, nationally and internationally, in the restless race to attract capital and foster growth, no matter the social and ecological cost. However, as Saskia Sassen reminds us, cities, more than nation-states, will be forced to actively confront the environmental challenges of the Anthropocene. Because cities are today at the center of the environmental problem, they must become part of the solution. Global cities have metabolisms that affect the entire planet and form a complex network with other cities. This network 'contains the site of power of some of the most destructive actors, but also potentially the sites at which to demand accountability of these actors'.[33]

For cities to become part of the solution, it is paramount to understand that they are open socioecological systems.[34] For cities to be sustainable, they must be both ecologically and socially regenerative. That implies thinking of urban policy and planning in terms of 'just sustainabilities', as Julian Agyeman suggests. Sustainable cities need to be designed not only to be environmentally sound, but also to improve the quality of life and well-being of their inhabitants while promoting justice and equality.[35] Without social equality and cultural plurality, cities are unlikely to become sustainable. Thus, 'achieving "just sustainabilities" will require a shift from current reformist strategies toward [urban] policy, planning, and practice for transformational change'.[36] Consequently, 'what is needed are [*sic*] positive, inclusive narratives of change in which the entire system is "reimagined"—narratives in which just sustainabilities are understood as a basis for security and in(ter)dependence'.[37] These narratives and their associated practices are what I call 'postgrowth urban imaginaries'.

In this context, municipalities are faced with the dilemma of either maintaining the inertia of neoliberal urbanization and eventually collapsing socially, ecologically, and financially—as environmental problems pile up and the supply of cheap food and cheap energy decreases and both become unaffordable—or transitioning from a Petropolis with a linear urban metabolism to an Ecopolis with a circular one. There are two main obstacles to achieving this postcarbon transition. The first is the inertia of the current

33 Saskia Sassen, 'Cities Are at the Center of Our Environmental Future', *S.A.P.I.E.N.* 2, no. 3 (2010), https://sapiens.revues.org/948.

34 Sassen, 'Cities Are at the Center of Our Environmental Future'.

35 Julian Agyeman, *Introducing Just Sustainabilities: Policy, Planning, and Practice* (London: Zed Books, 2013), 7.

36 Agyeman, *Introducing Just Sustainabilities*, 165.

37 Agyeman, *Introducing Just Sustainabilities*, 168.

infrastructure, which facilitates the perpetuation of growth-oriented practices and obstructs the implementation of other ways of inhabiting the city. To overcome this inertia, we could envision and cultivate what Dominic Boyer calls 'revolutionary infrastructure'.[38] The second obstacle is that global capitalist powers will oppose any attempt to move towards a convivial urban model by deploying all the weapons of their institutionalized arsenal: media disinformation and manipulation campaigns, capital networks, political bribery, neoliberal trade agreements, 'legal' instruments, lobbies, harassment, and military intervention. Every counter-movement initiated by an urban community will inevitably be precarious, given its inferior position in relation to the capitalist establishment, and its emergent imaginaries would certainly unleash unpredictable reactions and unintended consequences. Perhaps Madrid and Barcelona, whose mayors were elected on political platforms that emerged out of the 15-M movement, can lead the way. Ada Colau, mayor of Barcelona, began her tenure by challenging the neoliberal model of urbanization in several ways: rethinking tourism, enforcing environmental regulations, embracing co-ops and solar energy,[39] and opposing the unpopular transatlantic trade agreement secretly negotiated by elites. Interestingly, Barcelona en comú, Colau's party, 'won the election of the city without mentioning growth once in its programme'.[40] The mayor of Madrid, Manuela Carmena, also favors an urban model that fosters conviviality and equality rather than promoting capital accumulation for the well-off, while at the same time significantly reducing the debt of the city. Both mayors favor a very promising feminist urbanism at odds with the dominant growth imaginary. There may indeed be light at the end of the tunnel, but corporate media either ignores or misrepresents such light as darkness.

2.1.2. Towards Postgrowth Urban Imaginaries

One of the tasks I envision for urban ecocriticism is to track how counterhegemonic cultural processes challenge the dominant conception of cities as growth machines and envision postgrowth urban ecologies. I divide the study of post-2008 urban cultural manifestations into four distinct but non-exclusive categories, according to the way in which the socioecological

---

38 Dominic Boyer, 'Revolutionary Infrastructure', in *Infrastructures and Social Complexity: A Companion*, ed. Penelope Harvey, Casper Bruun Jensen, and Atsuro Morita (New York: Routledge, 2017), 174–186.

39 Sebastiaan Faber and Bécquer Seguín, 'Welcome to Sunny Barcelona, Where the Government Is Embracing Coops, Citizen Activism, and Solar Energy', *The Nation*, August 2, 2016.

40 Kallis, *In Defense of Degrowth*, 33.

metabolism of the city is conceived and depicted in relation to both the dominant imaginary of economic growth and its unsustainable energy regime. I hope other Iberian scholars find these interpretative categories useful for reading contemporary cultural manifestations through the lens of urban ecocriticism (beyond the multiple examples I provide in the following pages). The first of these interpretative categories explores the current negative social and ecological outcomes of neoliberal urban development in the context of the ongoing Spanish crisis by focusing on the discarded output of the urban linear metabolism: massive waste and precarious lives. The second category incorporates futuristic post-petroleum narratives, depicting the negative dystopian consequences of amplifying into the future the existing linear urban metabolic dysfunctions related to Petropolis. Relying on the fear generated by apocalyptic scenarios, these critiques are limited in their effectiveness because they do not offer any positive alternatives (on a related note, we will see in Chapter 4 why catastrophism may not be the best way to contest the dominant imaginary). The third category considers narratives that foreground the 'nonurban' geographies and cultures radically affected by the expansion of urban metabolisms. These narratives often envision a more or less forced neo-ruralization as a way of escaping the increasing unviability of urban life, but they may actually perpetuate (discursively) the rural-urban dichotomy that generated the metabolic rift in the first place. Finally, the last category focuses on the most effective strategy for criticizing the dominant urban imaginary, namely, cultural manifestations and social movements that dare to imagine, envision, articulate, and promote a postgrowth urban model that is socially desirable and environmentally sustainable. So-called 'nowtopians' intend to solve the problems caused by the metabolic rift by replacing urban linear metabolisms with circular ones (transition towns, slow cities); the measures they propose include urban agroecology and community gardens, child and health care cooperatives, urban permaculture, decentralized clean energy cooperatives, time banks, composting urban waste, collaborative economies, local currencies, open software, and participatory budgeting. Urban nowtopians often prefer to reimagine the city as a postgrowth settlement rather than promoting a counterproductive neo-ruralization that would perpetuate the rural-urban distinction that caused the metabolic rift in the first place.[41]

The suggested interpretative typology can be enumerated and summarized as the following four categories: The Crisis of the Urban

41 For the term 'nowtopians', see Chris Carlsson, 'Nowtopians', in *Degrowth: A Vocabulary for a New Era*, ed. Giacomo D'Alisa, Federico Demaria, and Giorgos Kallis (New York: Routledge, 2015), 182–184.

Growth Machine, Urban Collapse and Post-Petroleum Futures, Non-urban Spaces and Neo-ruralization, and Postgrowth Urban Imaginaries. Of course, some cultural expressions might fruitfully be read through more than one of these four categories at the same time. Nevertheless, this interpretative typology offers some guidelines for urban cultural critics as they rethink cities as socioecological open systems and refocus their analysis on the way in which urban metabolisms are represented. In the remaining pages, I will demonstrate the usefulness of this typology by applying it to a range of post-2008 Iberian literary and cultural manifestations.

2.2. Interpretative Typology

2.2.1. The Crisis of the Urban Growth Machine: Challenging Petromodernity

In the past few years, more and more cultural productions have challenged the grand narrative of progress equated with capitalist development and the acritical celebration of economic growth ingrained in the dominant imaginary. This chapter focuses on the urban ecocritical aspects of such challenges: namely, how the production and appropriation of space by the urbanization of capital creates an unsustainable social metabolism that is detrimental to both social conviviality and environmental health within and beyond the city limits. The built environment that characterizes modern cities and its functions is embedded in global material and symbolic networks of imperialism, toxicity, and destruction. From this perspective, it becomes obvious that the celebration of visible urban mega-infrastructures in Spain hides the proliferation of waste, pollution, and human/nonhuman displacement caused by neoliberal urbanization.

Out of many possible examples, I have selected three films that use different techniques and address diverse topics but are very effective in revealing the problems brought about by the neoliberal application of the growth imaginary to urban space. These are the documentaries *Sobre ruedas: el sueño del automóvil* (Keep It Rolling: The Dream of the Automobile, 2011), directed by Óscar Clemente, *Mercado de futuros* (Futures Market, 2011) by Mercedes Álvarez, and the experimental movie *Gente en sitios* (People in Places, 2013) by Juan Cavestany.[42] It seems to me that these films do not merely criticize the neoliberal management of the crisis, but the urban growth paradigm itself. Spanish literary and cultural production and criticism surrounding

---

42 Óscar Clemente, dir., *Sobre ruedas: el sueño del automóvil* (Seville: Labalanza, 2011); Mercedes Álvarez, dir., *Mercado de futuros*, DVD (Barcelona: Cameo, 2011); Juan Cavestany, dir., *Gente en sitios*, DVD (Barcelona: Cameo, 2013).

the financial crisis tends to focus on the social damage and human suffering it creates, rather than the unsustainable linear urban metabolism and 'petroculture' behind it. In the case of Spain, this focus on urban metabolism is especially relevant, since the nation's rapid passage from a rural economy to a neoliberal one involved a huge geographical transformation led by the proliferation of unsustainable agriculture, disastrous touristic and residential coastal constructions, and transportation infrastructures excessive even by Western European standards.

My goal here is not to catalogue the explicit environmental issues in the chosen films, but to understand how they reveal the socioecological shortcomings of the neoliberal urban model and how they articulate the resultant symbolic and material consequences in order to challenge the growth imaginary. Ecocinema critics generally agree, as noted by Stephen Rust, Salma Monani, and Sean Cubitt in *Ecocinema Theory and Practice*, that:

> all cinema is unequivocally culturally *and* materially embedded ... that the dominant, consumerist modus operandi often suggests a troubled state of affairs not only in human interactions but also with the nonhuman world ... and that *all* films present productive ecocritical exploration and careful analysis can unearth engaging and intriguing perspectives on cinema's various relationships with the world around us.[43]

Sobre ruedas exposes the unsustainable inefficiencies and socioecological pathologies generated by the massive spread of individual vehicles, as well as the energy-dependent urban model and the forced, futile mobility they provoked. Ivan Illich, one of the preferred philosophers of the degrowth movement, seems to be a source of inspiration for this documentary. Back in the early 1970s, Illich stated in his book *Tools of Conviviality* that beyond a certain threshold, when some modern tools (like the individual vehicle) continue growing in importance and efficiency, they stop serving their originally intended social purpose and become counterproductive, enslaving humans rather than helping them. At that point, the tools no longer enhance human autonomy or creativity and become impossible to control democratically; they become an end in themselves by structuring human relations and institutions to make societies dependent on the tools and the experts who manage and regulate them. The result of the proliferation of these non-convivial tools (for example, modern and

43 Stephen Rust, Salma Monani, and Sean Cubitt, 'Introduction: Cuts to Dissolves— Defining and Situating Ecocinema Studies', in *Ecocinema Theory and Practice*, ed. Stephen Rust, Salma Monani, and Sean Cubitt (New York: Routledge, 2013), 3.

institutionalized education, medicine, and modes of transportation) is a technocratic and fossil fuel-dependent society facing social fragmentation, structural dysfunctionality, and ecological collapse. Cars are one example of what Illich calls 'radical monopoly', that is, 'when one industrial production process exercises an exclusive control over the satisfaction of a pressing need, and excludes nonindustrial activities from competition ... Cars can thus monopolize traffic. They can shape a city in their image'.[44] Cars and the infrastructures that support them exclude other nonindustrial means of mobility (walking, biking) by creating distances (urban sprawl) that make it impractical or impossible to meet daily needs without an automobile. Because modern cities segregate urban functional spaces (housing, marketplace, working areas, entertainment venues, and social spaces), a car becomes necessary to compensate for the loss of multifunctional urban spaces.

Sobre ruedas also reveals the connection between the history of the car and the rise of productivist and consumerist culture. The documentary, which aims to be shocking yet pedagogically sound, combines numerous styles and formats to create a varied rhythm that captures the attention of the audience. It interweaves graphics and cartoons, background music, data charts, fragments of old documentaries and advertising, footage of Iberian urban environments dominated by vehicles and concrete, and extracts from interviews in which researchers and activists talk about the social and ecological downsides of cars and the urban model they support. The informed interventions of the interviewees and the disturbing facts they share contrast with the playful tone of the graphics and the sense of parody that the old documentaries and advertising generate. *Sobre ruedas* ends with guidelines on how to transition to a desirable and sustainable urban model designed for the convenience of humans rather than automobiles.

By showing how the infrastructures of petromodernity have (materially and symbolically) evolved in toxic ways, the documentary reveals the hidden energy regime behind the infrastructures that make humans' love affair with individual vehicles possible. It shines a bright light on the manufactured cultural associations that tie the automobile to progress, democracy, sexual desire, modern identity, and individual freedom. Stephanie LeMenager, in *Living Oil: Petroleum Culture in the American Century*, confronts the representational problems of 'materializing the ecologies of modernity', that is, mapping how the current pattern of 'modern living indebted to petroleum can have persistent damaging effects'.[45] 'Energy

---

44 Illich, *Tools of Conviviality*, 65–66.
45 Stephanie LeMenager, *Living Oil: Petroleum Culture in the American Century* (Oxford: Oxford University Press, 2014), 184, 183.

systems are shot through with largely unexamined cultural values, with ethical and ecological consequences'.[46] The petroleum culture impregnates every aspect of our urban daily lives, since 'oil itself is a medium that fundamentally supports all modern media forms concerned with what counts as culture ... [and] mediates our relationship, as humans, to other humans, to other life, and to things'.[47] The key question is how to craft 'counter-narratives to the petroculture' and its pervasive 'petroleum aesthetics' that permeate the dominant cultural imagination, and how to liberate ourselves from our destructive affective attachment to 'this profoundly unsustainable and charismatic energy system'.[48] *Sobre ruedas* provides an effective counter-narrative by showing both the false promises that the individual vehicle embodies and the cruel optimism that our attachment to petroculture entails. The documentary enumerates (through voice-overs and interviews) the increasing and ever more demanding sacrifices and losses we incur—both as individuals and as societies—to preserve our toxic attachment to cars and the oil energy regime. To illustrate the absurdity and futility of maintaining this attachment, the documentary notes some of the disturbing consequences that followed the massive introduction of individual cars: the disappearance of unaccompanied children and seniors from the streets, the segregation of urban space and its functions, the proliferation of parking lots and roads at the expense of green public areas, and the elimination of noncommodified spaces for social encounters, to name a few examples.

The film repeatedly uses the metaphor of the car as a 'devourer of space', and provides several illustrations of the expansive metabolism of car culture by pointing to its intensive materiality. A voice-over states that if all existing cars were placed in a line, it would circle the Earth 100 times; on another occasion, the narrator points out that the European highway system covers over 40,000 square kilometers, the equivalent of paving the surface of Switzerland with concrete. These statements are accompanied by animations that depict these disturbing facts with dark humor. A further example of petroculture's disproportionate human appropriation of net primary productivity is provided when the documentary attacks the shortcomings of the urban sprawl model by pointing out that it is an insatiable eater of space and disrupter of the geography, dependent on its continual appropriation of more and more territory and its biomass: an urban growth machine.

46 LeMenager, *Living Oil*, 4.
47 LeMenager, *Living Oil*, 6.
48 LeMenager, *Living Oil*, 195, 11.

Another effective metaphor used to visualize the expanding nature of this urban metabolism is that of an 'expanding bomb that multiplies the space' needed in order to manage our daily activities. The film shows how a stereotypical four-member Spanish family (the Pérez) living in the suburbs travels 24,140 kilometers every three months (the distance that Marco Polo traveled during his entire life!), just to carry out their daily routines within the city limits. Urban geography, as pointed out by philosopher Santiago Alba Rico, is divided into two categories: squares—spaces where people meet and interact—and corridors of transit. In modern cities, we spend more of our life in the corridors than in spaces for human encounter. But a democratic society needs plazas, as the 15-M movement reminds us through its reclamation of public spaces for politics. María Cifuentes, an urban architect interviewed for the film, states that Spanish cities devote an average of 62 percent of their space to the car, a machine that remains parked for 96 percent of its life. This results in a huge privatization of public space, as noted by the urban geographer David Harvey, who believes that 'streets are ultimately public spaces, and ... everyone in the community should have equal right to space within them, irrespective of whether they are in a car'.[49] It is unfair that a citizen who cannot afford or does not want a car is unable to use 62 percent of the city. To be able to fully access the urban space of Petropolis, fossil fuel needs to be bought and burned.

Sobre ruedas draws explicit connections between our unsustainable energy regime and the automotive petroculture. The individual car paradigm is embedded in an economic growth imaginary that does not recognize material limits to the endlessly expansive tendency of consumerist culture. Ironically it is a dominant imaginary that is impossible to universalize, because the more it succeeds, the more rapidly it diminishes its own possibilities for expansion due to energy and material peaks, entropy, and ecological devastation. The petroculture of linear growth is headed for a dead end because it is biophysically impossible to carry this urban model into the future. *Sobre ruedas* breaks with this dominant imaginary by taking all the positive symbols associated with it and exposing their destructive downsides. The film achieves, in some respects, what Stephen Rust claims that ecocinema concerned with climate change can accomplish, that is, to compel audiences 'to interpret historical images of oil, cars, and their related military-industrial complexes through the lens of global environmental risk'.[50] In the documentary, ecological economist Óscar Carpintero explains

49 Harvey, *Rebel Cities*, 97.
50 Stephen Rust, 'Hollywood and Climate Change', in *Ecocinema Theory and Practice*, ed. Stephen Rust, Salma Monani, and Sean Cubitt (New York: Routledge, 2013), 194.

how embracing the individual car as the default for the urban model is what is known in decision theory as feeding the idiocy: namely, adopting as a default the option with the greatest economic, social, and environmental costs. The problem is that this idiocy is the logic of capitalism itself and is now so ingrained in our economic, political, and cultural institutions that it is difficult not to see it as something given and unchangeable, instead of the result of historically emergent social constructions. *Sobre ruedas*, in conclusion, contributes to undermine and displace the dominant imaginary.

Mercado de futuros by Mercedes Álvarez also investigates the ills of neoliberal urbanization, but uses a very different cinematic strategy than *Sobre ruedas*. In this documentary the camera infiltrates the professional spaces of the principal engineers of the real estate and mortgage crisis—real estate agencies and fairs, the offices of financial speculators, and marketing and entrepreneurial conferences—and puts their spectacular paraphernalia of empty formulaic language, manufactured images, and fake scenarios on display. This close look at the urban growth 'experts' is both comical and infuriating to an audience that is immersed in the ongoing temporality of the financial crisis. The false promises of the dominant imaginary contrast dramatically with its dysfunctional and all too real urban metabolisms. Several sequences illustrate the proliferation of excessive traffic and concrete, abandoned construction sites, urban waste, and so on. The overall pace of the film is deliberately slow, enabling the audience to reflect on individual scenes and draw connections between multiple sequences. There are often long static shots of a given space or group of objects, highlighting their materiality. Human characters enter and exit the frame, but the camera remains still and does not prioritize their presence by focusing on them or following them. Some takes are unusually long and the film's rhythm is determined by the intensity of the characters' activity rather than by the frequency of the cuts. The overall slowness is subversive, since it enacts what the accelerated neoliberal temporality prevents us from doing: taking time to think, remember, evaluate, and decide whether an acceleration of our urban metabolism is socially desirable and ecologically viable. The film demonstrates that if people are granted the time to see, reflect, and make connections about the irrationality of neoliberal urbanization, they will do so on their own, without the need for complex technical explanations by self-proclaimed experts.

One of the most interesting things about *Mercado de futuros* is the absence of an authoritative narrator. The disembodied voice-over that is heard on a few occasions is more philosophical and lyrical than pedagogical and explicit. It deals with the art of memory and how our society may be losing it while the material world preserves it. Material transformations and changes in urban architecture are recorded memories. Objects have a persistent agency and they refuse to forget. One thinks of the massive geohistorical record imprinted on the biosphere during the Anthropocene that could be read by future archeologists. The Anthropocene, or 'Anthrobscene', as Jussi Parikka prefers to call it, is geological memory that 'describes the effects of the human species and its scientific-technological desires on the planet'.[51] As a result, the lack of historical memory in growth-oriented societies cannot prevent the Earth from recording the socioecological transformation brought about by capitalism's metabolic rift. Certainly, the ecological crisis and the mortgage crisis are nothing but a crisis of memory. Societies dominated by the growth imaginary quickly forget that 'it can take from 500 to 1,000 years to build an inch of new topsoil', as the Land Institute reminds us,[52] and that neoliberal fantasies can coerce us into killing it quickly with concrete and asphalt in the process of generating an unsustainable urban metabolism that is neither socially necessary nor desirable.

For the majority of the film, the camera allows the diegetic characters to express themselves in their own terms as they perform their professional activities without interference. The camera waits patiently until the growth-oriented fantasies expose themselves in their theatrical, manufactured, hyperrealist artificiality. In some cases, the spell is broken by the characters' regurgitation of nonsensical neoliberal speeches. When these discourses are critically analyzed, they prove to be delusional. The best example of this occurs at a real estate and tourism fair when a realtor talks to a couple of potential customers about a tourist resort in Latin America constructed in a biodiverse region that boasts mangroves. He conceives of the place as 'un derroche de naturaleza' [an excess of nature], as if one could have too much nature and as if humans were not part of the natural world. He recites a litany in praise of ecotourism and indigenous tribes without listening to his interlocutors. He celebrates the 'efecto de acoplarte con la naturaleza ... con aire acondicionado' [effect of coupling oneself with nature ... with air conditioning]. If we analyze his discourse ecocritically, numerous contradictions arise. The more successful these resorts become, the faster they deplete the biodiversity and cultural diversity they intend to commodify, and the more tourists learn to enjoy technologically mediated 'nature', the faster its biodiversity disappears. David Harvey describes the same paradox of the monopoly of rent, namely,

51 Jussi Parikka, *The Anthrobscene* (Minneapolis: University of Minnesota Press, 2014), 1.
52 Land Institute, https://landinstitute.org/about-us/.

that the more a commodified place becomes homogeneous and 'Disneyfied' (with swimming pools, air-conditioned hotels, corporate commodities, modern transportation infrastructures, etc.), the less unique it is and therefore the less valuable commercially.[53] And there is an ethical dilemma in the monopoly inherent in capitalist dynamics: corporations appropriate the value of 'the collective symbolic capital to which everybody has, in their own distinctive ways, contributed both now and in the past' by unfairly appropriating and monopolizing the symbolic and common creation of value by indigenous cultures and their cultural landscapes, while destroying the cultures (and biomes) that coevolved with and gave shape to the native landscape.[54]

Mercado de futuros does not provide any explanation of why so many apparently educated and well-dressed people insist on perpetuating discourses that seem to be parodic. In one scene, a realtor trying to sell property takes it for granted that the potential buyer wants to speculate with it, and becomes confused when his client explains that he is looking for a house in which to live. The reaction of the realtor is polite incomprehension. Rather than rethinking his own absurd profession—turning houses into places where most people cannot afford to live—he ends up preaching to the prospective customer about the need to open his mind (meaning, to consider speculating and investing in the mortgage markets which, as the audience knows, exacerbated the ongoing crisis). There are other examples in which characters shamelessly and aggressively talk (they rarely practice active listening) about the economic benefits of urban speculation and futures markets, the wonderful increase in gated communities, and how the capital movements they facilitate navigate and create crisis. All the while they act as if these pursuits did not have massive ethical, ecological, and social implications.

One remarkable sequence begins with a female voice-over and the image of an architectural mock-up. The emphatic voice celebrates a great opportunity to invest in Dubai and its macro-hotels, office buildings, and gigantic malls. Dubai is depicted as 'the ideal place to live and to work', and the voice-over swoons that 'something so beautiful and amazing appears from the desert'. A subsequent scene reveals that the speaker is talking to an apparently persuaded potential investor at a real estate fair. She mentions that Dubai has just opened the biggest shopping mall in the world and is now building one that will be twice as large. She remarks that everything is bigger and better in Dubai, and that in Dubai 'all dreams

53 Harvey, *Rebel Cities*, 103–112.
54 Harvey, *Rebel Cities*, 105.

come true'. However, the material reality is not compatible with this urban neoliberal fantasy, for Dubai is an extreme example of a Petropolis with an unsustainable linear urban metabolism.[55] The spectacular growth of cities in the Arabian Gulf (a desert) equipped with eccentric engineering and architectonic features (artificial lakes, pharaonic sports facilities and shopping centers, skyscrapers) proceeds without attending to all the elements necessary for livable and sustainable urban spaces: community parks, public schools, squares, and so on. In addition to the social corrosion and lack of social resilience in Dubai and other Arabian Gulf 'growth' cities, these urban models depend on intensive energy input and generate disturbing amounts of waste and pollution; their 'per capita use of fossil fuel—and greenhouse gas emissions—is among the highest in the world'.[56] Furthermore, 'their utter dependence on desalinated water and imported food', both energy-intensive goods, further complicates the future viability of these cities.[57] The more successful these cities are, the faster they deplete the energy upon which their functions depend. The magnificent dreams that the real estate agent celebrates are likely to become a nightmare in the near (post-petroleum) future. *Mercado de futuros* goes on to show disturbing images of the material consequences of these urban atrocities.

The unveiling of neoliberal contradictions in the film is also achieved by the unexpected intrusion of visual elements and the relationships created between seemingly unassociated sequences by the soundtrack. For example, one shot shows a desolate landscape of concrete pavement and benches (a place devoid of vegetation and shade) in which people appear to be listening to the sounds of the sea. Subsequent shots are close-ups of a poster about tourist beach resorts. These resorts are located in Murcia and Alicante, along the overwhelmingly overdeveloped and ecologically depleted Spanish Mediterranean coast. We come to realize that the sea sounds are supplied by a recording accompanying an advertising campaign that is being staged on the periphery of a city near an airport, far from the sea. In the next scene, posters bearing paradisiac images, such as an attractive white heterosexual couple walking on a deserted beach, are paired with a marine soundscape, but the view is suddenly interrupted by workmen passing before the camera. They are building the infrastructure of what seems to be an urban fair promoting tourism, and the noises made by their tools invade the scene. The cacophony of power tools and an exotic view frequently interrupted by mundane elements are a much

---

55 Girardet, *Creating Regenerative Cities*, 56–59.
56 Girardet, *Creating Regenerative Cities*, 57.
57 Girardet, *Creating Regenerative Cities*, 56.

more realistic representation of what a tourist might expect to find on the overcrowded Mediterranean coast. The most disruptive moment occurs when a door opens in the wooden wall to which the poster is attached and a person walks out of it. This metaleptic moment calls our attention to the artificiality of marketing paraphernalia and how human and nonhuman phenomena alike insist on disturbing neoliberal fictions.

The massive transformation of landscapes generated by the new financial technologies engineered by neoliberal capitalism (including the futures markets to which the film's title refers) results in unnecessary and dysfunctional urban developments, futile transportation infrastructures, and real estate over-construction, accompanied by loss of biodiversity and overall ecological depletion. In this light, the image of the 'successful' people who deliver hyperbolic and empty speeches throughout *Mercado de futuros* suffers a radical shift. Their positive identification with the dominant imaginary, celebrated and admired as a model of economic success, is replaced by a negative association with the mortgage crisis. They are no longer perceived as the entrepreneurial heroes who will grow the economy and generate a trickle-down effect making everyone more prosperous, but as unethical plunderers of the Earth who engineered the financial crisis and promoted dysfunctional urban development. They destroyed not only the wealth generated by communities and ecosystems, but also the conditions necessary for the production of wealth in the future. They committed the crime of ecocide against present and future generations of humans and the nonhuman alike. As David Orr puts it, on our already overstressed planet we cannot define success in capitalist terms, since

> the planet does not need more successful people. But it does desperately need more peacemakers, healers, restorers, storytellers, and lovers of every kind. It needs people who live well in their places. It needs people of moral courage willing to join the fight to make the world habitable and humane. And these qualities have little to do with success as our culture has defined it.[58]

The world needs the kind of people who try to heal the metabolic rift by creating a more circular and cyclical urban metabolism. Two examples of such people appear in *Mercado de futuros*.

The two characters are an urban gardener and a scrap dealer. Because they do not contribute to the growth of the GDP, they are marginalized and displaced by the dominant imaginary, although they make a significant difference

---

58 David W. Orr, *Earth in Mind: On Education, Environment, and the Human Prospect* (Washington, DC: Island Press, 2004), 12.

to the urban common good. The urban gardener reduces the metabolic rift by growing food in the city (instead of stealing soil nutrients from the countryside) and makes the city a more self-sustainable and breathable place. The scrap dealer reduces the pressure on landfill by repurposing and reintroducing discarded materials into the urban metabolism. Let us take a closer look at these two figures and their film sequences in turn. One scene shows a couple of small food gardens overwhelmingly surrounded and threatened by transportation infrastructures (a railroad, several streets, and a highway). The gardens look like a biotic oasis resisting the tidal wave of abiotic asphalt and iron. The uneasy feeling generated by the scene is intensified by the unpleasant sound of vehicles. All of this contrasts with the tranquility of the gardener as he gathers fruits and vegetables and waters the produce by hand. At one point he sits down and eats some of his fruit. Later, walking slowly, he carries his produce home and, accompanied by a dog, navigates the inconveniences and dangers of roads not designed to be crossed by pedestrians. The gardener resists being swept up by the rapid pace of the logic of growth.

The scrap dealer has a small garage in the *rastro de los Encants* in Barcelona, where people gather to buy and sell used books, secondhand furniture, and other odds and ends. We know his name, Jesús, because another character states it; he is the only character identified by name in the film, which grants him an authentic personality as opposed to the nameless, unauthentic people parroting the dominant imaginary. He sits in front of his garage and relaxedly chats and jokes with whoever stops by. He is unmotivated by the capitalist logic of maximizing economic profit, and he refuses to sell a number of things because they are not easy for him to retrieve. The materials that a consumerist society discards are kept by a person who does not embrace the logic of growth. The gardener and the scrap dealer are the kind of people who are needed to create regenerative cities with circular metabolisms. They resist, materially and symbolically, the accelerated urban model imposed by neoliberal reason. Their attitude is sober and calm; they seem to know that nothing should be considered trash, because all things have agency. Their tranquil personalities and their unhurried movement contrast with the frenzied and inflated body language and speech of the market-oriented characters.

Another significant scene in *Mercado de futuros* focuses on an abandoned and crumbling block of apartments. The desolate setting is suddenly peopled by a group of teenagers gracefully entering the frame. Using the ruins as a space to practice acrobatics, they improvise beautiful shapes with their bodies as they interact with the decaying space. The acrobats are repurposing the neoliberal wasteland in order to create something beautiful and artistic that does not require any exosomatic energy and does not commodify or privatize the space. For a desirable non-growth-oriented city to emerge from the neoliberal ashes, this kind of creativity in the reappropriation of space is key. As Matthew I. Feinberg and Susan Larson point out in relation to spaces that have been culturally repurposed in Madrid in the wake of the economic crisis, this reinvented 'use of previously discarded, abandoned or otherwise unused city spaces ... suggest[s] that there are viable urban alternatives to the accumulation strategy of debt-driven financial capital'.[59]

Mercedes Alvarez's documentary joins the crop of new Spanish films that 'acknowledge the relations between film-makers and filmed social actors'.[60] As Moreno-Caballud observes in relation to other Spanish documentaries dealing with 'the issue of urban transformation', *Mercado de futuros* allows the social actors to perform, 'questioning the authority of a neutral and disembodied source of knowledge about the world ... The "performative" turn brings back the embodied and subjective positions that classic authoritarian documentaries wanted to erase'.[61]

Gente en sitios, directed by Juan Cavestany, is an experimental film comprised of seemingly unrelated short stories set in Spanish urban spaces (often in Madrid). The title's reference to people in places is ironic, because most of the characters in the film feel out of place, alienated by both the built environment and other people. In fact, most of the characters convey an uneasy sense of disorientation through their behaviors, expressions, and acts of miscommunication. The places where the characters find themselves never encourage positive emotional attachment or meaningful human interaction, but are spaces of dislocation and alienation. Many characters appear to each other as untranslatable, unrecognizable, estranged, and incoherent. There are many instances of rapidly alternating close-ups that show the characters' facial expressions as they chat without listening to or understanding each other. The uninhabitable neoliberal urban spaces can only produce awkward and disturbing social relations. They do not foster conviviality, empathy, reciprocity, and communication, but rather aggression, competition, fear, and social fragmentation. Constant tension is the norm. In one of the sequences, Juan Carlos Monedero, an influential social and political activist linked to Podemos who signed the 'Última llamada' (Last

---

59 Feinberg and Larson, 'Cultivating the Square'.

60 Luis Moreno-Caballud, 'Looking Amid the Rubble: New Spanish Documentary Film and the Residues of Urban Transformation (Joaquim Jordá and José Luis Guerín)', *Studies in Spanish & Latin American Cinemas* 11, no. 1 (2014): 62.

61 Moreno-Caballud, 'Looking Amid the Rubble', 63.

Call) manifesto mentioned in Chapter 1, delivers a philosophical speech from inside a taxi. He claims that a decent life is one in which a person can develop a life without damaging others, but that just the opposite is true in modern society. Here individualism, consumerism, and competition are society's guiding behavioral principles.

One sentence that is repeated several times is key to understanding the film as an expression of a pathological linear urban metabolism: 'Antes, todo esto era campo' [Before, all this was countryside]. This expression is well known to Spaniards, as it was a common utterance during the last decades of rapid urbanization. By highlighting this phrase, the film forces the audience to think more deeply about it, and a new meaning emerges. Usually, the sentence does not carry negative connotations; it crops up in everyday conversations as a formulaic, superficial remark, like an observation about the weather, and does not allude to a critical or controversial issue that might trigger an urban planning debate. But following the real estate and mortgage crisis in Spain, the phrase sounds much more problematic. The same is true of conversations about the weather in the context of rapid anthropogenic global warming. Language is never innocent. By moving a casual reference to the countryside to the foreground, the film obliges us to interpret it as a subtle critique of neoliberal urban metabolism and its socioecological downsides. The importance of the phrase as a unifying motif in *Gente en sitios* is evident: it even appears on the DVD packaging in capital letters, competing with the actual title of the film.

In one sequence, a character is discussing possible titles for a novel and 'Antes, todo esto era campo' is one of the preferred options, suggesting that the title of the film itself, *Gente en sitios*, might be replaced by *Antes, Todo Esto Era Campo*. The places where people are now used to be countryside; putting people in modern urban places requires erasing the countryside. Unfortunately, these modern spaces are socioecologically depleting spaces where people live miserable and alienated lives.

The phrase appears for the second time in a sequence in which a middle-aged man with a backpack (played by Santiago Segura) is looking for something in a store full of colorful plastic objects—low-quality items made mostly in China. He looks nervous and suspicious as he holds a hammer that he eventually decides to purchase. Later on he appears in the rear seat of a vehicle, carpooling with other people. One character tries to engage him in small talk, recounting how well he himself navigated the crisis due to the fact that he works for a firm unaffected by the recession, which sells clothing for dogs. In the course of his monologue he remarks, 'Antes, todo esto era campo'. The increasingly disconcerted man in the rear seat, whose gestures suggest that he is about to use the hammer to silence his talkative travel companion, replies '¿Qué?' to express his growing confusion. When the salesman repeats his sentence, the nervous man demands that the car stop at a nearby gas station and he jumps out. Several short shots and a rapidly moving camera indicate the character's disorientation as he finds himself in a gas station surrounded by noisy freeways. Again, the unpleasant urban space is perceived psychosomatically by the characters. A pathological space produces pathological societies and vice versa. As Ivan Illich and Henri Lefebvre understood well, tools and environments built by humans are not unidirectional transformations of the nonhuman world by human agency. Rather, they transform and mold humans in turn. It is a codetermined process.

Over the course of *Gente en sitios*, 'Antes, todo esto era campo' becomes a statement about the disturbing increase of the ecologically devastating human appropriation of net primary productivity, as the rapidly expanding urban metabolism devours Spanish territory in order to produce the pathological and unlivable places where the people in the movie spend their tormented existences. These places are devoid of green spaces and trees, populated instead by airports, highways, industrial warehouses, parking lots, apartments, gas stations, and so on. The only character whose facial expressions and body language reflect comfort and well-being appears in one of the last sequences of the film. Like the apprehensive passenger with the hammer, she too occupies the rear seat of a car, but she is looking at a tree-filled landscape through the open window—a place that is still countryside. As *Sobre ruedas* points out, it seems that the only way to escape the horrible urban model generated by the rise of the automobile is by driving one of them. A perverse paradox.

As in *Mercado de futuros*, a wise voice emerges from a socially marginalized character, a man (Coque Malla) who is committed to finding a gift in a scrapyard for the person he has been dating. Again, a beautiful act emerges from the waste of consumerist society. While evaluating the gift potential of random parts of dysfunctional cars, the man recognizes that 'El mundo va mal. Vamos hacia un sinsentido' [The world is going in the wrong direction. We are heading towards senselessness]—an accurate description of our current direction, as the next section will emphasize.

These three films, produced with small budgets and deploying very different cinematic techniques, clearly expose the socioecological implications of current urban alienation. They all explore, explicitly or implicitly, the unsustainable expansion of neoliberal urban metabolisms in post-2008 Spain and the various drawbacks of the urban growth imaginary.

2.2.2. Urban Collapse and Post-Petroleum Futures

The previous section explored a number of urban narratives that depict the Spanish crisis of the current growth model without making projections about the future. The second category of the interpretative typology includes cultural productions that take the growth crisis as a given and speculate on the consequences of adhering to the current dominant imaginary and maintaining its metabolic dysfunctions into the future. As is widely recognized by cultural scholars, science fiction provides a fruitful venue and creative intellectual laboratory for understanding the present social and ecological situation by extrapolating it into the future. With the help of speculative fiction, we can envision how the dominant imaginary and some of its currently normalized socioecological materializations might determine future developments. In other words, by projecting into the future the planetary urbanization of capital addicted to economic growth, we can examine the traumatic social disruptions that will result from severe energy restrictions and extreme ecological depletion. I will discuss two novels in this section, focusing exclusively on their vision of the socioecological implications of pursuing our current unsustainable linear urban metabolism.[62]

El peso del corazón (The Weight of the Heart, 2015), a work of science fiction by Rosa Montero, continues the story of Bruna Husky, the charismatic protagonist of her previous novel, *Lágrimas en la lluvia* (Tears in the Rain, 2011).[63] Both novels are critical dystopias that take place mainly in Madrid (which has been part of the United States of the Earth since 2098) in the year 2109, after an era of devastating global wars and in the context of a chronic social and ecological crisis. Critical dystopias often suggest alternative possibilities, latent within the dystopian grand narrative, for counter-imagining the hegemonic trajectory. In addition to human agents, Montero's future world includes extraterrestrial beings as well as artificially intelligent anthropomorphic androids ('reps') created for commercial and military purposes. These new 'others' force humans to renegotiate human exceptionalism and social identities. They also trigger the emergence of new fundamentalist groups, including human supremacists, that define their identities in aggressive opposition to the new others by translating differences into hierarchies—another iteration of the anthropological machine. Bruna

---

62 For more examples, see the essay 'Decrecimiento o barbarie: ecocrítica y capitalismo global en la novela futurista española reciente', *Ecozon@: European Journal of Literature, Culture and Environment* 3, no. 2 (2012): 74–92, in which I discuss several Spanish futuristic novels published in 2011 from a degrowth-inspired ecocritical approach.

63 Rosa Montero, *El peso del corazón* (Barcelona: Seix Barral, 2015).

Husky herself is a rep with an existentialist personality. After serving as a combat rep for a few years, she became a private detective and earns a frugal living. In both novels, the crises of the future are amplifications of aspects of the current socioecological degradation resulting from the intensification of neoliberal globalization: worsening environmental issues that have dramatic consequences for daily life; the management, monopoly, and privatization of vital resources by the multinational corporations that caused them to become scarce; the massive increase of environmental injustices in which the people who suffer the most from ecological deterioration are those least responsible for it; and the extreme dehumanization of society. In Montero's future, technocratic management of populations, a hierarchical and uneven social distribution of risks, and technologies that monitor life and bodies are so pervasive that extreme neoliberal biopolitics are the norm.

El peso del corazón could be categorized as an environmental thriller, given that the main plot is determined by Bruna Husky's investigation of a corrupt framework embedded in a complex network of geopolitical environmental issues. Many areas of the Earth are classified as 'Zone 0' and are hyper-contaminated. This situation provokes, on the one hand, a rapid deterioration in the health of people who are forced to live in hyper-contaminated spaces if they cannot afford to pay for clean air, and on the other, the corporate privatization and assimilation of breathable areas as living spaces for the wealthy. Living in Zone 0 areas is especially harmful, and even fatal, for children.[64] In El Retiro, the central park of Madrid, there is an 'ecological' area with artificial trees constructed by Texaco-Repsol (a giant energy oligopoly), while the traditional gardens of the park are in terminal decline due to continuous drought.[65] The corporations which in the reader's present have profited most from exacerbating environmental deterioration (while actively obstructing any proposed solutions for climate change) are portrayed in the novel as benefiting disproportionally from chronic catastrophic situations. The narrator explains that for a long time the air was the property of the big energy corporations, which charged a fee for breathing it, but this practice was declared illegal just a few months ago. Unfortunately, that has not solved the environmental justice problem, because the clean areas quickly imposed a residential tax that only the well-off can afford, generating an enforced gentrification.[66]

In the United States of the Earth, the new borders are determined not by nations but by the degree of pollution, and they are maintained by the

64 Montero, *El peso del corazón*, 207.
65 Montero, *El peso del corazón*, 36.
66 Montero, *El peso del corazón*, 13, 259.

gated and militarized limits that separate environmentally unsafe spaces from zones that have been depolluted, which are only accessible for a price. This system results in the technocratic, militarized, and neoliberal management of populations and spaces, as well as extreme segregation based on income (in the next chapter we will discuss how this is already happening). Neoliberal reason is carried to its logical extreme, since the least fortunate—who seem to be the majority of the population—are fully exposed to the worst effects of ecological degradation, generated by the capital accumulation they did not benefit from, and they receive no public support. As Wendy Brown points out, under current neoliberal tendencies, 'responsibilized individuals are required to provide for themselves in the context of powers and contingencies radically limiting their ability to do so'.[67] Yet it is difficult to justify the claim that children with cancer dwelling in Zone 0 are responsible for their plight because they have not pulled themselves up by their own bootstraps and have not invested their human capital wisely enough to improve their living conditions. The very expression 'pulling oneself up by one's own bootstraps', fully embraced by the dominant imaginary, is a biophysical impossibility that defies gravity and, as with many neoliberal fantasies, ignores not only physical laws but also the asymmetrical distribution of power, wealth, and privilege, as well as the socioecological contexts in which individuals are inextricably enmeshed.

That the desperate situation in 2109 is the result of continuing the present inertia into the future is made explicit by historical archives included in the novel which describe events familiar to the contemporary reader. This helps to connect the dots between the temporalities. The narrative strategy makes visible the slow violence that Rob Nixon describes as 'attritional catastrophes that overspill clear boundaries in time and space [and] are marked above all by displacement'.[68] One of the main challenges of holding accountable those who perpetrate slow violence is the difficulty of tracking its multiple and diverse temporalities. Showing how our current lifestyle endangers the health of the children of the future could be a good starting point. Slow violence invites us to redefine displacement, as Nixon argues, for 'instead of referring solely to the movement of people from their places of belonging, [it] refers rather to the loss of the land and resources beneath them, a loss that leaves communities stranded in a place stripped of the very characteristics that made it inhabitable'.[69] This displacement is currently more intense in the global South but, as the novel warns, it could be the norm everywhere

---

67 Brown, *Undoing the Demos*, 134.
68 Nixon, *Slow Violence and the Environmentalism of the Poor*, 7.
69 Nixon, *Slow Violence and the Environmentalism of the Poor*, 19.

in the near future if the current dominant imaginary is not challenged and the metabolic rift increases.

The temporal dimension of slow violence is not fully discernible or easily comprehended. One character in *El peso del corazón* expresses this ineffability when talking about an enormous cemetery of nuclear waste: 'Las primeras pinturas rupestres sólo tienen treinta mil años, y la toxicidad de algunos residuos dura tres veces más que eso' [The first cave paintings are only thirty thousand years old, but the toxicity of some nuclear waste lasts three times longer than that].[70] Of course, this violence (not perceived as such by the dominant logic that perpetuates it) affects the more vulnerable members of society disproportionally, as advocates of environmental justice insist, because they are much more exposed to anthropogenic environmental risks and less able to afford to deal with the related problems. However, nobody is immune to a degraded environment. The novel shows how the syndrome of chemical sensitivity has become much more aggravated in the future due to generalized and continuous contact with synthetic chemical substances that alter the human immune system.[71] This disruption of the body's natural defenses also reminds us that, despite capitalist fantasies which claim that human individuals are independent from social and ecological systems, '"human" and "environment" can by no means be considered as separate' and therefore we should think of 'human corporality as trans-corporeality, in which the human is always intermeshed with the more-than-human world … By emphasizing the movement across bodies, trans-corporeality reveals the interchanges and interconnections between various bodily natures'.[72]

Stacy Alaimo elaborates on the topic of multiple chemical sensitivities in her outstanding book *Bodily Natures: Science, Environment, and the Material Self*. Trans-corporeality, she argues, erodes 'the foundations of human exceptionalism', since things are also agents affecting our bodies rather than just passive objects to be utilized by humans. This material turn 'inspire[s] a trans-corporeal, posthuman environmentalism' that entails a different ethical approach.[73] Significant modifications to environmental conditions always have consequences for human bodies and therefore these alterations need to be considered ethically. However, the neoliberal tendency to ignore the origins of problems, thereby reducing them to nonpoliticized obstacles to be overcome by entrepreneurial individuals

70 Montero, *El peso del corazón*, 330.
71 Montero, *El peso del corazón*, 54.
72 Alaimo, *Bodily Natures*, 2.
73 Alaimo, *Bodily Natures*, 111.

competing in the global market, does just the opposite. The environment, rapidly depleted by market competition, is perceived, if at all, as an irrelevant background independent of human economic dynamics and the system of social reproduction that is damaging it. For example, the disproportionate amount of research on genetics and cancer treatments 'deflects attention from environmental carcinogens'.[74] The insistence on blaming individual choices, psyches, or genes 'absolves government, industry, and indeed the entire material/political world from blame'.[75] The fact is that finding an effective way to deal with multiple chemical sensitivities, or with the disturbing proliferation of cancer, could never be an 'individual matter, but instead would entail a staggeringly thorough overhaul of nearly all military, industrial, manufacturing, agricultural, domestic, and consumer practices'.[76] The many issues related to environmental and public health cannot be solved by individuals targeting symptoms within the context of a growth imaginary that dominates the conditions of material and symbolic reproduction and worsens ecological problems, but rather by a collective transition to a postgrowth society led by a repoliticized culture.

The urban environments of *El peso del corazón* are radically affected by climate change and other ecological issues, but urban planning still follows a growth-oriented blueprint that relies on a linear metabolism. The grossly insufficient ways of dealing with pressing ecological problems are still based on market-oriented logics (reform environmentalism, eco-modernism, eco-efficiency, green capitalism) which only succeed in increasing an already intolerable inequality and securing the power of a global super-oligarchy.[77] Of course, to manage the massive slow violence generated by environmental injustices without changing the dominant imaginary requires extreme biopolitical control[78] and, conversely, the anthropological machine accelerates and multiplies its exclusionary and aggressive distinctions.[79] The main urban lesson is that post-petroleum neoliberal urbanism, the continuation of the logic of growth in a post-peak oil world characterized by scarce energy and a depleted environment, undermines the conditions of possibility for any socially desirable urban society. For that reason, it seems urgent to challenge this predominant urban model before it is too late and to politicize uneven urban metabolic processes, as urban political ecologists recommend: 'Political ecology attempts to tease out who (or

74 Alaimo, *Bodily Natures*, 105.
75 Alaimo, *Bodily Natures*, 119.
76 Alaimo, *Bodily Natures*, 115.
77 Montero, *El peso del corazón*, 98, 175.
78 Montero, *El peso del corazón*, 12–14, 133.
79 Montero, *El peso del corazón*, 312.

what) gains from and who pays for, who benefits from and who suffers (and in what ways) from particular processes of [urban] metabolic circulatory change'.[80] Montero's novel does a good job of showing the future victims and winners of the ongoing urban metabolism, but by presenting such a trajectory as inevitable, it underplays the possibilities for a more affirmative politicization. Envisioning desirable postgrowth urban imaginaries would be a good starting point for this much-needed politicization, as will be shown later in this chapter.

In recent years, new research combining fields such as artificial intelligence, big data, geographical computation, and urban planning has investigated the potential for using big data to create 'smart cities'. The idea is to use the massive digital data collected by the so-called 'internet of things' (by tracking citizen movements, feelings, transactions, entertainment habits, calories burned, web pages surfed, home energy usage, and so forth) to understand how people are using the city so that the city can respond to such demands accordingly in real time. Some rudimentary versions of this 'smart' city are depicted in *El peso del corazón*, although this theme is developed further in Montero's previous novel. The outcome is less ideal than the one pictured by the supporters of smart cities. Many futuristic novels contradict the techno-optimistic vision behind this kind of research when they contextualize these technologies in a complex social, economic, cultural, and ecological context. This high-tech urban paradigm is highly problematic in a number of ways, because these smart cities molding and adapting to citizens' behavior are also reinforcing, influencing, and channeling such behavior by facilitating it. These technologies can make existing urban processes more efficient, but they question neither the asymmetrical power relations that created them nor the current logic of the urban model itself. This tendency is inherent to techno-managerial reform environmentalism, as discussed in Chapter 1. This mindset often forgets that nothing is neutral, and that the urban adaptations envisioned and programmed into smart city processes—and the identity and power position of those who make these choices—matter immensely. As Montero's novel reveals, if we just make our cities 'smart' so that they effectively and efficiently perpetuate the ongoing urban neoliberal dynamics, the result will be 'stupid' cities reproducing unsustainable urban metabolisms programmed to facilitate and reinforce consumer

80 Nik Heynen, Maria Kaika, and Erik Swyngedouw, 'Urban Political Ecology: Politicizing the Production of Urban Natures', in *In the Nature of Cities: Urban Political Ecology and the Politics of Urban Metabolism*, ed. Nik Heynen, Maria Kaika, and Erik Swyngedouw (New York: Routledge, 2006), 12.

habits, thus exaggerating current power asymmetries and accelerating the ongoing biological annihilation. This could easily generate a vicious circle: the ingrained neoliberal logic disseminated by the dominant imaginary exerts a powerful influence on how people behave in the existing urban spaces in which they coevolve, and if we used these behaviors to model the city, it would further condition people's neoliberal behavior and the city would become a more aberrant urban space of total commodification. Decolonizing the dominant imaginary will become more and more challenging given this vicious circle.

Another problem with this 'smart city' approach also visible in Montero's novel entails the widespread consolidation of urban biopolitics that will not only manage, monitor, and control populations in real time, but also manage the built environment in which they are embedded, thus limiting, manipulating, or channeling future behavior. The cybernetic construction of the smart city will rule out the possibility of political challenges to its regime as citizens are excluded from the debate over what kind of urban model ensures a good life. Under these circumstances, we can assume the exclusion or marginalization of everybody and everything that does not fit into the smart city's processes. The smart neoliberal city, by transforming urban space into a synchronized cybernetic mega-growth machine to facilitate fluid commodity circulation and consumer convenience, leaves no space for urban politics to flourish. This will hinder urban social movements that seek 'to convert public space into a political commons'.[81] In other words, making our current growth-based urban model smarter is not a smart thing to do. While dystopian futuristic novels like *El peso del corazón* provide powerful critiques of the neoliberal urban model and the dominant imaginary of growth, they fail to portray alternative postgrowth urban models that are desirable and sustainable. Narratologists recognize that exposure to certain stories can have effects on readers' political and ethical perspectives, and if a narrative presents a future undesirable urban development as inevitable, it may considerably limit the power of the story to trigger political activism and instead encourage passivity, withdrawal, and resignation. There are thus obvious limitations on the capacity of critical dystopias to envision postgrowth imaginaries and to articulate an effective urban political ecology able to advance a new, emancipatory common sense.

The next example is a brilliant novel by Lara Moreno titled *Por si se va la luz* (In Case the Power is Cut, 2013).[82] This is a post-peak oil or post-petroleum

---

81 Harvey, *Rebel Cities*, 161.
82 Lara Moreno, *Por si se va la luz* (Barcelona: Lumen, 2013).

narrative set in the near future; unlike Montero's novel, it takes place in a 'nonurban' space (this novel could also be read through the next category of the typology elaborated here). The book portrays an urban-rural relocation, orchestrated by an undefined entity called 'the organization', due to social and ecological issues that intensified after the financial meltdown and transformed modern capitalist cities into precarious and dysfunctional spaces. Like Montero's novel, it is a systemic narrative. The story in *Por si se va la luz* emerges out of the multiple perspectives provided by four autodiegetic narrators (Martín, Nadia, Enrique, and Damián), as well as an extradiegetic alternation of internal and external focus on the seven main characters. The reader is led to assume that the story unfolds a few years ahead of the present moment, given the analeptic references to the financial crisis and to the emergence of social movements that are recognizably incarnations of the 15-M movement.[83] The novel extends the duration of the financial crisis several years into the future, affirming what many people already suspect today, namely, that we are immersed in a systemic crisis.

Nadia, an artist, and Martín, a researcher, are a couple of urban dwellers who move to a semi-abandoned village where they interact with the new environment and its few inhabitants. Living in the village are two long-time locals (Damián and Elena) and a seasoned philosopher (Enrique) who moved there some time ago and now owns the only operational—yet dysfunctional—business, a poorly supplied bar. Later, Ivana, a Russian political activist, and a child in her custody, Zhenia, join the group. Many symptoms of global warming are affecting the regional climate, including extreme drought and unusual ecological changes.[84] Damián, who has spent his whole life living off the land, notices the changes more than anyone else. In the context of the village, the abstract knowledge brought by Nadia and Martín is not functional, while Damián and Elena have practical experience with resilient agricultural methods that can assure survival under current conditions. The complex and irrational neoliberal economy of integrated global markets and financial speculation that has dominated the geopolitics of past decades means nothing in a localized context of bartering and subsistence activities. When meeting material needs is the priority, and water, electricity, and food supplies cannot be taken for granted, 'use' value displaces 'exchange' value. Trade with outsiders takes place irregularly, when a group of gypsies arrives with a van carrying various goods and, occasionally, with passersby. Nadia observes: 'Los porteadores son gitanos, no hay más remedio de que así sea, nos llevan tanta ventaja ahora' [The

83 Moreno, *Por si se va la luz*, 115, 162.
84 Moreno, *Por si se va la luz*, 44–45, 155–156, 188, 232–234, 237, 238, 247.

traders are gypsies, it couldn't be otherwise, they are way ahead of us].[85] Interestingly, traditional peasants and gypsies, representatives of groups whose cultures have been diminished and erased by the imaginary of economic growth, become crucial actors in this postgrowth society. Under the new socioecological conditions, as Nadia puts it, 'Todo ha pasado de moda' [Everything is out of fashion].[86] Where massive inputs of fossil fuel are not available, the local biophysical resources at hand are the only option[87] and outputs are necessarily limited.[88] A more circular metabolism must be created, and thus all organic waste is repurposed as compost to fertilize the soil.[89]

Details about exactly what happened in the cities are not provided, but there are plenty of clues that point to progressive urban decay resulting from vast socioeconomic structures that have become difficult to maintain.[90] The constant injections of energy and materials needed to fuel the urban linear metabolism of Petropolis become less and less available as the global growth machine approaches its biophysical limits. As the politically engaged Spanish nonfiction writer and degrowth promoter Fernández Durán points out, metropolitan spaces are islands of apparent order generating oceans of disorder elsewhere in order to function.[91] One example of this unsustainable metabolic expansion is provided by Martín when he talks about the collapse of the city:

Lo monstruoso. La frivolidad del ensanchamiento, esos kilómetros llenos de construcciones, de pequeñas ciudades que nunca terminaron de existir, bloques simétricos con sus instalaciones de luz y agua, urbanizaciones parásito. Hombres parásito. Virtualidad y desorden ... Ahí empieza el precipicio.[92]

[Monstrosity. The frivolity of sprawl, kilometers full of buildings, full of little cities that never completely existed, symmetric blocks of apartments with their power and water installations, parasitic suburbia. Parasitic men. Virtuality and disorder ... The beginning of the end]

85 Moreno, *Por si se va la luz*, 118.
86 Moreno, *Por si se va la luz*, 120.
87 Moreno, *Por si se va la luz*, 51.
88 Moreno, *Por si se va la luz*, 241–242.
89 Moreno, *Por si se va la luz*, 243.
90 Moreno, *Por si se va la luz*, 41, 73, 101, 102, 104, 114, 115, 116, 162, 205, 242, 248, 290.
91 Fernández Durán, *El antropoceno*, 21.
92 Moreno, *Por si se va la luz*, 101.

The urban-agro-industrial system is completely dependent on a centralized energy regime and a giant infrastructural fabric that disproportionally appropriates biomass and is unsustainable:

Este lugar sigue conectado a un generador, igual que otros miles de lugares en el mundo, tentáculos olvidados donde ya no vive un alma, fábricas inservibles, parques temáticos, centros comerciales, hospitales, seguirán conectados a la máquina aunque nadie encienda los interruptores. Millones de cables recorren la Tierra ... ese gran despliegue de progreso destruido. También las inmensas ciudades parásito que han sido construidas en las faldas de las inmensas ciudades parásito tienen sus conductos de agua y sus cables conectados a la máquina, aunque los edificios estén completamente vacíos.[93]

[This place continues to be connected to the generator, just like a thousand others in the world, forgotten sprawl where nobody lives anymore, useless factories, theme parks, malls, hospitals will still be connected to the machine even if nobody turns on the switches. Millions of cables cover the Earth ... that huge display of progress destroyed. The immense parasitic cities that were constructed on the outskirts of other parasitic cities also have their water conduits and their cables connected to the machine, even though their buildings are completely empty]

The rest is easy to imagine: the price of everything escalates,[94] pets become an unaffordable luxury and the city fills with pestilential abandoned dogs,[95] vital goods are scarce and stores close,[96] basic services are discontinued,[97] energy unreliability becomes the default,[98] and malnutrition, pollution, disease, and generalized chaos proliferate.[99] In summary, 'El mundo construido se convertirá en un campo de concentración' [The man-made world will become a concentration camp].[100]

Por si se va la luz challenges the perverse, cannibalistic dominant growth imaginary: 'Hablamos de progreso. Un progreso que se lo ha comido todo'

93 Moreno, *Por si se va la luz*, 104.
94 Moreno, *Por si se va la luz*, 41.
95 Moreno, *Por si se va la luz*, 73.
96 Moreno, *Por si se va la luz*, 114–115.
97 Moreno, *Por si se va la luz*, 116.
98 Moreno, *Por si se va la luz*, 163, 205, 242.
99 Moreno, *Por si se va la luz*, 248.
100 Moreno, *Por si se va la luz*, 104.

[We talk about progress. A progress that has devoured everything].[101] Martín remembers that scientific publications in the academic journals to which he contributed were not read by anyone, since everyone was busy feeding 'las necesidades irreales de un sistema autodestructivo' [the unreal necessities generated by a self-destructive system].[102] Continuing along the path laid out by the dominant imaginary of economic growth is likely to lead us to some version of the undesirable forced urban degrowth depicted by the novel. The obvious moral is that degrowing in a system designed to grow is always catastrophic, and thus it is necessary to design a prosperous postcapitalist society that is not addicted to growth. The task is not to weigh the pros and cons of the rural versus the urban, but to ask the question, as I believe the texts discussed in the next section do, What can we do about 'the epistemological privileging of the city since the 19th century', which ignores the interdependency between the urban and the nonurban?[103]

In my view, the most interesting aspect of these two critical dystopias is that they challenge audience expectations that catastrophe should unfold in a spectacular and instantaneous fashion. Instead, disaster capitalism is more about an accumulation of chronic problems unfolding at different scales and temporalities, not a big cataclysmic occurrence. In other words, the represented future dystopia is actually already unfolding, and for colonized people it has been here for centuries! In this sense, the experiences of the characters in these novels are not very different from the quotidian phenomenology of many colonized and disenfranchised people in the past and present alike, all victims of the deleterious effects of economic growth and capitalist accumulation by dispossession.

2.2.3. Non-Urban Spaces and Neo-Ruralization: Escaping the Urban Growth Machine?

By now it should be clear that the social metabolism of capitalism that radically transforms and produces modern urban and rural spaces (the urban-agro-industrial system, as Ramón Fernández Durán likes to call it)[104] can never be understood by focusing on either the urban or the rural as impermeable, separate entities, but only by considering the flow of materials, energy, bodies, and discourses that circulate through the urban-agro-industrial system. The growing metabolic rift is the result of the unsustainable linear material interchange entailed by the capitalist

---

101 Moreno, *Por si se va la luz*, 162.
102 Moreno, *Por si se va la luz*, 162.
103 Resina, 'The Modern Rural', 8.
104 Fernández Durán, *El antropoceno*.

rural-urban dialectic movement: it is the material manifestation of the planetary urbanization of capital in its differentiated articulations and uneven geographical developments. It is a system in which the urban process depends on massive inputs of energy and vast displacements of inanimate materials as well as biotic beings (including humans), and ends up disrupting planetary ecological cycles, creating refugees, accelerating entropy, and producing unmanageable quantities of waste and pollution. The expansion of this dysfunctional and unsustainable planetary urbanization—since it only functions by undermining its future conditions of possibility—requires the application of a capitalist logic to the food system: namely, implementing industrial agriculture in its different stages as the dominant (institutionally supported and incentivized) mode of food production. Industrial agriculture also leaves the food system addicted to fossil fuels and biotechnologies, resulting in the eradication of traditional peasant cultures and the massive relocation of people.

Today we know we cannot sustain the current global population for much longer using industrial agriculture since it is a system of production that contributes heavily to the ongoing transgression of three planetary boundaries: climate change, biodiversity decline, and the disruption of nitrogen and phosphorous cycles. It is also dependent on a fossil fuel input that will no longer be cheaply and abundantly available in the near future:

> One farmer using fossil energy for fuels and fertility, for example, can feed some 75 people. Such numbers, however, conceal the fact that it takes 11 calories of fossil fuel to put 1 calorie on the consumer's plate ... Subsistence farmers, operating at far lower 'efficiency' levels, invest 1 calorie to produce 50 calories of food.[105]

In other words, industrial agriculture 'works well if energy is cheap and ecological costs are ignored'.[106] In the context of peak oil and climate change, however, ecological costs are more and more difficult to ignore and the availability of cheap energy is likely not going to last much longer. Furthermore, since industrial food is centrally produced, it depends on long-distance transportation, exorbitant packaging, and refrigeration. All this contributes to the consolidation of macro-corporations that control and monopolize the food supply while undermining democracy worldwide. This centralization also undermines food security and triggers the instability of food prices and access: 'Marx described how capital creates a rupture in the "metabolic interaction" ... that is only intensified by large-scale agriculture,

---

105 Orr, *Earth in Mind*, 188.
106 Orr, *Earth in Mind*, 188.

long-distance trade, and massive urban growth'.[107] The industrial approach to food obeys a single rule: 'producing ever more quickly and cheaply'.[108] But this growth-oriented agricultural method cannot be sustained much longer since 'we simply cannot organize the agricultural produce market according to the same criteria used for the industrial sector ... Agricultural production cannot be increased indefinitely because the availability of land is not unlimited'.[109] In addition, the industrial agriculture model causes rapid degradation of the topsoil, destroying the conditions necessary for the possibility of agriculture itself.

The rapid transition from traditional rural cultures to industrial agriculture and urban growth in Spain required a vast change in land use and distribution, new economic policies, agrarian reform, new energy policies and infrastructures, and the rapid transformation of traditional landscapes and cultures into operational landscapes to support the planetary urbanization of capital. Such changes do not happen spontaneously, but are orchestrated from above and entail a forced relocation of people and an enormous intensification of ecological degradation. Óscar Carpintero's study of the metabolism of the Spanish economy during the second half of the twentieth century clearly shows that in those years the Spanish economy rapidly increased the material and energy intensity of its activities, significantly affecting ecological systems and grossly overshooting its territorial biocapacity.[110] The role of Franco in the implementation of this capitalist modernization and its dominant imaginary cannot be overlooked, as pointed out by Jo Labanyi and Helen Graham.[111] Moreno-Caballud notes that 'within the broad meaning of "culture" (production and circulation of meaning, ways of life, creation of subjectivity), the capitalist implementation instigated by Francoism undoubtedly implies a complete economic revolution—but it also implies a cultural one'.[112] Following Jesús Izquierdo, Moreno-Caballud explains Francoism's effective 'task of dismantling rural traditional cultures',[113] whose strategy included:

the marginalization and disarticulation of community-based rural cultures; the implementation of a middle-class, individualist, urban,

---

107 Foster, Clark, and York, *The Ecological Rift*, 77.
108 Hermann Scheer, 'Region Is Reason', in *Slow Food*, ed. Carlo Petrin (White River Junction, VT: Chelsea Green, 2001), 9.
109 Hermann Scheer, 'Region Is Reason', 9.
110 Carpintero, *El metabolismo de la economía española*.
111 Graham and Labanyi, 'Culture and Modernity: The Case of Spain', 16–17.
112 Moreno-Caballud, *Cultures of Anyone*, 41.
113 Moreno-Caballud, *Cultures of Anyone*, 42.

consumerist social model; and finally, a significant part of that implementation, the launch of a whole series of liberal economic policies ... that will establish the foundations of the neoliberal model still to come.[114]

Eugenia Afinoguénova eloquently explains how the slippery concept of 'quality of life' was constructed during late Francoism to justify socially undesirable and environmentally destructive economic policies based on unsustainable growth and the overdevelopment of tourism.[115] Once capitalist growth and quality of life are presented as synonyms, it becomes quite difficult to criticize the former without being accused of opposing the latter. Thus, neither right- nor left-oriented political discourses dare to oppose the suicidal addiction to economic growth once it is equated with 'quality of life' by a vast segment of the population, no matter how wrong and contradictory that association may be. Hence, any radical ecological project is easily marginalized and diminished. The result was a dominant economic and cultural context programmed to embrace without much resistance what Isidro López calls 'consensonomics: the economic ideology of the CT' which has dominated the Spanish social imaginary over the last few decades. According to López, the most effective bait deployed by the cultural authorities to promote mass acceptance of this ideology was to equate it with European integration. Actually, the neoliberalization of Spain was significantly intensified after its entry into the European community.[116] The Transatlantic Trade and Investment Partnership (TTIP) agreement, which has been under negotiation between the European Union and the United States since 2013, promotes the culmination of the neoliberal project and threatens a corporate-orchestrated disarticulation of what remains in Europe of small and medium-sized farming. This dismantling entails dire socioecological consequences. Research journalist and activist Esther Vivas warns that since the onset of the global financial crisis, the same speculators who provoked the real estate bubble are now generating a food bubble by speculating with the food supply.[117] Extracting capital first by expelling people from their houses and now by taking food from their mouths: this is the culmination of the life-capital conflict excoriated by feminist and ecological economics.

---

114 Moreno-Caballud, *Cultures of Anyone*, 46.
115 Afinoguénova, 'Tourism and "Quality of Life" at the End of Franco's Dictatorship'.
116 López, '*Consensonomics*: la ideología económica en la CT', 84–85.
117 Esther Vivas, 'De la burbuja inmobiliaria, hemos pasado a la burbuja alimentaria', *Esther Vivas*, October 21, 2013, https://esthervivas.com/2013/10/21/de-la-burbuja-inmobiliaria-hemos-pasado-a-la-burbuja-alimentaria/.

One of the most rarely challenged pillars of the CT's dominant economic and cultural paradigm is the notion that economic growth driven by capitalist development is the only path to progress and therefore should be society's priority. Whatever economic cultures are incompatible with capitalist modernity—and its intense, unsustainable material regime— are systematically condemned and discarded. If the only way to progress as a modern, normalized European country is through economic growth and capitalist urbanization, all ways of life that do not contribute to it are to be undermined materially and symbolically. Non-market-oriented communitarian ways of life, where the culture of sharing and frugality are the default, are to be disposed of and fragmented, leaving the market as the only way to fulfill the needs previously supplied by the community itself. It is well known that lonely individuals fearing their neighbors in neoliberal urban environments are much more dependent on commodified products than people living in coherent communities. Indeed, if the priority of society is economic growth, a fragmented urban environment full of disempowered, overstressed, fearful individuals is preferable to cohesive and convivial communities. In the dominant semiotic realm, however, the urban is often associated with the desirable, setting the standard for quality of life, and the rural is constructed as its denigrated opposite: capitalist urban growth is taken for granted and equated with progress. Subsistence economies are disallowed and the word 'subsistence' (which means to have the autonomy, as a community, to be able to sustain your own life) becomes a derogatory term. As Amaia Pérez Orozco reminds us, under capitalism, by definition, capital accumulation is a process that is socially guaranteed (on a material, symbolic, and political level) over the reproduction of life.[118] Thus, the maintenance of life is not a social priority and it becomes ignored, feminized, and privatized. Today, planetary life is being annihilated— species are becoming extinct at a rate hundreds of times faster than what was previously the norm—in the intensified conflict between capital and life inherent to capitalism.[119]

Let us explore how some recent cultural manifestations (fiction and nonfiction writings, op-eds, web series, and documentaries) are challenging the dominant imaginary by focusing on the rural-urban metabolic rift from the vantage point of the 'nonurban'. In these cultural productions, crucial nonurban spaces, often ignored by the city-centric dominant imaginary, are moved to the forefront. These spaces—Neil Brenner calls them 'operational landscapes'—where the conflict between capital and life and its slow violence

---

118 Pérez Orozco, *Subversión feminista de la economía*, 133.
119 Pérez Orozco, *Subversión feminista de la economía*, 181.

are especially virulent, reveal how the metabolism of cities depends on extra-urban spaces that encompass the whole planet. As such, planetary urbanization operationalizes and transforms 'the entire planet, including terrestrial, subterranean, fluvial, oceanic and atmospheric space, to serve an accelerating, intensifying process of industrial urban development'.[120] These conflicting geographies tend to be completely obliterated—at least in their problematic socioecological aspects—by the dominant urban imaginary. In other words, the applauded urban monuments of industrial and postindustrial modernity come with a huge global socioecological cost (within and without the geography of the city) and, frequently, the more pharaonic and spectacular monuments are, the more disturbing the dimensions of such costs become.

Distintas formas de mirar el agua (Different Ways of Looking at Water, 2015), a short choral novel by Julio Llamazares, narrates how a number of family members gather by a reservoir to deposit the ashes of their deceased grandfather, Domingo.[121] The reservoir was one of the many hydraulic projects undertaken by the Franco regime to fuel urbanization, industrialized agricultural irrigation, touristic infrastructures, and economic growth. As a result, Domingo's hometown was flooded and he and his family were relocated in one of the rapidly sprouting 'colonization towns', where they found a mass-designed 'non-place' with completely different ecological and agrarian conditions to which their traditional knowledge and practices were not always appropriate. They were forced to abandon a more or less coherent community with a cartography of memories and emotional attachments for a culturally and historically unfamiliar place full of unknown people. This affected not only the life of Domingo, who never overcame a deep and silent nostalgia due to his lost sense of place, but his entire family as well. The novel fictionalizes some of the specific consequences of Franco's technocratic project in Spain and its authoritarian, biopolitical management of populations. Moreno-Caballud beautifully describes the manifold social and cultural implications of these 'technical' decisions:

> The technocrat draws the line where the dam will be built: everything that falls on one side will perish under the water. This includes, of course, hunger, endless days of manual labor, patriarchal violence, ecclesiastical control, and other scourges of the countryside. But it also

120 Neil Brenner, *Critique of Urbanization: Selected Essays* (Basel: Birkhäuser, 2017), 200.
121 Julio Llamazares, *Distintas formas de mirar el agua* (Barcelona: Alfaguara, 2015).

includes traditional knowledge, and the many material and symbolic capacities that guaranteed subsistence peasant cultures but would not be considered 'productive'—particularly knowledge and skills associated with the reproduction of life, care, emotional and domestic work, the tasks usually assigned to women in a patriarchy.[122]

The ecological implications of these engineering works, often overlooked, are also enormous.

Distintas formas de mirar el agua is a systemic narrative, and the reader reconstructs the story of Domingo's family from the internal monologues of 17 intradiegetic narrators. Each person perceives his or her own circumstances in relation to both the reservoir's meaning and Domingo's life. The different ways of looking at water referred to in the title could be interpreted as different ways of understanding Spanish economic development and the various assessments of its benefits and costs. This polyphonic novel challenges the one-dimensional logic of the CT 'consensus' and its singular view of Spanish capitalist modernization. What is not mentioned by CT supporters is that without a proper debate, there can never be a consensus, but only enforcement, manipulation, propaganda, or marketing. There was never any public discussion about what kind of growth is desirable in Spain: growth of what, for what, for whose benefit, orchestrated by whom, and at what cost? These questions were always excluded from the political menu in Spain both during and after the Franco regime, and simply raising the questions could be viewed as opposing progress and improvement of the quality of life. The testimony of Virginia, Domingo's widow, shows how the expropriation and forced relocation they suffered did not lead to a better quality of life at all.[123] For Teresa, Virginia and Domingo's older daughter, the disappearance of the village and the elimination of its historical geography is sad.[124] Other members of the family, who never experienced life in the village and have no direct emotional memory of it, can maintain a certain distance and either enjoy the aesthetic qualities of the engineered landscape and disdain Domingo's *machismo*, like Teresa's son,[125] or celebrate capitalist modernity as if it were an inextricable teleological progression towards human betterment, as Teresa's daughter does.[126] In both cases, we have an ahistorical and unproblematic explanation of the present reality in line with the CT.

---

122 Moreno-Caballud, *Cultures of Anyone*, 277.
123 Llamazares, *Distintas formas de mirar el agua*, 11.
124 Llamazares, *Distintas formas de mirar el agua*, 36.
125 Llamazares, *Distintas formas de mirar el agua*, 51, 56.
126 Llamazares, *Distintas formas de mirar el agua*, 65, 67.

José Antonio, Virginia and Domingo's son, introduces more complex historical and cultural nuances. He is vividly aware of how the river's history, measured in geological time, was interrupted by the contingency of the dam,[127] and of how the engineer's hubristic interventions had unintended consequences: alterations to the riverbed and to the course of many people's lives,[128] including the destruction of an ancestral peasant culture, and even change to the climate of the region.[129] José Antonio claims that his parents deserve the respect denied them by the landowners and engineers implicated in their forced relocation.[130] Ironically, Daniel, José Antonio's son, works as an engineer. As one might expect, he justifies his profession, which brings progress and an improved quality of life to unspecified 'inhabitants', dismissing its critics as ignorant and irrational individuals: 'por encima de los sentimientos está la razón. Y papá no es ningún idiota. Sabe que su país necesita obras de ingeniería que favorezcan la vida de sus habitantes. Y que esas obras producen daños' [reason is above feelings. And father is not an idiot. He knows that his country needs engineering works that improve the life of its inhabitants. And that these works cause harm].[131] Of course, this argument is specious, since almost nobody attacks engineering as a practice to be eliminated. Rather, the problem is deciding which kinds of interventions serve the community and which do not. Are the interventions to be determined by the communities affected or imposed from above? What are the specific socioeconomic purposes and interests behind them? Who benefits and who suffers, and is there another way to achieve the same goal that reduces socioecological harm?

Interestingly, it is Alex, Daniel's brother, who raises some of these issues when he mentions that the successors of the people responsible for the dam's construction are still enjoying the benefits derived from it, although they now live in León and Madrid: 'Beneficios que nunca han visto aquellos que, como mis abuelos, sacrificaron todo lo que tenían para que se pudieran empezar a producir' [Benefits never seen by those who, like my grandparents, sacrificed everything they had so that the benefits could start to appear].[132] Alex, who is much more empathetic than his brother towards other people's suffering and more sensitive to environmental injustices, states: 'El progreso económico no lo justifica todo' [Economic progress does

127 Llamazares, *Distintas formas de mirar el agua*, 73, 77.
128 Llamazares, *Distintas formas de mirar el agua*, 76, 77.
129 Llamazares, *Distintas formas de mirar el agua*, 79, 133.
130 Llamazares, *Distintas formas de mirar el agua*, 80.
131 Llamazares, *Distintas formas de mirar el agua*, 97.
132 Llamazares, *Distintas formas de mirar el agua*, 115–116.

not justify everything].[133] He also notes the rotten smell released by the stagnant water of the reservoir,[134] which is a symptom of some of the many ecological problems associated with it. But it is another son of Domingo and Virginia, Agustín, considered by some members of the family to be of little intelligence, who displays the deepest posthumanist ethics. He describes how many people see the water as a mere resource to be utilized, and therefore mistreat it, but he has learned from his father to see the water with emotion and respect, and to feel pain when others disrespect it.[135]

Llamazares's novel focuses on one of the many nonurban spaces that have been operationalized by the urban linear metabolism and its energy-devouring regime. But it does so not through the usual celebration of human ingenuity and its techno-scientific control, associated with these spaces by the dominant imaginary, but a multiperspectival narrative that includes many heterogeneous and intergenerational voices contesting the celebratory paradigm of growth—voices that, in this novel at least, are emitted at the same frequency as the omnipresent voices that promote modern consumerist societies through the obdurate repetition of prefabricated messages. The dominant imaginary of urban growth can only achieve a celebratory rhetoric by erasing memory, as Llamazares's novel shows (the same conclusion is extracted from the ecocritical interpretation of *Mercado de futuros*). As one character points out, old people loyal to their memories are perceived with uneasiness in such conflicting geographies, 'porque recordaban lo que los demás no saben o ignoraban voluntariamente' [because they remembered that which others either do not know or voluntarily ignore].[136] As Helen Graham and Antonio Sánchez rightly assert, referring to the many government-sponsored and internationally visible macro-events in Spain during 1992, 'these popular celebrations of Spain's new status tended to neglect the past and glorify the present. Indeed this seemed to be part of an official attempt to represent Spain's new, "modern", democratic national identity as if it were built on a *tabula rasa*', thus avoiding confrontations and historically unresolved issues.[137] In Spain, the self-congratulation accompanying these devastating movements of the 'urban growth machine', which David Harvey describes in *Rebel Cities* (following the lead of John Logan and Harvey Molotch), avoids the fact that this process not only 'entails the

133 Llamazares, *Distintas formas de mirar el agua*, 117.
134 Llamazares, *Distintas formas de mirar el agua*, 120.
135 Llamazares, *Distintas formas de mirar el agua*, 182.
136 Llamazares, *Distintas formas de mirar el agua*, 129.
137 Helen Graham and Antonio Sánchez, 'The Politics of 1992', in *Spanish Cultural Studies: An Introduction*, ed. Helen Graham and Jo Labanyi (Oxford: Oxford University Press, 1995), 406.

dispossession of the urban masses of any right to the city whatsoever',[138] but also the marginalization and dissolution of any other alternative—including nonurban—ways of relating to the territory that do not accelerate the process of planetary urbanization.

The extinction of these ways of life and their memories—parallel to the massive loss of biodiversity, since the loss of cultural and biological diversity go hand in hand—also marks the loss of ancestral knowledge, technologies, and skills perfected over centuries to optimize the use of limited resources and to facilitate the survival of the community within specific ecologies. As noted in the previous section, these bodies of knowledge could mean survival in a future in which, most likely, ecological degradation and energy restrictions will be the default. Cultures of survival are mostly found in nonurban (in neoliberal times also infra-urban) spaces and have experienced constant attrition marked by the material and symbolic dispossession orchestrated by different powers since the 1950s (from Franco's agricultural rationalization to the European Union agrarian laws and transnational trade agreements). However, the past few years have witnessed an increased revalorization of these cultural modes, prompted by a sense of urgency that stems from both the situation of these cultures at the edge of extinction and the pressing social and environmental issues brought about by the global financial crisis.

As pointed out by Joan Ramon Resina in his introduction to the edited volume *The New Ruralism: An Epistemology of Transformed Space*, 'the new ruralism is not synonymous with the late nineteen sixties movement of "return to nature" ... [but rather] the return of a social consciousness of the dignity and importance of the non-urban'.[139] There is currently a wave of projects of all kinds—including collections of rural memories and traditions published in book form or online, regional websites, and documentaries—devoted to conserving for posterity specific local cultural knowledge throughout the Iberian territory. Unfortunately, certain practices cannot be preserved in a textual, visual, or digital format for future use, since they depend on specific socioecological conditions that have vanished. Nevertheless, these works show a deep respect for cultures marginalized by the dominant imaginary, and could be evidence of an increasing suspicion that the paradigm of growth and capitalist development is not really functional in a limited biosphere and may indeed be on the verge of collapse.

---

138 Harvey, *Rebel Cities*, 22.
139 Joan Ramon Resina, 'The Modern Rural', in *The New Ruralism: An Epistemology of Transformed Space*, ed. Joan Ramon Resina and William Viestenz (Madrid: Iberoamericana/Vervuert, 2012), 8.

If, as Moreno-Caballud suggests, 'traditional knowledge is denied the very status of *being* knowledge' through the usual mechanism—'the negation of intelligence in those who are dedicated to ensuring the reproduction of material life, and the construction of a monopoly on authorized knowledge'— what does it mean that more and more people are now searching for meaning in *non*-authorized sources of knowledge?[140] Is this another indication of the current fracture of the growth imaginary? There are two recent books that I consider important in this regard: *La voz de los sabios* (The Voice of the Elders, 2013) by Elena García Quevedo, and *Palabras mayores: un viaje por la memoria rural* (Older Words: A Journey through the Rural Memory, 2015) by Emilio Gancedo.[141] Both of these are based on conversations with elders in which the writers truly listen; they are open to learning from and being transformed by the interaction. Both books present testimonies that rarely appear on the mainstream media radar, since they recount livelihoods and cosmovisions that do not match the modern capitalist agenda. Frequently these forgotten voices offer wise, humble, and complex interpretations of reality in ways that contrast with the oversimplified and arrogant verbiage generated by the dominant imaginary.

Gancedo's book is a delightfully written work that brings together diverse oral traditions, ancestral memories, and philosophies of life from Iberian rural geography. The author allows people to express themselves in their own terms, always respecting the pace of their storytelling and the flow of their memories. He traveled to remote villages to converse with elders who have experienced a variety of ways of being in the world. Gancedo talks little, because he prefers to listen. In many respects, these meaningful voices are those that have been swept away by the rapid advances of Spanish consumerist culture and its associated values. Many of these people embrace a notion of time that does not coincide with the hectic, accelerated pace of capital accumulation and spectacular media. For them, seasonal changes and communal gatherings mark the rhythms of their life and labor.

Palabras mayores is rich in descriptions of *naturecultural* landscapes, which are understood as a socioecological symbiotic coevolution of humans and the nonhuman. The agency of the nonhuman is never disregarded. This does not imply that nonurban spaces are more natural and less cultural than cities, but rather that in such spaces the inextricable socioecological interdependence

---

140 Moreno-Caballud, *Cultures of Anyone*, 36.
141 Elena García Quevedo, *La voz de los sabios* (Barcelona: Ediciones Luciérnaga, 2013); Emilio Gancedo, *Palabras mayores: un viaje por la memoria rural* (Logroño: Pepitas de calabaza, 2015).

of humans and their environment is not intentionally hidden and negated by unsustainable fossil fuel depletion and their petromodern fantasies. The linguistic diversity displayed in the book is significant, as each elder speaks with a different regional dialect full of distinct nuances and expressions. Some have a telluric lexicon that vividly describes the changing aspects of their environment with remarkable precision. The global, rapid modern shift from diverse languages to fewer linguistic variations parallels the ongoing extinction of cultures and species. This is not mere coincidence. If everything is a commodity or resource to fuel the capitalist economy, only the language of neoclassical economics, the vocabulary of marketing, and entrepreneurial and corporational stories need to be developed and disseminated. Other variations are nothing but an obstacle to economic growth and can be exterminated without remorse, even if they are, in fact, the very stories 'we will need ... to survive by'.[142] That is why the stories that Gancedo gathers are so important, because they challenge the monologic of the dominant imaginary not only philosophically and practically, but also linguistically. Many times Gancedo notes his interlocutors' refusal to give up their linguistic heritage: 'Lucha este hombre alto, y con todas sus fuerzas, para evitar la extinción definitiva de las palabras que definieron su mundo' [This tall man fights with all his might to prevent the definitive extinction of the words that defined his world].[143]

Many of the elders remember frugal living conditions and hard manual labor, but they also remember a widespread sense of community, solidarity, and conviviality that no longer exists.[144] A generalized good life is never possible (in any geography or for any culture) under a regime of exploitation and inequality (no matter whether we are talking of a rural aristocracy or an urban capitalist class). 'Inequality is socially corrosive', as Wilkinson and Pickett remind us, and desirable progress implies a system of social reproduction that abolishes all forms of exploitation and inequality.[145] Gancedo's book, through its focus on the elders' memories, offers an embodied and historical document of multiple geographical, demographic, and cultural perspectives in Spain that resisted the trendy exodus to cities. Economic development, which for the dominant imaginary is an unequivocal symptom of progress, is presented with complexity and nuance in Gancedo's book. This resistance to oversimplification is properly summarized by one elder: 'Ni aquello fue todo lo malo, ni esto es todo lo bueno' [neither was

---

142 Stibbe, *Ecolinguistics*, 183.
143 Gancedo, *Palabras mayores*, 129.
144 Gancedo, *Palabras mayores*, 52, 135, 145, 174.
145 Wilkinson and Pickett, *The Spirit Level*, xiv.

that all bad, nor is this all good].[146] Of course, many of those interviewed appreciate some of the improvements in their physical living conditions— the eradication of some forms of exhausting manual labor, and access to formal educational opportunities—but they also recollect positive aspects that have been lost and values that have been left behind. Ángeles González, for example, is critical of the way in which children are educated today, claiming that we are spoiling them: 'Por no enseñarles la raíz de las cosas, de dónde vienen los alimentos o cómo se llaman los componentes que engranan la asombrosa máquina del paisaje' [Because we are not teaching them the root of things, where food comes from or the names of the components that fit together in the awesome machine that is the landscape].[147] The abstract education denounced here entails a loss of understanding and communitarian control as a result of technocratic centralization and faith in a growth-oriented technical system that cannot be sustained. But it would be wise, as says Lines, another of Gancedo's interlocutors, not to put all one's eggs in one basket:

> Aquí hubo quien dijo: 'Yo ya tengo luz eléctrica, yo tiro el candil'. Y se pusieron a quitar las cosas antiguas. Pero vamos a ver—se reafirma— ¿cómo sabes que no tendremos que volver a lo de antes? Y si se va una noche la luz, ¡habrá que prender el candil otra vez![148]

> [Some people said: 'I have electric power, I'll throw away the candle'. And they started removing old things. But let us see—she emphasizes— how do you know that we will not have to get back to what we had before? What if one night the power goes off? In that case, we would have to light the candle again!]

Indeed, if we pay close attention to the world energy situation, it is easy to conclude that, in a not-too-distant future, energy restrictions are likely to become commonplace.

Most of the elders featured in the book are cognizant of the erosion of social cohesion and are sensitive to the environmental deterioration brought about by the changes they have experienced. They feel uneasy about the hubristic cultural attitudes thriving under the auspices of these transformations, which lack any commonsensical precautionary principles. Perhaps because of their intimate understanding of the cycle of nutrients that traditional food production methods involve, many of these elders

146 Gancedo, *Palabras mayores*, 56.
147 Gancedo, *Palabras mayores*, 35.
148 Gancedo, *Palabras mayores*, 48.

express concern about the problematic scale of the changes associated with the linear metabolism of economic growth. There is a clear comprehension of the fact that nothing can grow forever. For example, we find some highly critical statements regarding the irrationality of many agro-industrial practices,[149] complaints about the loss of food sovereignty that the new model entails,[150] and explanations of the integrated virtues of circular agroecological practices that were displaced by modern developments.[151] Currently, industrial agriculture is destroying topsoil at an astonishing rate by grossly simplifying complex ecological systems. Permaculture produces food by doing exactly the opposite, but it is wholly ignored by the dominant imaginary. An ironic comment of a clam fisherman provides a concrete example of the disruption of the cycle of nutrients that the metabolic rift entails:

> Desde que salieron las depuradoras, la aportación de materia orgánica al mar ha desaparecido. Sale el agua muy limpia, muy perfecta, sí, pero ... Vamos, que si tú en un campo no echas estiércol, aquello no produce nada. Y en una piscina cristalina no criarás un pez en la vida. Sin materia orgánica desaparecen las especies filtradoras, como son la almeja y el mejillón, que aquí antes llegamos a pescar la almeja cincuenta barcas, ojo. Claro, las lejías, los jabones, los metales pesados, eso no es nada bueno, pero la materia orgánica sí. ¡Banderas azules! ¿Qué es lo que quiere el pueblo? Una bandera azul. Es que cincuenta pescadores comparados con el turismo, amigo ... ¡no son nada![152]

> [Since they installed water treatment plants, the contribution of organic matter to the sea disappeared. Water comes out very clean, perfect, yes, but ... if you do not put manure in a field, it is not going to produce anything. And in a really clean pool you will never grow a fish. Without organic matter the filtration species disappear, like clams and mussels. Here before there use to be fifty of us fishing for clams! Of course, bleach, soaps, heavy metals, are not good at all, but organic matter is. Blue flags! What do people want? A blue flag. Fifty fishermen are nothing in comparison with the tourist industry!]

In relation to the ongoing destruction of soil, another character remarks: 'Si uno deposita un puñado de semillas sobre un ladrillo, no arraigarán, pero

149 Gancedo, *Palabras mayores*, 37, 78–79, 108–109.
150 Gancedo, *Palabras mayores*, 188, 197, 314.
151 Gancedo, *Palabras mayores*, 71, 78, 189.
152 Gancedo, *Palabras mayores*, 167.

sí lo harán sobre el suelo negro y prieto' [If you put a handful of seeds on a brick, they are not going to establish themselves, but they will in a black, rich soil].[153] The ongoing life-capital conflict ingrained in the dominant imaginary is clearly expressed in the subtext of such sentences.

Some elders remember the circularity of a social metabolism that did not generate waste and was based on a rational and efficient use of resources: 'Antes no había basura' [before there was no garbage],[154] 'no se desperdiciaba nada' [nothing was wasted],[155] 'antes se aprovechaba la paja y se aprovechaba todo' [in the past we used the straw and all],[156] 'todo se aprovechaba y reciclaba' [everything was used and recycled].[157] There are also some complaints about the complex legal obstacles to small rural business that have increased during their lifetimes[158] and become more stringent following integration into the European Community.[159] While some inhabitants from mountainous and inner regions often yearn for the past vibrancy of their communities, island and coastal dwellers have an ambiguous reaction to tourists but explicitly lament the disturbing over-construction and radical transformation of their ancestral geographies.[160]

In a consumerist, unsustainable society, the elderly are seen as—or turned into—problems. The dominant imaginary does not know how to describe them in politically correct terms. In CT Spain, with the exception of rich senior citizens, old people are perceived as undesirable creatures who do not contribute to GDP growth, tend to consume frugally, and rely on pensions that depend on capital that cannot be fully appropriated by the capitalist class (unless the retirement system is privatized, as neoliberal policymakers would prefer). Consider the proposed solutions to the inverted demographic pyramid in Spain, the result of the disproportionate increase in retirees in relation to people of working age: cutting pensions and/or increasing birth rates. The first is socially unsustainable and the second ecologically unviable; neither solves the problem and will only aggravate it in the future. For Gancedo, in contrast, elders are purveyors of priceless knowledge and experience and should be a vital part of the solution to socioenvironmental issues. A fascinating study by Judy Aubel notes an interesting connection between the degree of a society's sustainability

---

153 Gancedo, *Palabras mayores*, 22.
154 Gancedo, *Palabras mayores*, 324, 329.
155 Gancedo, *Palabras mayores*, 53.
156 Gancedo, *Palabras mayores*, 79.
157 Gancedo, *Palabras mayores*, 305.
158 Gancedo, *Palabras mayores*, 78–79, 108.
159 Gancedo, *Palabras mayores*, 78–79, 196–197, 312–314.
160 Gancedo, *Palabras mayores*, 187, 196, 223.

and its treatment of elders.[161] The less a society appreciates and respects its elders, the less sustainable it becomes. Thus, listening carefully to seniors and considering them full members of society does not mean going backwards, but rather leads to the possibility of a desirable future in which we learn how to live better with less and prepare ourselves for a low-energy society with a circular metabolism. As Lines says: 'What if one night the power goes off? In that case, we would have to light the candle again!'

Some other cultural manifestations seem to be more optimistic in their depiction of a new Iberian ruralism because their characters are motivated not by survival, but by voluntary existential or ideological choices that inspire them to join rural intentional communities. Such is the case with the documentary *La extraña elección* (The Odd Choice, 2015) and the web series *Libres* (The Free Ones).[162] *La extraña elección*, which is associated with a companion TV show and a transmedia collaborative project, declares as its guiding principle, 'Colocamos el pueblo en el centro de todo y analizamos el mundo' [We place the village at the center of everything to analyze the world]. As this motto and the film's title clearly indicate, the project challenges the city-centric dominant imaginary by epistemologically privileging the village. The documentary features the experiences of several people who have chosen to move to the countryside. The locus of enunciation (and source of meaning-making) is, as in Gancedo's book (or the documentary *Desde que el mundo es mundo*),[163] not the city. However important these new rural experiences may be in deeply transforming the lives and thinking of their participants, they nevertheless do not suffice to modify the power relations of global capitalism. A 'new ruralism can only refer to a critical form of disenchantment, or better yet detachment, that challenges modernity's epistemic superiority and culture's alleged dependence on the city's tempo and intensity of exchanges'.[164] In other words, the urban-agro-industrial metabolism cannot be escaped simply by retreating from its urban core since, in the age of planetary urbanization and the Capitalocene, its transformative economic, cultural, political, and ecological processes affect the entire globe. All the planet is now an operational landscape of the growth-oriented urban-industrial complex.

161 Judi Aubel, 'Nuestros mayores: un recurso cultural para promover el desarrollo sostenible', in *La situación del mundo 2010: cambio cultural: del consumismo hacia la sostenibilidad*, trans. Isabel Bermejo and Mar Garzón (Barcelona: Icaria, 2010), 99–108.
162 Carmen Comadrán, dir., *La extraña elección* (2015); Alex Rodrigo, dir., *Libres* (2013).
163 Günter Schwaiger, dir., *Desde que el mundo es mundo* (Since the World is World, 2015).
164 Resina, 'The Modern Rural', 15.

Presently, new rural projects can be easily co-opted, reappropriated, or disarticulated by urban growth dynamics. As Nick Srnicek and Alex Williams have recently pointed out, 'this form of politics has focused on building bunkers to resist the encroachment of global neoliberalism. In so doing, it has become a politics of defense, incapable of articulating or building a new world'.[165] An online series about rural occupation, *Libres* reflects on the limitations of such politics. Written and directed by Alex Rodrigo, *Libres* presents a group of seven people who have decided to move from the city to the countryside in order to occupy an abandoned house in the rural Aragonese Pyrénées of northern Spain. They have diverse sociocultural backgrounds and personal histories, as revealed in intertwined flashbacks that link the collective present to the recent or remote past in the life of each. Most of them are motivated by a mix of anticapitalistic ideology and the desire to escape the ongoing intensification of neoliberal urban precarity in Spain. The members of the group embrace environmental values— solar power, ecological gardening, and recovering and repurposing existing infrastructure—and try to organize and regulate their social interactions by means of a horizontal and self-managed form of decision-making. The story avoids idealizing rural life or the characters' solidarity by centering the plot on the many material and convivial challenges faced by the group. The extremely frugal living conditions that the seven experience are sometimes pressing, even though they do not spend the winter months in the village; in fact, given the winter climate typical of that region of Spain, it is unlikely that the group would have made it through the colder months. Furthermore, their insistence on consensus-building is sometimes paralyzing or subject to manipulation by dominant personalities. Eventually, after months of hard work refurbishing the house, they cannot escape the unfair legal system that overtly favors private property and capital accumulation over use value and socioecological improvements, and the group is evicted and sued. Again, the claims made by Srnicek and Williams about the limitations of this form of politics seem accurate:

> In seeking the direct and unmediated cancelation of social relations of domination, these movements either tend to ignore the more subtle forms of domination that persist, or else fail to construct persistent political structures able to maintain the new social relations in the long term.[166]

In the case of *Libres*, both criticisms apply.

165 Srnicek and Williams, *Inventing the Future*, 3.
166 Srnicek and Williams, *Inventing the Future*, 27.

Although the new ruralism has evoked some empathic op-eds,[167] which is no small achievement in a corporation-dominated media environment, the truth is that these projects have a marginal impact on regional, national, or global ecologies and politics. Srnicek and Williams call the preference for local, small-scale, and personal solutions a 'folk politics' that dominates current political thinking on the left.[168] They claim that 'there is a preference for the everyday over the structural, valorizing personal experience over systemic thinking ... Given the nature of global capitalism, any postcapitalist project will require an ambitious, abstract, mediated, complex and global approach—one that folk-political approaches are incapable of providing'.[169] In the case of the new ruralism, it seems obvious that prefigurative politics are mainly a symbolic process, for its small, costly, and transient gains pale in comparison with the ongoing surge of legal implementations and supranational trade agreements that disproportionally benefit agro-energy-corporations and the capitalist elite. While a few hundred houses are occupied and a few small ecovillages heroically resist the advance of the growth machine, foreign capital is buying entire towns and private financial interests are acquiring vast forests and land (sometimes previously protected and publicly owned), while rich people are enclosing communal spaces for the sake of their private entertainment. The question remains: could postgrowth imaginaries combine the phenomenological and the structural in politically efficacious ways?

Ursula Heise has made a point very similar to that of Srnicek and Williams in regard to the inadequacy of folk politics *vis-à-vis* environmental ethics. In *Sense of Place and Sense of Planet: The Environmental Imagination of the Global*, Heise claims that the traditional tendency of environmental criticism to focus on the local may not be an effective strategy in the context of a global capitalism where the local is always overrun by transnational and supranational economic and political powers. Heise urges us to develop 'an ideal of "eco-cosmopolitanism" or environmental world citizenship' to deal with 'the increasing connectedness of societies around the world' and the technological mediations of cultures, economies, and risks.[170] 'Rather than focusing on the recuperation of a sense of place, environmentalism needs to foster an understanding of how a wide variety of both natural and cultural places and processes are connected and shape each other around the world,

---

167 E.g., Isabel Martínez, 'Vivir en comunidad: un fenómeno alternativo que se extiende', *La Vanguardia*, February 19, 2015, http://www.lavanguardia.com/vida/20150219/54427385216/vivir-comunidad-fenomeno-alternativo-auge.html.

168 Srnicek and Williams, *Inventing the Future*, 10.

169 Srnicek and Williams, *Inventing the Future*, 11–12.

170 Heise, *Sense of Place and Sense of Planet*, 10.

and how human impact affects and changes this connectedness'.[171] If the arguments made by Heise and by Srnicek and Williams are considered closely, it seems that an effective political ecology today needs to be more imaginative and less reactive to localized symptoms if it is to envision and enact a systemic transformation of power relations. 'Resistance is futile' or even counterproductive if it is not accompanied by counterhegemonic projects.[172] Politics that do not confront the global, large-scale neoliberal system are 'simply a salve for the problems of capitalism, not an alternative to it'.[173]

Postgrowth and postcapitalist alternatives to the urban growth machine are urgently needed, along with a massive mobilization of new languages, new logics, new imaginative projects, and integral strategies able to move beyond a timid, insufficient reruralization to a regenerative Ecopolis with a circular metabolism where the urban-rural dichotomy becomes obsolete. If cities are acting as destructive terraforming agents, why not turn them into benign metabolisms to enhance diverse socioecological systems? Such a move would entail radically transforming the cultural imaginary, disarticulating what Zygmunt Bauman calls the 'modern power-knowledge complex', and embracing postgrowth counterhegemonic ways of thinking. If socialization in a linear metabolic order produces, normalizes, and self-perpetuates the cultural values of the growth imaginary, perhaps socialization in a circular social metabolism will be able to bring about new cultural modes based on sufficiency, conviviality, and the recognition of limits. In any case, I concur with David Orr that 'it is foolish to think that we can reinhabit rural areas sustainably without also changing the way we inhabit urban areas. Rural prospects mirror those of cities, and one cannot be improved much without improving the other'.[174] Stretching our political imagination is crucial to shrinking the metabolic rift. This will require (among other things) 'stretching our ecological imagination to break down the dichotomy between urban and rural and allow rural things ... into the urban world'.[175] The cultural manifestations included in the following section strive to break down that dichotomy while embracing postgrowth urban imaginaries.

---

171 Heise, *Sense of Place and Sense of Planet*, 21.
172 Srnicek and Williams, *Inventing the Future*, 46.
173 Srnicek and Williams, *Inventing the Future*, 38–39.
174 Orr, *Earth in Mind*, 199.
175 Orr, *Earth in Mind*, 200.

2.2.4. Postgrowth Urban Imaginaries: Imagining and Performing the Ecopolis

The last section of the typology explores cultural manifestations that not only challenge the urban growth imaginary, but suggest desirable alternatives to it. If pursuing continual growth through the urbanization of capital in an already overstressed biosphere leads to a dead end, a possible alternative could be to design non-growth-oriented cities that can operate without plundering the ecologies in which they are embedded. Because modern global cities are socioecological open systems with a global reach, as Saskia Sassen reminds us, 'Cities will be forced into the frontlines by global warming, energy and water insecurity, and other environmental challenges'.[176] They will quickly feel many of the current consequences of the Anthropocene crises 'because of the often extreme dependence of cities on complex systems'.[177] City leaders will not be able to avoid addressing these problems once they begin to affect urban supplies and living conditions. Cities cannot afford to wait until states or international agreements come to terms with climate change, for it will be too late. Today,

> cities are complex systems in their geographies of consumption and waste-production. This complexity makes them essential for the creation of solutions ... Eliminating cities would not necessarily solve the environmental crisis. We need to understand the functioning of, and possibilities for changing, specific systems of power, economic systems, transportation systems and so on, that entail modes of resource use that are environmentally unsound.[178]

Transforming the metabolism of cities, therefore, can have a large-scale systemic socioecological impact (in both urban and nonurban spaces) and even the potential to change structural power relations, especially if alliances and networks of transformative global cities arise. Global alliances and collaborations of these cities with nonurban movements, such as Via Campesina, could also significantly turn the tide against neoliberal power. One example is the Climate Alliance of European Cities, uniting 1,700 member municipalities across Europe committed to reducing their carbon emissions and acting in solidarity with the indigenous peoples of the Amazon to protect the rainforests. Unfortunately, to date Barcelona is the only member from the Spanish state. Another example is the recently

176 Saskia Sassen, 'Cities Are at the Center of Our Environmental Future', *S.A.P.I.E.N.* 2, no. 3 (2010), https://sapiens.revues.org/948.
177 Sassen, 'Cities Are at the Center of Our Environmental Future'.
178 Sassen, 'Cities Are at the Center of Our Environmental Future'.

constituted Global Parliament of Mayors, a call for cities worldwide to become proactive and collaborate in developing effective urban responses to climate change, migration, and governance.[179] Other relevant city networks include the Compact of Mayors, the Mayors Climate Protection Agreement, the Urban Sustainability Directors Network, the Carbon Neutral Cities Alliance, the C40 Cities Climate Leadership Group, and ICLEI-Local Governments for Sustainability.

Herbert Girardet writes that 'In the age of climate change and peaking oil supplies, Petropolis is an outmoded model of urbanisation'.[180] During the shift from Petropolises to regenerative cities or Ecopolises, as Girardet recommends, municipalities will be the main actors. In order to minimize future disasters, to create the conditions for a good life, and avoid potential collapse, they must 'minimize fossil fuel dependency ... reduce their ecological footprint ... reconnect to their local countryside for efficient food supplies ... regenerate regional soils and ecosystems ... and facilitate the creation of new green business and job opportunities'.[181] The main challenges for successfully engaging in this transition are how to navigate the existing 'rules of economic globalization' and 'challenge the perceived financial benefits of it'.[182] Municipal urban policies can have immediate and noticeable consequences for the quality of life of their residents. There are many examples of inspiring cases on different scales, from neighborhoods and small towns to great metropolises, and from very simple and inexpensive changes that generate a spiral of social and ecological benefits to complex legal and technical implementations.[183] These changes share an integral, multifunctional, and systemic approach to city planning (as opposed to the dominant imaginary's focus on corporate interests, foreign investment, and GDP growth) and are motivated by the daily socioecological needs of their inhabitants, rather than by global market signals or the desire to attract tourists and compete for foreign investment. Ecopolises should be thought of as integral parts of the territory hosting them. Their main objectives, other than becoming functional and pleasant living spaces for their communities, should be to reduce waste (moving towards zero waste and total composting) and to incorporate concepts of industrial ecology, biomimesis, and permaculture in order to think about urban planning as an integrated system. In order for these transitions to have a chance,

179 http://www.globalparliamentofmayors.org/.
180 Girardet, *Creating Regenerative Cities*, 96.
181 Girardet, *Creating Regenerative Cities*, 96.
182 Girardet, *Creating Regenerative Cities*, 119–120.
183 A number of examples can be found in Girardet, *Creating Regenerative Cities*, and Agyeman, *Introducing Just Sustainabilities*.

municipalities must not be managed by mainstream neoliberal politicians, but by leaders with socioecological sensibilities who are able to think systemically and capable of gaining massive support from urban social movements, as well as from their emerging citizens' political platforms. Such was the case in Barcelona, Madrid, Cadiz, and A Coruña during the 2015 municipal elections in Spain. Today, 50 Spanish municipalities, including Barcelona, have declared themselves free of the TTIP—the secretly negotiated neoliberal trade agreement designed to serve the interests of large corporations—in order to make their own decisions about crucial issues affecting their territories.

The ongoing struggle of transforming Petropolis into Ecopolis includes a competition between urban models representing opposing worldviews of what a city should be: a farm for economic growth or a space for collectively deciding what a life worth living entails. For the dominant imaginary, a city should facilitate capital accumulation, but from the ecopolitan point of view, the urban model should promote socioecological well-being and a sustainable good life for all. A transition from Petropolis entails, as David Harvey puts it, challenging the capitalist control and production of space that molds the city and its social relations in the image of its ideological desires while appropriating the collectively generated urban symbolic capital. Meaningful municipal debates trigger 'localized questions about whose collective memory, whose aesthetics, and whose benefits are to be prioritized'.[184] Postgrowth urban social movements reclaim what Lefebvre called 'the right to the city', which must 'be construed not as a right to that which already exists, but as a right to rebuild and re-create the city as a socialist body politic in a completely different image—one that eradicates poverty and social inequality, and one that heals the wounds of disastrous environmental degradation'.[185] Since 2008, Spain has seen a great rise in cultural practices and processes that are trying to rebuild and recreate, symbolically and physically, the city as a place where the social reproduction of life, not capital, is collectively prioritized. Thanks to the 15-M movement, 2011 marked the visibility of alternative urban models and a growth in the number of communitarian experiments with urban practices, narratives, and spaces. In spring 2015, *La revista de eldiario.es* published a special issue on municipalism titled *Qué ciudad queremos*. This publication, especially the contributions by Elena Cabrera and Yayo Herrero, focuses on urban metabolisms, socioecological justice, and the need for postgrowth urban models.[186]

184 Harvey, *Rebel Cities*, 106.
185 Harvey, *Rebel Cities*, 138.
186 *Qué ciudad queremos* (Madrid: Roca editorial, 2015).

One example of the new cultural practices that have emerged in Spain is the design of urban projects by Carmen Blasco and Ángeles Souto, based on ephemeral architecture, to improve some areas of Madrid. These projects have proposed inexpensive and effective alternative socioecological solutions to revitalize and regenerate a number of degraded urban spaces in Madrid, namely the Plaza de Jacinto Benavente, the Lago de la Casa de Campo and its environs, and the Parque Lineal Manzanares Sur. The solutions proposed meet four criteria: they conserve pre-existing features of local identity; they do not alter the harmony of the place, they are ephemeral, self-sustained, and ecological installations; and they accomplish the socioecological revitalization of degraded spaces.[187] These three projects propose simple but highly creative ways to make the city a more livable place, as opposed to the neoliberal urban model that has dominated Madrid in past decades, which is obsessed with macro-investments and mega-infrastructures. The ephemeral architectural designs proposed by Blasco and Souto are intended to meet the daily needs of local people while encouraging communitarian interaction in healthy social and environmental urban spaces.

One of the most interesting features of these installations is that they are designed to be highly flexible and easily repurposed by users to match their diverse needs. In other words, the urban space is not forced upon the people, conditioning and limiting their behaviors, but mutates to facilitate new social interactions and functions; the spaces evolve with their users. These installations empower and invite people to reclaim and modify public space as an inclusive place for horizontal encounter and conviviality, where access and interactions among people and the environment are not mediated by commodification and soft pollution. As Blasco and Souto state, their alternative model of urban intervention is versatile, inexpensive, and sustainable, and it fosters citizens' participation in communitarian management. Furthermore, it has the potential to change the perception of urban space and democratize its use.[188] This non-growth-oriented urban model could be implemented at any time to dramatically improve quality of life, since it does not require the city to brand itself and compete for massive investments on the global market.

Similarly, a number of recent street-art interventions in Spain have challenged the urban growth paradigm by exposing its aesthetic, symbolic, and material wrongs and revealing issues that neoliberal rationality strives

187 Carmen Blasco and Ángeles Souto, 'Proyectos efímeros para la mejora de lugares degradados en la escena urbana de Madrid', in *Arte y Ecología*, ed. Tonia Raquejo and José María Parreño (Madrid: UNED, 2015), 308.
188 Blasco and Souto, 'Proyectos efímeros', 339.

to hide. An interesting example is the Guerrilla Gardening project in Madrid,[189] whose mission is to plant gardens in abandoned or neglected public spaces to call attention to issues related to urban political ecology, such as the connection between inadequate land use, social inequality, gentrification, disregard for social well-being, non-commodified beauty, and the environmental degradation endemic in capitalist urbanization. These actions show how small, inexpensive modifications in the urban environment improve the socioecological conditions of all and can be made by anyone. Unfortunately, 'el modelo urbanístico actual premia el ocio consumista y limita el espacio público' [the current urban model rewards consumerist leisure and limits public space], as Pablo Rivas points out in an informative op-ed playfully titled 'El día en que una terraza se comió tu plaza' [The Day a Bar Terrace Ate Your Square].[190] The title refers to the rapid proliferation of private businesses that have taken over public spaces in Spain over the last few years. In many squares, traditional benches near trees where people could meet and chat have been replaced by private *terrazas* where one must pay to sit. During the past few years most cities in Spain have been transformed beyond recognition to serve touristic demands and the interests of the private sector, at the cost of making public urban spaces inaccessible to local residents. Of course, there is resistance to this oppressive urban model, such as the paradigmatic cases of the Ésta es una plaza and El Campo de Cebada projects in Madrid. These are two examples of locally initiated participatory urbanism studied by Feinberg and Larson to show how 'culturally repurposed spaces ... [can offer] viable urban alternatives to the accumulation strategy of debt-driven financial capital'.[191] Another example of creative resistance is *#femPlaça*, a monthly happening staged in different Barcelona squares to generate communitarian cohesion and conviviality while reclaiming the public space for all to enjoy.[192]

Two noteworthy examples of collaborative platforms that have recently emerged in Madrid with the goal of mapping and promoting citizen-generated initiatives to repurpose the city space are Plazas P2P: A Southern European Network and Vivero de Iniciativas Ciudadanas (VIC). Plazas P2P promotes citizens' occupation and appropriation of urban spaces for communitarian

---

189 http://guerrillagardeningmadrid.blogspot.com/.

190 Pablo Rivas, 'El día en que una terraza se comió tu plaza', *Diagonal*, June 22, 2015, https://www.diagonalperiodico.net/libertades/26976-dia-macroterraza-se-comio-tu-plaza.html.

191 Feinberg and Larson, 'Cultivating the Square', 136.

192 See Megan Saltzman, 'Las formas de control y la cotidianidad en la ciudad global: *#femPlaça*, una intervención para reclamar el uso abierto del espacio público', *Journal of Contemporary Spanish Literature and Film* 2 (2014–2015): 189–224.

and convivial purposes, while VIC is an open-source platform and collaborative project for rethinking architecture and urbanism. Another interesting platform is Masqueunacasa, whose goal is to promote alternative and participatory forms of collective living. Other emerging architecture collectives, such as ZULOARK and TXP Todo por la praxis, combine horizontal structures, collaborative learning and design, experimental urbanism, and cultural resistance in order to empower citizens to create more liberating urban spaces. Fortunately, many of the newly elected mayors coming from the social movements and political platforms developed after 15-M are joining forces with some of these small communitarian experiments to challenge the neoliberal urban model.

Another example of cultural production that challenges the urban growth imaginary and proposes postgrowth alternatives is a recent graphic novel that explicitly criticizes the addiction to growth inherent in our urban consumerist society. The fragmented and multicentered stories of *Memorias de la tierra* (Memories of Earth, 2012), by Miguel Brieva, are tied together by the conceit that they are the memories of an extraterrestrial alien who visited the Earth long ago (approximately during the years 2009–2012).[193] The strategy of employing the perspective of an outsider to expose the absurdities of our daily habits has been successfully used by many authors, from Voltaire to Cadalso. In this case, the alien reflects on the critical situation of the human species at the moment of her visit, since civilizational collapse is imminent due to the rapid depletion of resources.[194] According to the observer, the vast majority of humans seem to ignore this threat due to a collective delusion. Only a few are aware of the gravity of the situation,[195] and the alien includes selections from actual texts written by contemporary authors to shed light on the pressing problems they foresee. Some of these authors—Yayo Herrero, Amaia Pérez Orozco, Jorge Riechmann, and Ramón Fernández Durán—are degrowth supporters discussed earlier in Chapter 1.

Memorias de la tierra comprises nine chapters and an epilogue. Each chapter begins with the alien's description of an aspect of humanity's critical situation. The rest of the chapter, with the exception of one page devoted to the previously mentioned fragments of visionary texts written by humans, then consists of disconnected comic vignettes that were supposedly recorded by the alien during her visit to serve as disturbing parodies of the individual and collective human behaviors that caused the problems referred to at

---

193 Miguel Brieva, *Memorias de la tierra* (Barcelona: Random House Mondadori, 2012).
194 Brieva, *Memorias de la tierra*, 6.
195 Brieva, *Memorias de la tierra*, 6.

the beginning of the chapter. The first few chapters expose the overriding myths embraced by humanity at that time: the pathological and hubristic linear notion of 'progress' that celebrates material expansion, which in turn depletes the environment that supports human survival; the belief that no alternative exists to an economic system based on capital accumulation and growth; and the idea that individuals cannot do anything to alter this collective madness. The fifth chapter reveals the way in which humans waste their creativity, technological innovation, and storytelling energy on consolidating the myths that support the dominant imaginary. The sixth chapter deals with the systemic and structural violence consistently deployed against the biotic community (humans and nonhumans) to maintain the irrational mandates of mainstream economics. The hierarchical nature of the system and the inequalities it perpetuates is the subject of the seventh chapter. The eighth chapter wonders whether humans will end up changing direction or continue on to their inevitable collapse. And the final chapter reveals possible paths to a socially desirable and ecologically sustainable postgrowth society.

The fragmented aesthetic of *Memorias de la tierra* does not result in a chaotic fluctuation of attention but, on the contrary, serves as a recurring reminder of the systemic crisis of the growth paradigm from different perspectives. The novel's fragments are unified and framed by an overt and explicit critique of the socioenvironmental damage caused by an economic system addicted to growth. Of particular interest here is the last chapter, which envisions a positive urban postgrowth imaginary. The first set of vignettes in this chapter, 'Saludos desde el futuro' (Greetings from the Future), features a middle-aged man speaking in 2136 with a very relaxed attitude about the positive changes embraced by humanity, which include a reduction of working hours and of superfluous production and consumption, in order to produce only necessary goods; using technology to enhance socioecological well-being; and eliminating unnecessary mobility. Some of the drawings show a reverse human appropriation of net primary productivity in which vegetation takes over obsolete and unnecessary infrastructure (highways, gas stations) or enhances current urban spaces. Other drawings depict decentralized and localized clean-energy production, agroecological practices, and the displacement of individual vehicles by public transportation and biking.[196] The next series of drawings explicitly proposes degrowth as a way to escape the maladies of capitalism and to create a just and sustainable society for all, free of soft and hard pollution. The main vignette features a very appealing town whose streets are vibrant

196 Brieva, *Memorias de la tierra*, 163.

public spaces where all people can enjoy a pleasant, non-commodified life.
The four smaller vignettes that follow in this section indicate how to achieve
that kind of life: liberate the mind from hegemonic prejudices, reduce
overproduction and working hours, socially guarantee what is needed for
the reproduction of a good life, and enjoy what you have.[197] The following
series, 'Instrucciones para cambiar el mundo' (Instructions for Changing
the World), recognizes the need to combat the current model of economic
growth and recommends employing critical thinking, avoiding exposure to
discourses that poison the mind (advertising, corporate media), reducing
consumption, rethinking mobility, opposing neoliberal political parties,
and channeling collective energy to imagine a different world.[198] The page
in Chapter 9 that contains genuine quotes from authors includes several
critiques of the growth paradigm and an invitation to create and embrace
a degrowth society.[199]

Another section of the final chapter, 'El gran salto revolutivo' (The Big
(R)evolutionary Jump), combines the words for revolution and evolution
in its title and urges us to adopt an ecological economics paradigm with
ecofeminist roots in which we learn to take care of each other and live better
while reducing entropic activity. Again, an invitation to expand the political
limits of the possible through a decolonized imagination is extended:

> Todo nuestro potencial creativo dedicado a ensanchar lo imaginable,
> y no a vendernos una y otra vez la misma moto estropeada ... Toda
> nuestra inventiva y nuestra ciencia centrada en resolver los verdaderos
> problemas (salud, recuperación ambiental, energías renovables) y no en
> fabricar más y más chismes inútiles.[200]

> [All our creative potential dedicated to expand the imaginable, and
> not to sell us the same broken motorcycle over and over again ...
> All our ingenuity and science focusing on the real issues (health,
> environmental restauration, renewable energies) and not on producing
> more and more useless stuff]

In the last vignette of this chapter, two characters escape from the frame that
contains them and begin to think outside the epistemological limitations of
the dominant imaginary. After naming many Spanish degrowth activists
and thinkers in the acknowledgments, Miguel Brieva extends his thanks

197 Brieva, *Memorias de la tierra*, 164.
198 Brieva, *Memorias de la tierra*, 165.
199 Brieva, *Memorias de la tierra*, 166.
200 Brieva, *Memorias de la tierra*, 167.

a todas aquellas mujeres y hombres que piensan y sienten el mundo como un hogar común, hermoso y único, que merece ser salvaguardado de la estupidez devoradora de nuestro sistema actual y preservado para las generaciones futuras.[201]

[to all those men and women who think of and feel the world as a common home, beautiful and unique, that deserves to be protected from the devouring stupidity of our current system and preserved for future generations]

Memorias de la tierra does not advocate reruralization, but a new metabolic order in which humans learn to live better by creating just communities with reduced material and energy intensity.

Many cultural practices today rethink the city model by revisiting the food system. A recent book by Daniel López García, *Producir alimentos, reproducir comunidad* (Produce Food, Reproduce Community), elaborates on the need to radically change the global food system, emphasizing the many social and ecological virtues of agroecology and providing examples.[202] Agro-industrial practices are the greatest contributors to the metabolic rift and the increased unsustainability of the linear rural-urban model. The main problem is the conception of the rural as the space where food is produced and the urban as the locus of its consumption; Germán Labrador observes 'that the social circulation of food and food images is a decisive contributing factor in the symbolic landscape of the crisis'.[203] Challenges to the prevailing view of agriculture as a strictly rural phenomenon include the spread of communitarian urban gardening in Iberian cities since 2008 as well as organic agricultural co-operatives that integrate producers and consumers (community-supported agriculture) to create an urban food system that is socioecologically sound. These projects can engage in broad exchange practices beyond food and significantly transform socioeconomic relations, as in the case of the Cooperativa Integral Calatana (CIC).

In *El jardín Escondido: espacios verdes en la ciudad* (The Hidden Garden: Green Spaces in the City, 2013), Pilar Sampietro and Ignacio Somovilla celebrate 12 successful urban gardens in Barcelona.[204] Madrid also boasts a number of successful examples, among them BAH (¡Bajo el asfalto está

201 Brieva, *Memorias de la tierra*, 175.

202 Daniel López García, *Producir alimentos, reproducir comunidad* (Madrid: Libros en acción, 2015).

203 Labrador Méndez, 'The Cannibal Wave', 244.

204 Pilar Sampietro and Ignacio Somovilla, *El jardín Escondido: espacios verdes en la ciudad / The Hidden Garden: Green Spaces in the City* (Barcelona: Pol·len Edicions, 2013).

la huerta!) [Under the Asphalt Is the Garden!], which has been operating since 2000. BAH is a participatory project developed and self-managed by local collectives operating outside of capitalist institutions. It promotes education in agroecology and organizes workshops and convivial activities for the community. The name of the collective explicitly points to the need to change the linear urban metabolism in order to generate a more resilient and circular one: if asphalt disrupts the cycle of nutrients and water, the ecological garden enhances it. Another example is the Network of Urban Gardens in Madrid, a group of collectives of urban agriculture devoted to sharing knowledge, support, and agricultural supplies. If the dominant imaginary is 'based on the masking of the biopolitical links connecting nutrition, economy and society', as Labrador suggests, the agroecological urban practices mentioned above contribute, instead, to connect these dots and make the links visible.[205] Once the connections are made, the neoliberal fantasies and their ideology of disconnection are exposed. Labrador also deconstructs the neoliberal rationality deeply ingrained in some television cooking shows that have become very popular during the ongoing crisis.[206] The hegemonic imaginary is rooted even in our gastronomic cultural imagination!

Many other examples of postgrowth urban imaginaries have emerged across the Iberian Peninsula. The 15-M *acampadas* (encampments) proliferating in public squares have been interpreted as collective creations of alternative urban spaces. The Acampada Sol in Madrid, for instance, has been described as a 'nonneoliberal city within the neoliberal city'.[207] Luis Moreno-Caballud explains that 'in Sol, a city was built in four days. In spite of the urgency, they created a daily life rich with activities'.[208] This multifunctional inclusive city (which included a library, kitchen, flower garden, and communications center), employed the collective intelligence and diverse knowledge and skills of its participants to create a space where mutual care and collaboration was prioritized over competition and accumulation.[209] The 15-M *acampadas* created spaces where specific solutions to real problems were collectively negotiated and solved without the mediation of capitalist institutions. Of course, these spaces were transient and impossible to maintain for extended periods, but they created networks and synergies for new political platforms and transformative projects. The camps also showed the possibility of

205 Labrador Méndez, 'The Cannibal Wave', 244.
206 Labrador Méndez, 'The Cannibal Wave', 246–251.
207 Moreno-Caballud, *Cultures of Anyone*, 197.
208 Moreno-Caballud, *Cultures of Anyone*, 195.
209 Moreno-Caballud, *Cultures of Anyone*, 194–197.

developing desirable postgrowth urban practices despite their embedment in a hostile neoliberal city.

Perhaps the most consistent effort to envision and put into practice a desirable postgrowth urban imaginary is found in the transition towns movement. This movement started in 2005 in Totnes (Devon, UK) with the goal of transforming towns and cities addicted to fossil fuel into resilient socioecological systems that can respond to the challenges brought about by peak oil and climate change. In *The Transition Handbook: From Oil Dependency to Local Resilience*, Totnes resident Rob Hopkins outlines the steps for beginning the transition to self-reliance in any community (not just towns, but virtually any human settlement).[210] Currently, there are hundreds of transition projects in over 50 countries. The transition movement strategically creates the conditions for a community to improve its resiliency (the capacity of a system to recover, adapt, and thrive in the face of disruptions) by applying permaculture principles that improve the socioecological well-being of the local community while decarbonizing its operational capacities. These projects are initiated by community members and can only flourish by gaining the support, participation, and engagement of the local population and its institutions. The outcome is usually a much more pleasant and egalitarian urban environment for the community. The movement embraces an assertive and positive attitude that emphasizes the benefits of transitioning (improving quality of life, fostering social cohesion, enhancing the environment) and employs research on the psychology of change and participatory methodologies to facilitate collective and horizontal communication, synergy, and self-management.

The first book about the transition movement written in a language other than English, *Guía del movimiento de transición: cómo transformar tu vida en la ciudad* by Juan del Río, was published in Spain in 2015.[211] Much like Hopkins's book, it outlines the resources and steps needed to begin a transition movement in any town, based on the knowledge produced by current initiatives and experiences. The first Spanish transition groups emerged in 2008–2009. The number of initiatives increased after the 15-M movement, and by 2015 more than 50 groups had been established and three Iberian Transition Conferences had been held.[212] These groups interact, cooperate, and share experiences and knowledge through the Red de

---

210 Rob Hopkins, *The Transition Handbook: From Oil Dependency to Local Resilience* (Totnes: Green Books, 2008).

211 Juan Del Río, *Guía del movimiento de transición: cómo transformar tu vida en la ciudad* (Madrid: Catarata, 2015).

212 Del Río, *Guía del movimiento de transición*, 80–82.

Transición España. In Spain, the transition movement is closely aligned and integrated with other movements with similar goals, such as the degrowth, ecovillages, and permaculture movements. The transition movement also collaborates with the Postpetroleum Municipalities wiki and its magazine for a new civilization, *15/15\15*.[213] It has created a number of workshops and activities to nourish and foster communitarian creativity, such as Jorge Carrasco's 'art for the transition' workshops, whose goal is the creation of transition stories.[214] For, as Del Río recognizes,

> Las palabras, nuestro lenguaje e historias son en cierta medida el límite de nuestra imaginación, y actualmente las historias dominantes hablan del poder de la tecnología, del crecimiento económico sin límites y de la cultura de la separación, de uno mismo de los demás y del mundo que nos rodea. Precisamos de la creación de nuevas narraciones, más apropiadas para los tiempos que corren.[215]

> [Words, languages, and stories are in a way the limits of our imagination, and currently the dominant stories talk about the power of technology, limitless economic growth, and the culture of separation from oneself, others, and the world around us. We need to create new narratives that are more appropriate for our current context]

Two examples of these new postgrowth narrations can be found in a collection of post-transition stories titled *Tapas de un futuro pospetróleo* (Covers of a Post-petroleum Future) and the first issue (issue 0) of *15/15\15*.[216]

The inaugural issue of *15/15\15: Revista para una nueva civilización* (Journal for a New Civilization) was financed by crowdfunding and published in 2015 under a Creative Commons license.[217] This first issue, named *2030-05*, contains contributions in five Iberian languages (Basque, Catalan, Galician, Portuguese, and Spanish). The magazine has the explicit intention of creating a critical and independent media platform able to break away from the inertia of the dominant imaginary of economic growth. The three fifteens (15/15\15) in the name of the magazine, along with the subheading (2030-05), are meant to suggest that the publication is celebrating its fifteenth anniversary in 2030, when only 15 percent of global fossil fuel remains, and its contributors are reflecting on the last 15 years. This is the

---

213 Del Río, *Guía del movimiento de transición*, 83.
214 Del Río, *Guía del movimiento de transición*, 120–127.
215 Del Río, *Guía del movimiento de transición*, 127.
216 Del Río, *Guía del movimiento de transición*, 127.
217 The issue is available for download at https://www.15-15-15.org/webzine/num-0-mayo-2030-es/.

end of the fossil fuel regime, 'la energía con la que el petróleo había venido sosteniendo la Civilización del Crecimiento' [the energy that has sustained the Growth Civilization], as the editorial introducing the magazine points out.[218] The 29 contributions, grouped in sections on analysis, practice, and creation, provide fictional perspectives on the 15-year period that marks the end of the age of capitalist petromodernity and the transition to the new economic, cultural, social, and ecological system that is emerging from its ruins. The tensions between the desire to construct a new functional society and the cruel optimism of those who refuse to let go of the old paradigm are described, sometimes in the form of intergenerational conflicts. While most of the texts point out the many social difficulties brought about by the demise of capitalism, such as rapid energy decline, tightened material restrictions, environmental deterioration, and the injustices ingrained in the dominant imaginary, none of the narratives depicts an apocalyptic or dystopic future. The postgrowth transition is viewed as a worthwhile but continual work-in-progress facing innumerable obstacles.

The magazine's pages are not populated with individual heroes, benevolent elites, technological miracles, or rapid panaceas, but rather collective, patient efforts to unlearn hegemonic habits and relearn forgotten communal knowledge and skills that will enable us to repurpose existing technologies and institutions to solve pressing problems. The expert knowledge of neoliberal technocrats (useful only if cheap energy is widely available) is replaced with a much more open and flexible collective intelligence that functions in diverse ways to meet the specific needs of each community. New noncapitalist modes of social reproduction are organized along decentralized and resilient lines favoring communal and collective property over private ownership. There is no homogeneous image of the transition, as different stories focus on specific local and regional examples and their peculiarities. But in most of these narratives, although the dominant imaginary and its power have not been completely eradicated and the possibility of ecofascist reactions is still latent, a process of economic deglobalization is empowering communities to create new social structures. A renovated lexicon also marks the ongoing epistemological decolonization, as the euphemistic and misleading rhetoric disseminated by neoliberal media (creation of wealth, growth, development, financial crisis, unemployment, markets, externalities) is replaced by clear and critical terms describing the material and symbolic reality of the hegemonic order—*La Gran Estafa* (The Big Fraud), *final de la Era del Petróleo* (the end of the Fossil Fuel Period), *Decrecimiento* (Degrowth), *Caos Climático* (Climatic Chaos), *declive energético* (energy decline), etc.

218 'Editorial: 2015+15', *15/15\15 Revista para una nueva civilización* o (2015): 1.

Some of the stories depict new rural communities without implying the disappearance of the urban world. Of course, without fossil fuels, urban models and lifestyles are unlikely to resemble those of a Petropolis. Henrique Pérez Lijó speaks of the 'urban peak' and the need to revisit our use of territory.[219] He refers to the 'desintegración do urbano en multiples configuracións de novidosos estilos de vida, dificilmente etiquetábeis baixo a dicotomía rural-urbano' [breakup of cities into multiple configurations of new lifestyles that are difficult to classify under the rural-urban dichotomy].[220] In similar terms, Adrián Almazán describes a series of urban mutations:

> Los grandes aglomerados urbanos han tenido que restructurarse casi íntegramente ante la disminución crítica de combustibles fósiles. En la mayoría de las ciudades los barrios han recuperado su autonomía tanto política como espacial, volviendo a generarse cinturones verdes entre las zonas urbanizadas encaminados a la producción de alimentos (mediante el cultivo y mediante la creación de bosques comestibles).[221]

> [The big metropolitan areas have had to drastically restructure themselves, given the critical decline of fossil fuels. In most cities the neighborhoods have regained their political and spatial autonomy, generating green belts between urbanized areas to produce food (through the creation of food gardens and edible forests)]

These narratives target both the material and the symbolic hegemony for, as David Harvey reminds us, the city we inhabit molds our current subjectivities and conditions our daily possibilities, and thus neoliberal urbanization reduces the possibility of a desirable postcapitalist society from emerging. In theory and in practice, the transition movement claims that living spaces should be the product of a participatory process shaped by the communities inhabiting them with the goal of enhancing their well-being through the use of decentralized and convivial tools managed and determined by each community.

On Juan del Río's website, the section titled *Tapas de un futuro pospetróleo* includes seven transition stories by different authors. The purpose of these stories is to reactivate our political imagination in order to envision

---

219 Henrique Pérez Lijó, 'O cénit da concentración urbana. Análise das mudanzas nos asentamentos humanos no inicio do colapso', *15/15\15 Revista para una nueva civilización* o (2015): 34.

220 Lijó, 'O cénit da concentración urbana', 35.

221 Adrián Almazán, 'Amoeiro', *15/15\15 Revista para una nueva civilización* o (2015): 92.

a post-petroleum future.[222] The stories are followed by references to counterhegemonic books that inspired the authors and which the reader can consult. Some questions function as starting points to trigger the imaginative process:

¿cómo podría ser la vida en unas décadas, después de años de transición hacia una sociedad más local, resiliente y menos dependiente de los combustibles fósiles? ¿Cómo satisfaríamos nuestras necesidades básicas? ¿Cómo nos organizaríamos? ¿Cómo sería el proceso de cambio?

[What would our lives be like in a few decades, after a few years transitioning towards a more local and resilient society less addicted to fossil fuels? How are we going to satisfy our basic needs? How are we going to organize? What would the process of change look like?]

The project recognizes the power of stories to change the imaginary: 'Las narraciones y las historias tienen el gran poder de crear un nuevo imaginario, y esto es clave para la construcción de un futuro alternativo' [Narratives and stories have great power to create a new imaginary, and this is key to constructing an alternative future].

The stories comprising *Tapas de un futuro pospetróleo* describe a variety of possible measures to be adopted during the transition to a postgrowth society. In 'Barcelona 2030. Territorio comestible' (Barcelona 2030: Edible Territory), Pilar Sampietro envisions a regenerative Barcelona where the disproportionate amount of urban space previously monopolized by individual vehicles is now occupied by edible landscapes, including urban gardens and small forests (a reverse human appropriation of net primary productivity that liberates previously human-appropriated ecological space for the use of other species).[223] The city has a circular metabolism that not only does not pollute, but also helps the healing process by enhancing sink capabilities and natural purification and detox processes, thereby shrinking the metabolic rift. In 'La sociedad post-tecnológica' (The Post-technologic Society), Jordi Pigem depicts life in 2039, after the systemic crisis of 2008 spelled the end of the growth society and its paradigm.[224] The homodiegetic narrator reports that cities collapsed as soon as they lost their daily injections of food and energy, and that the larger the metropolis,

222 Juan Del Río, *Tapas de un futuro pospetróleo*, http://juandelrio.net/tapas-de-un-futuro-pospetroleo/.
223 Pilar Sampietro, 'Barcelona 2030. Territorio comestible', http://juandelrio.net/tapas-de-un-futuro-pospetroleo/barcelona-2030-territorio-comestible/.
224 Jordi Pigem, 'La sociedad post-tecnológica', http://juandelrio.net/tapas-de-un-futuro-pospetroleo/la-sociedad-post-tecnologica/.

the less able it was to adapt to the transition. 'Ahora son almacenes de materiales' [Now cities are warehouses of materials], the narrator says, referring to the unsustainable linear metabolism characterizing modern cities and their tendency to accumulate material inputs instead of reusing them in a circular fashion. In Quim Nogueras's 'Velas y recuerdos' (Candles and Memories), an elderly man remembers the past and explains to his grandchildren the widespread changes that humanity experienced after the collapse of petromodernity.[225] In this case, the transition succeeded thanks to the implementation of an agroecological food system and the reduction of superfluous consumption. Àngels Castellarnau's 'Si las paredes hablaran' (If Walls Could Talk) describes the paradigm shift in architecture that accompanied the transition her story narrates, a change from massive over-construction that pillages materials and energy to biodesigns based on local breathable materials, energy sufficiency, comfort, and adaptation to regional climatic conditions.[226] The envisioned futures articulated by these stories grow from the many counterhegemonic seeds planted during the last few decades that have been nourished by countless ongoing collective initiatives.

One of the most overlooked crises of our time is the widespread privatization of public urban space. In an informative and disturbing op-ed piece published in *The Guardian* in November 2015, Saskia Sassen warns us of the post-2008 tendency towards large-scale 'corporate buying of urban buildings and land', which has 'significant implications for equity, democracy and rights'.[227] Sassen confirms that 'foreign corporate buying of properties from 2013 to 2014 grew by ... 180% in Madrid'. This process entails foreclosing on modest buildings and replacing them with exclusive luxury mega-projects with vast footprints and no public access or social utility for locals. The resultant privatized and de-urbanized city prevents any relevant political, cultural, or social use of urban space at all. The small but meaningful marginal spaces once inhabited by powerless people within modern capitalist cities are now completely appropriated by the new extreme neoliberal metropolis. In corporate cities no epistemological or cultural diversity can flourish outside the dominant imaginary. If postindustrial neoliberal cities offer no place for the peasants of the world—who were and still are forced to migrate *en masse* to the city after being dispossessed

---

225 Quim Nogueras, 'Velas y recuerdos', http://juandelrio.net/tapas-de-un-futuro-pospetroleo/velas-y-recuerdos/.
226 Àngels Castellarnau, 'Si las paredes hablaran', http://juandelrio.net/tapas-de-un-futuro-pospetroleo/si-las-paredes-hablaran/.
227 Sassen, 'Who Owns Our Cities'.

of their livelihood by global capitalism—what spaces are going to sustain these surplus populations? We do not know. But we do know that capitalism is generating more and more surplus population without providing it with a place or a function in the dominant system. On the one hand, this creates the potential for emancipatory movements to emerge, yet on the other it may foster reactionary tendencies (more on this in Chapter 3). The outcome depends on what kind of imaginaries are activated and how. Some communities strive to strategically produce their own spaces instead of remaining passive and reactionary. Such activism entails not only challenging the material order, but collectively imagining and practicing new ways of thinking and of inhabiting the world, namely, postgrowth urban imaginaries. It is time to recognize that the spaces which the dominant imaginary celebrates as monuments of progress are only made possible by the accelerated and intensified production of planetary landscapes of violence and extractive geographies (the massive biological annihilation and social exploitation brought about by the Capitalocene). It seems to me that moving towards postgrowth urban imaginaries is a necessary condition for the flourishing of regenerative radical geographies of justice and prosperity for all earthlings.

PART III

Waste, Disaster, Refugees, and Nonhuman Agency

CHAPTER THREE

Nonhuman Agency
and the Political Ecology of Waste

The Anthropocene has reversed the temporal order of modernity: those at
the margins are now the first to experience the future that awaits all of us.
—Amitav Ghosh[1]

T he more waste modern societies produce, the less their members want
to think about it, and thus dominant cultural narratives are dedicated
with increasing vigor to obliterating the link between growth and pollution.
As Zygmunt Bauman points out, 'we dispose of leftovers in the most radical
and effective way: we make them invisible by not looking and unthinkable
by not thinking'.[2] Usually, waste is left out of the dominant 'distribution
of the sensible' (as Rancière would put it) and its symbolic order, which
determines and prearranges what can be visible or thinkable in advance and
therefore significantly limits our epistemological, imaginative, and political
possibilities. In this chapter I claim that if we are to 'reconfigure the map of
the sensible', we need to create a political ecology of waste that persistently
disrupts and disturbs the growth imaginary with narratives and practices
that redefine what can be thought, said, and seen.

Capitalist economic processes are transforming material and energy into

1 Amitav Ghosh, *The Great Derangement: Climate Change and the Unthinkable* (Chicago,
IL: University of Chicago Press, 2016), 62–63.
2 Zygmunt Bauman, *Wasted Lives: Modernity and its Outcasts* (Cambridge: Polity
Press, 2004), 27.

waste with increased velocity. This entropic and carcinogenic economic system not only reduces the future availability of such resources for other economic inputs, it generates toxic outputs that will alter the biogeochemistry of the Earth for millennia to come. The longevity of capitalism's 'toxic progeny' leads Heather Davis to label plastic pollution the 'bastard child that will certainly outlive us'.[3] In this chapter I will approach the problem of waste from several angles: How should we think—ethically, aesthetically, and politically—about the agency of such toxicity operating in different temporalities and on different scales? What politics of representation are useful to connect this toxic progeny with the growth imaginary in a critical way? How might we mobilize a poetics of waste in such a way that it is not co-opted by neoliberal reason, but instead encourages the emergence of postgrowth imaginaries?

In 2010, José Luis Pardo, one of Spain's most thought-provoking philosophers, published a collection of essays under the title *Nunca fue tan hermosa la basura* (Never Was Trash so Beautiful). At the beginning of the eponymous essay, Pardo reformulates the first sentence of Karl Marx's *Das Kapital*, replacing the word 'commodity' with the word 'trash': 'The wealth of societies in which the capitalist mode of production prevails appears as "an immense accumulation of trash"'.[4] According to Pardo, modern society has produced such quantities of waste that they now threaten the survival of modern institutions.[5] The crisis of modernity is marked by the end of the utopia of a world without waste:

> un mundo ordenado, en el cual cada cosa esté en su sitio ... La entrada en crisis de este modelo, el despertar de este sueño, fue por tanto ese momento en el cual llegamos a pensar que la basura acabaría devorándonos. Que era el fin del progreso.[6]

> [an organized world in which each thing is in its own place ... The crisis of this model, the awakening from this dream, was the moment in which we started thinking that waste would end up devouring us. This meant the end of progress.]

Interestingly, Pardo suggests that the end of the teleological notion of progress coincides with the moment in which modern societies realize

3 Heather Davis, 'Toxic Progeny: The Plastisphere and Other Queer Futures', *PhiloSOPHIA: A Journal of Continental Feminism* 5, no. 2 (2015): 232.

4 José Luis Pardo, *Nunca fue tan hermosa la basura* (Barcelona: Galaxia Gutenberg, 2010), 163.

5 Pardo, *Nunca fue tan hermosa la basura*, 163.

6 Pardo, *Nunca fue tan hermosa la basura*, 167–169.

that things in general and waste in particular have an unexpected agency that might destroy us. Progress perceived as constant economic growth is therefore nothing but an epistemological trap with dire semiotic and material consequences. The most obvious example is the transformation of Earth's ecological systems into a toxic landfill that suffocates life. But redefining progress in a postgrowth fashion is difficult given the tenacity of the dominant imaginary and its dream of unlimited growth.

Now that trash is everywhere—expressing itself in different fashions, from global warming and plastic patches the size of Mexico floating in the ocean to heavy metals in mothers' breast milk—one of the newest strategies to hide it is to look at it with aesthetic joy. Trash is actually beautiful:

> ¿Y si lo que llamamos basura no lo fuese en realidad? Entonces no tendríamos que preocuparnos porque nos devorase, no nos sentiríamos asfixiados por los desperdicios si dejásemos de experimentarlos como desperdicios y los viviéramos como un nuevo *paisaje urbano.*[7]

> [What if that which we call garbage were not really garbage? Then we would not have to worry about being devoured by it, and we would not feel asphyxiated by waste if we stopped perceiving it as waste and saw it as a new *urban landscape*]

If modern waste were to be seen for what it is, a toxic byproduct of economic growth and the result of a pathological social metabolism, the dominant imaginary would need to be changed; however, if trash is presented as something with aesthetic and monetary potential, the problem disappears and the capitalist mode of production and consumption can continue. Compare the media celebration of Northern European countries that produce energy out of waste, or the increasing popularity of industrial ecology and eco-design using industrial waste as raw material, to the 'invisibility' of communities around the planet whose lifestyles and systems of social organization never produced industrial waste to begin with. Why are the former highlighted and celebrated as models of human ingenuity while the latter are trivialized and erased from memory? Why does the clever reuse of waste materials hold so much appeal for the most progressive sectors of the dominant imaginary? The answer is simple: this reform environmentalism keeps the dream of constant growth alive by implying that a few technological fixes and changes in management can solve the problem without addressing its structural and epistemological causes. Unfortunately, technology is not a panacea. In fact, it often exacerbates the existing problem.

7 Pardo, *Nunca fue tan hermosa la basura*, 170.

ECOALF by Boamistura, picture by Luis I Prádanos

In May 2013, the ground floor facade of one of the buildings facing Santa Bárbara Square in Madrid was painted with graffiti by Boamistura, a group of street artists based in that city.

The mural, measuring ten meters square, consists of an amorphous Earth—labeled *mundo* (world) in large capital letters—full of anthropogenic materials (car tires, buildings, bottles, and an industrial chimney). Interestingly, neither biomass nor humans are visible in this global allegory of massive human appropriation of net primary productivity. The perturbing image implies that humans have been devoured by their material pollution, but the integrated text (semiotic pollution?) offers a strained optimism with the sentence 'Aceptando el mundo comienzas a cambiarlo' [By accepting the world you can start changing it], as if humans have not sufficiently changed the world already. The word 'recycle' crowns the mural. Furthermore, the enigmatic word play in the phrases 'in trash we trust' and 'tras(h)umanity' appear respectively above and below the word *mundo*, and the whole functions as a textual sandwich in which the world is the main ingredient to be consumed. Is this a piece of street art intended to make people aware of the unsustainable proliferation of waste created by capitalism or, as Pardo would suspect, a neoliberal reminder that 'there is no alternative' to the current wasteful capitalist dynamics? Is it a challenge to growth or an invitation not only to accept capitalism's toxic progeny, but to love it by seeing the potential beauty of trash? Is this a call for political activism or for passive acceptance?

The context of the mural can shed some light on these questions. Near the bottom right corner of the wall appear the words 'ECOALF by Boamistura'. ECOALF is a clothing store established in 2009 and located near the mural. According to its website, 'the idea was to create a fashion brand that is truly sustainable', and thus ECOALF manufactures and sells clothes and accessories using recycled materials. ECOALF has its own 'manifesto tras(h)umanity' that states:

> Tras(h)umanity is a paradoxical concept. Like the 21st century. Like you. We must stop the continuing pollution of the environment. But ECOALF isn't willing to settle for just that, it wants to invert the process. *New technologies allow us to do that, revolutionizing the idea of raw material.*
>
> Tras(h)umanity accepts that trash is an *inherent* feature of our species.
>
> By accepting the world you can start to change it. Only then can we think of ways to clean up that reality in an intelligent, useful way.
>
> Tras(h)umanity isn't a utopian term. It's an awareness of trash. We are looking for a *new generation of conscious consumers* who are not willing to reject their *aesthetic values.*
>
> We create objects that make your life more enjoyable without damaging our relationship with nature. And we do it by erasing part of the ecological footprint that is fouling the world.
>
> ECOALF wants to share with you its passion for beautiful, useful *products that clean up the planet.* Help us *take the concept of trash into the future.*
>
> This time, *trash is good news.* (my emphasis)[8]

This could very well be a manifesto produced by a neoliberal think tank attempting to convince us that trash is beautiful. A critical discourse analysis quickly unveils the document's neoliberal rhetoric of reform environmentalism. The affirmation that 'new technologies allow us to do that, revolutionizing the idea of raw material' is not only a celebration of techno-optimism, but an invitation to participate in a conceptual

8 As of November 2016 the ECOALF manifesto was not available on the company's English- or Spanish-language websites. An archived version from February 18, 2015, is available at http://web.archive.org/web/20150218172250/http://ecoalf.com/us_en/about/manifiesto/.

revolution (rather than a political revolution) that will invert the process of environmental degradation. Apparently, for ECOALF the problem has nothing to do with capitalism, colonialism, power asymmetries, racism, socioecological injustice, gender inequality, wealth distribution, hubristic individualism, or anthropocentrism. The problem is that we got the idea of raw material wrong! If we could only understand and accept that 'trash is an inherent feature of our species', we could right all wrongs. And the protagonists of these changes are not to be concerned (politically organized) citizens but rather a 'new generation of conscious consumers who are not willing to reject their aesthetic values'. By consuming we can solve the problems of overconsumption! Because there are 'products [rather than ecological cycles] that clean up the planet'. Moreover, we should, according to ECOALF, 'help take the concept of trash into the future', as if global warming or nuclear waste, with deep temporalities unthinkable on a human scale, were not already part of our future. The final sentence, 'trash is good news', sounds like black humor, considering, for instance, the massive number of birds and fish dying every day from ingested plastic, and the cancerous lungs of children informally recycling e-waste in African countries, India, and China. In sum, ECOALF proposes to solve environmental problems by repurposing industrial waste (good luck with nuclear waste!) and relying on consumers to make ethical choices. This well-intentioned discourse undermines the possibility for more radical responses—namely, collective politics that challenge the dominant imaginary.

Make no mistake, I agree that we need both technology and an economy that closes the cycle of materials in a circular fashion, but a growth-oriented economy is ill-equipped to make this happen since it is, by definition, an organization of ecological relations that 'becomes more wasteful over time'.[9] The representation of waste in cultural texts and media is a crucial arena in which to do battle with the dominant imaginary. How waste is represented and narrated matters because such representations can enhance or undermine the effectiveness of a postgrowth political ecology. A recycling economy is not a circular economy, as discard studies shows and as Josh Lepawsky and Max Liboiron remind us:

recycling captures a fraction of waste, uses virgin materials in its process, creates pollution, and naturalizes disposables and other forms of harmful waste under the guise that recycling 'takes care' of things. In short, recycling as it is currently structured perpetuates growth

9 Jason W. Moore, 'Nature in the Limits to Capital (and Vice Versa)', *Radical Philosophy* 193 (September–October): 15.

and dominant economies rather than providing a social or technical avenue for change.[10]

A politically effective representation of waste must understand the deep temporalities and perverse socioecological entanglements that play out in the emergence of modern waste and attempt to track its physical as well as discursive networks. Rather than reducing waste to an ahistorical, post-political, and isolated material waiting to be repurposed and revaluated by the growth economy—as ECOALF proposes—the 'political ecology of waste' I propose functions, instead, as an entry point to expose the historical, political, material, and semiotic network of power relations that encircle modern waste. An efficacious political ecology of waste does not celebrate trash, because it does not overlook its dire social and ecological consequences.

'El número de objetos de basura espacial que rodean a la Tierra se ha duplicado en 15 años' [The number of discarded objects orbiting the Earth has doubled in the last 15 years] is the title of an article published in November 2015 in the Spanish newspaper *eldiario.es*.[11] The author explains that in the previous week, two of these orbiting pieces of refuse landed in a meadow in Murcia, Spain, and another was expected to fall into the Indian Ocean the next Friday. Another 100 million such objects orbit the Earth! Humans are not only filling the Earth with trash, but also outer space. According to the journalist, however, the possibility that any of these discarded objects will wreak a lethal revenge seems unlikely, so readers can rest assured that, most probably, cosmic debris will not strike them down while they are reading the news and enjoying their coffee. The most disturbing revelation comes later in the report, when the reader finds out that in 2009 a collision between an abandoned satellite and an operating one produced 2,000 new objects, thereby multiplying the risk of future collisions:

> el consultor de la NASA Donald Kessler planteó un escenario en el que la enorme cantidad de basura en órbita podría empezar a colisionar entre sí, y con los sistemas actualmente operativos, creando una reacción en cadena que terminaría por destruir la mayoría de los

10 Josh Lepawsky and Max Liboiron, 'Why Discards, Diverse Economics, and Degrowth?', *Society & Space* (2015), http://societyandspace.org/2015/08/14/why-discards-diverse-economies-and-degrowth-josh-lepawsky-and-max-liboiron/.

11 Teguayco Pinto, 'El número de objetos de basura espacial que rodean a la Tierra se ha duplicado en 15 años', *eldiario.es*, November 11, 2015, http://www.eldiario.es/sociedad/basura_espacial-astronomia-ciencia_0_451105767.html.

objetos en órbita, incluyendo satélites de comunicaciones, plataformas científicas o incluso estaciones espaciales.

[NASA consultant Donald Kessler suggested a scenario in which the enormous number of pieces of orbiting waste could start crashing into each other, and into currently operating machinery, creating a chain reaction that would end up destroying the majority of orbiting objects, including communication satellites, scientific platforms, or even space stations]

Again, this example suggests that objects set in motion by humans can unexpectedly reveal their own agency and cause unimagined damage. Global warming, ocean acidification, desertification, toxic chemical synergies, pandemics related to industrial agriculture, mass extinctions, and the imminent threat of a post-antibiotic (and maybe also post-satellite, according to Kessler) world are just a few of the proliferating dire, unintended consequences of capital accumulation. The growth-oriented imaginary grossly ignores the agency of the nonhuman at society's peril, while setting in motion socioecological processes that function as threat multipliers and can neither be controlled nor reversed.

Thinkers working on the philosophy of science urge us to abandon the epistemological dichotomies established at the core of industrial modernity between nature and culture, human and nonhuman, and active subject and passive object. Bruno Latour, Donna Haraway, and Karen Barad, among others, compellingly argue that such rigid distinctions are not only grossly inaccurate accounts of how material processes operate across different temporalities and scales, they are also vastly dysfunctional when dealing with current socioecological issues. New materialisms have proliferated in recent years and are convincingly claiming that ignoring or rejecting the agency of the nonhuman is no longer advisable, or even possible, at the current geohistorical moment. Humans are not individual and autonomous creatures whose behaviors are determined solely by rational economic choices. They do not control and exploit environments that are radically separated from themselves, as neoclassical economics implies. Rather, humans are transcorporeal beings, as Stacy Alaimo notes, because 'we inhabit a corporeality that is never disconnected from our environment ... we are permeable, emergent beings, reliant upon the others within and outside our porous borders'.[12] We always exist in constant and inextricable co-transformative relations with other species and things. Presently, many

12 Alaimo, *Bodily Natures*, 156.

health problems in consumerist societies are associated with the loss of biodiversity (bacteria and worms) in our own guts![13]

We are not just embodied beings. 'We are, rather, *an array of bodies*, many different kinds of them in a nested set of microbiomes'.[14] As Donna Haraway and Bruno Latour remind us, we are *naturecultures*, intersecting in multiple semiotic and material networks composed by human and nonhuman actors, where everything can have agency, but nothing acts alone.[15] All actions are 'intra-actions', as Karen Barad beautifully puts it, since individual agencies are co-constituted and only emerge through connections with other agencies.[16] In Jane Bennett's words, 'human agency is always an assemblage of microbes, animals, plants, metals, chemicals, word-sounds— indeed, ... insofar as anything 'acts' at all, it has already entered an agentic assemblage'.[17] I believe that cultural criticism could benefit from recognizing that humans are not the only actants, to use Latour's term, and that cultural scholarship could be significantly enhanced by paying attention to the agency of the nonhuman in all cultural domains.

Timothy Morton suggests in *Ecology without Nature*, and again in *The Ecological Thought*, that 'in order to have 'ecology', we have to let go of 'nature ... [and start] thinking of interconnectedness',[18] since nature is nothing but a reification of a myth of 'the lump that exists prior to the capitalist labor process'.[19] This myth implies that capitalist societies and their transformations are something radically different and autonomous from the ecological and historical processes in which they are entangled. Similarly, Latour invites us to be cautious with the concept of nature in its possible articulations by political ecology because, too often, nature has been used precisely 'to abort politics'.[20] So both ecological thought and political ecology have to let go of 'nature' in order to become transformative enough to transcend the dominant

13 William Parker, 'If Being Too Clean Makes Us Sick, Why Isn't Getting Dirty the Solution?', *The Conversation*, January 13, 2016, https://theconversation.com/if-being-too-clean-makes-us-sick-why-isnt-getting-dirty-the-solution-50572.

14 Bennett, *Vibrant Matter*, 112–113.

15 Donna Haraway, 'Anthropocene, Capitalocene, Plantationocene, Chthulucene: Making Kin', *Environmental Humanities* 6 (2015): 159–165; Bruno Latour, *Politics of Nature: How to Bring the Sciences into Democracy*, trans. Catherine Porter (Cambridge, MA: Harvard University Press, 2004).

16 Karen Barad, *Meeting the Universe Halfway* (Durham, NC: Duke University Press, 2007).

17 Bennett, *Vibrant Matter*, 120–121.

18 Timothy Morton, *The Ecological Thought* (Cambridge, MA: Harvard University Press, 2010).

19 Morton, *Hyperobjects*, 113.

20 Latour, *Politics of Nature*, 19.

imaginary of the growth paradigm. What interests me most, however, is how the much-needed change of thinking advocated by new materialists is advanced in recent Spanish cultural manifestations, and how an ecologically oriented cultural criticism can help to facilitate the emergence of postgrowth imaginaries. Morton recognizes that 'one of the things that modern society has damaged, along with ecosystems and species and the global climate, is thinking',[21] but, paradoxically, the 'current ecological disaster ... has torn a giant hole in the fabric of our understanding',[22] which creates an opportunity to open up refreshing new imaginaries and possibilities for thinking beyond capitalism and, as such, for reconfiguring the distribution of the sensible and the thinkable, in Jacques Rancière's sense. As Morton writes, 'The ecological thought must imagine economic change; otherwise it's just another piece on the game board of capitalist ideology. The boring, rapacious reality we have constructed'.[23]

In the remainder of this chapter, I will explore how recognizing the agency of waste helps us imagine radical economic change by exposing the nonsensical and uneconomical dynamic of a social system oriented towards constant economic growth. In the last few years, Spanish cultural manifestations that focus on discarded materials and degraded spaces have multiplied greatly, placing objects and processes that the dominant system usually keeps out of sight at the center of our attention. This has a number of aesthetic, semiotic, and political consequences that could be better understood from a material ecocritical perspective. I believe that by moving to the foreground the agency of the massive waste generated by our linear socioeconomic metabolism, these cultural expressions are challenging the dominant narratives of progress as unlimited economic growth. How can converting the biosphere into an uninhabitable landfill and a toxic, acidified seascape be equated with progress? If the byproduct of growth is widespread toxic waste that depletes the life-supporting systems of the planet, then the ability to progress towards a healthy society that can thrive in a healthy environment lies in developing a postgrowth society. Note my intentional semantic shift in recontextu-alizing the verbs 'to progress' and 'to develop' in order to detach them from the growth-oriented imaginary that has monopolized their semiotic and rhetorical possibilities for too long. Progress and development could be radically redefined in order to be unlinked from economic growth.

Drawing on Jane Bennett's book *Vibrant Matter: A Political Ecology of Things*, I refer to 'the political ecology of waste' as the rhetorical strategy

21 Morton, *The Ecological Thought*, 3.
22 Morton, *The Ecological Thought*, 14.
23 Morton, *The Ecological Thought*, 19.

Brieva 'Chabola'

of foregrounding the things which the growth economy discards. Waste stubbornly problematizes its own existence by showing off its agency. This proliferation of the visibility of wasted bodies, materials, and discourses discarded by the economy of growth signals the tipping point past which dominant imaginaries can no longer sustain their aseptic fantasies and solipsist aesthetics of disconnection. A cartoon by Miguel Brieva vividly expresses the effectiveness of displaying 'the political ecology of waste' in order to unveil neoliberal fallacies.

At the center, a man and a woman, easily identified as a stereotypical North American heterosexual, patriarchal, middle-class couple from the 1950s, smile while standing in front of a dilapidated house located on a desolate piece of suburban property. Their property is entirely fenced in and guarded by a host of security devices and symbols (electrified fencing, surveillance cameras, and warning signs). The husband, wearing a self-satisfied smile, states, 'Somos felices porque protegemos lo nuestro' [We are happy because we defend what is ours]. The neoliberal discourse that views individual property as an arena for competitive self-realization and hyperbolized autonomy is disrupted by the scene of socioecological devastation surrounding the house. The perturbing contrast immediately calls attention to the toxic physical consequences of the articulated semiotic pollution: the house, which is actually a shack, is surrounded by a landscape of waste and industrial pollution. In the end, individual greed and the commodification of reality did not translate into well-being and prosperity for all, just the opposite. Interestingly, the two characters in Brieva's vignette are both victims and perpetuators of the dominant imaginary. The hegemonic discourse which the married couple embraces shifts public concern to individual anxiety or, as Zygmunt Bauman says, 'from the economic and social roots of trouble and towards concerns for personal (bodily) safety'.[24] This movement benefits the security and military industries (two of the most profitable and wasteful corporate complexes), which easily align themselves with the managerial and individualistic neoliberal ideology, while preventing any meaningful collective political reaction from challenging the systemic causes of the safety issues that such an ideology exacerbates.

Brieva's drawing suggests that the hegemonic, obsessive, managerial regime of total command and control represented by the fenced-in property causes massive disorder elsewhere; the couple's internalized neoliberal biopolitics create a deadly geography. The omnipresence of material waste and semiotic pollution on the global level shows that there is no getting away

24 Bauman, *Wasted Lives*, 7.

from the ecological process of the biosphere, and that so-called 'economic externalities' are not only vast market miscalculations, but irrefutable proof of the fantasy out of which the mainstream economic imaginary arises. Nothing is external because everything is interconnected. Pervasive waste and toxic discourse flow through and over everything to reveal that an economy based on growth becomes a frenetic machine of garbage production, social corrosion, and ecological depletion. A political ecology of waste points to the fact that the current crisis—which the dominant imaginary attributes to lack of growth—can only be overcome by discarding the growth model, and not by reactivating growth. To do so requires a new economic culture that minimizes waste not by recycling (which is a neoliberal notion bound up with the need of humans to constantly reinvent—recycle—themselves according to the changing moods of the market) but by changing production and consumption patterns, modifying power relations, closing the cycle of materials, and minimizing the material and energy throughput of the social metabolism.

As William Connolly suggests, we need to 'render the fragility of things more visible and palpable' in order to expose neoliberal fantasies and account for the vast nonhuman forces unleashed, but hidden, by the material and semiotic infrastructure supporting and perpetuating such ideology.[25] According to Connolly, 'the *fragility* of the late modern order seems insufficiently articulated in radical theory today'.[26] Degrowth researchers and activists, as I point out in Chapter 1, are doing just that by articulating a radical critique of the modern order based precisely on its social and ecological fragility. If we subscribe to Jane Bennett's brilliant reformulation of political theory in light of a new materialist perspective, it becomes clear that politics is always a collective assemblage of the human and the nonhuman, as well as a congregation of distributive agencies implicated in events.[27] An effective political ecology thus 'give[s] up the futile attempt to disentangle the human from the nonhuman' and pays more attention to shared environments in which we all participate.[28]

It seems to me that an emancipatory radical politics for the Anthropocene—one that cannot be co-opted by the logic of growth—can articulate itself through the lens of a radical ecology and a new way of understanding materiality. I claim that radical politics can reduce the risk of co-optation by resisting anthropocentricism as well as teleological and hierarchical illusions.

25 Connolly, *The Fragility of Things*, 37.
26 Connolly, *The Fragility of Things*, 32.
27 Connolly, *The Fragility of Things*, 20–21.
28 Connolly, *The Fragility of Things*, 116.

Unless we adopt a non-anthropocentric postgrowth political perspective, human prospects do not look good, as Mick Smith notes when commenting on the irony of state and corporate powers using the ecological crisis to further their agenda (this point will be elaborated upon in the following chapter), the crisis is presented '*as the latest and most comprehensive justification for a political state of emergency, a condition that serves to insulate those powers against all political and ethical critique* ... [and] to further extend the state and corporate management of biological life, including the continuing reduction of humanity to bare life'.[29] Apparently, we must let go of a few things to avoid destructive, totalitarian biopolitics and envision emancipatory postgrowth imaginaries. We have to let go of nature, human exceptionality, and growth, but in order to do this we must disable the anthropological machine, which reproduces the fantasies that justify the growth inertia. A political ecology of waste could help to get rid of these pervasive fantasies, because a postgrowth poetics of waste—unlike the ECOALF poetics of neoliberal recycling—makes plain that nothing is unaffected by economic processes (there is no nature), humans are not exempted from the ecological messes they set into motion (they are not exceptional), and pursuing growth on an overstressed planet with billions of vulnerable bodies—human and nonhuman—is as unethical and violent as putting poison in people's food (which industrial agriculture is already doing). Put otherwise, as long as the main objective of societies is confined to pursuing economic growth, the possibility of engaging in meaningful politics—namely, intervening in the vastly asymmetrical architecture of power, tracking its historicity, and modifying it in favor of the most vulnerable and powerless constituencies—is deactivated. Under the dictate of growth, there is no room for collective debates and decisions on how we should gather and live together, but only pre-framed discussions about the best way to grow under current circumstances. A growth-oriented society generates a post-political hegemonic culture, where the norm becomes fighting on the individual level to secure one's survival at all costs in an ecologically crumbling competitive society—as the family in Brieva's vignette does—rather than collectively changing the rules of the destructive and suicidal game of neoliberal globalization.

If the anthropological machine makes distinctions and marks what is worthy and what is not, what can be spared and what can be exploited, the growth machine does the same thing by using a reductive economic language of valuation, as political ecology reminds us. The anthropological machine is nothing but an engine of valuation and devaluation that transforms differences into inequalities. To subvert this order of things, we should include

29 Smith, *Against Ecological Sovereignty*, 126.

different languages of valuation in a nonhierarchical way, as proposed by Joan Martínez-Alier[30] or, even better, recognize that everything that exists is priceless, that no value can be assigned to it. In other words, the worst strategy to protect something is to assign economic value to it (the main purpose of environmental economists), because it can then be devaluated, depreciated, and wasted without ethical or political consideration, or transformed beyond recognition by the industrial process to extract its value.

A postgrowth political ecology refuses utilitarian and monetarized notions of value and thinks instead in terms of non-anthropocentric agency and relational ontology. The key is to extend not monetarized value but ethics and empathy to the more-than-human. Here there is no room for hierarchies, exceptionalisms, or rigid distinctions, but rather different arrangements of things becoming 'matters of concern', to use Latour's term. Matters of concern can be ethically and politically thinkable. If in the Anthropocene our trash and pollution acquires a virulent agency that exercises a 'slow violence' that massively kills human and nonhuman beings, what prevents us from thinking about it legally, politically, and ethically? According to Rob Nixon, 'a major challenge is representational: how to devise arresting stories, images, and symbols adequate to the pervasive but elusive violence of delayed effects. Crucially, slow violence is often not just attritional but also exponential, operating as a major threat multiplier'.[31] To counter such unfolding environmental violence, Nixon suggests, it is critical to revise our narrow notion of violence to include the 'discounted casualties ... that result from war's toxic aftermaths or climate change'.[32]

> Violence is customarily conceived as an event or action that is immediate in time, explosive and spectacular in space, and as erupting into instant sensational visibility. We need, I believe, to engage a different kind of violence, a violence that is neither spectacular nor instantaneous, but rather incremental and accretive, its calamitous repercussions playing out across a range of temporal scales. In so doing, we also need to engage the representational, narrative, and strategic challenges posed by the relative invisibility of slow violence.[33]

I argue that a political ecology of waste engages the representational challenges of tracking and linking flows of toxic materials and neoliberal

30 Joan Martínez-Alier, *El ecologismo de los pobres: conflictos ambientales y lenguajes de valores*, 3rd ed. (Barcelona: Icaria, 2004).
31 Nixon, *Slow Violence and the Environmentalism of the Poor*, 3.
32 Nixon, *Slow Violence and the Environmentalism of the Poor*, 2–3.
33 Nixon, *Slow Violence and the Environmentalism of the Poor*, 2.

discourses while rendering visible the slow violence perpetrated by the massive waste resulting from consumerist societies, individualist cultures, and growth economies.

Material ecocriticism is perhaps the most persistent attempt to incorporate new materialist concerns into the arena of cultural studies. One of its main precursors, although not environmentally oriented, is the 'thing theory' articulated by Bill Brown, in which things are recognized to have an important role in forming human subjectivities and in mediating relations among humans. However, the most important aspect of thing theory for material ecocriticism may be, as Matthew Zantingh points out, its attention to the 'myriad ways that objects refuse to simply act by the codes that have been assigned them by consumer culture'.[34] The ecological crisis 'is a crisis of urgent materiality ... [Materiality] refused to play the passive role assigned to it by nation-states and corporations'.[35] Only when things behave unexpectedly do we pay attention to their agentic properties. In the Anthropocene, where 'hyperobjects' emerging out of industrial byproducts—like global warming and nuclear radiation—proliferate everywhere, not paying attention to such things becomes suicidal. A proper and consistent theorization of the 'material turn' by ecocritical scholars has only emerged in the past few years, with the publication of a cluster of essays on the topic in the summer 2012 issue of *ISLE* and an edited volume on material ecocriticism that appeared in 2014.[36] Interestingly, both contain contributions that focus on waste and excrement and their agentic capabilities. Such is the case with Heather I. Sullivan's 'dirt theory' and Dana Phillips's 'excremental ecocriticism'.[37]

Green is the color usually associated with the reductive and selective environmental imagination of a pristine, undisturbed, and balanced nature that never existed. It is the color of pastoral romantic landscapes, bourgeois environmental thinking, and packages of commodities produced by green capitalism, but is by no means the color of a postgrowth radical ecology. Green cannot be the color of a transformative political ecology for the

---

34 Matthew Zantingh, 'When Things Act Up: Thing Theory, Actor-Network Theory, and Toxic Discourse in Rita Wong's Poetry', *ISLE* 20, no. 3 (2013): 624.

35 Zantingh, 'When Things Act Up', 625.

36 Serenella Iovino and Serpil Oppermann, eds., *Material Ecocriticism* (Bloomington: Indiana University Press, 2014).

37 Heather I. Sullivan, 'Dirt Theory and Material Ecocriticism', *ISLE* 19, no. 3 (2012): 515–531; Dana Phillips, 'Excremental Ecocriticism and the Global Sanitation Crisis', in *Material Ecocriticism*, ed. Serenella Iovino and Serpil Oppermann (Bloomington: Indiana University Press, 2014), 172–185. *ISLE* vol. 20, no. 3 (2013) includes a special cluster on the topic of waste.

Anthropocene, for the current geohistorical moment demands that we face the dark, unpleasant, and disturbing side of ecology if we want to escape the fantasies of individualistic and consumerist green growth and its ideology of disconnection. A variety of articulations of a post-green ecocriticism can be found in the delightful volume *Prismatic Ecology: Ecotheory beyond Green*, edited by Jeffrey Jerome Cohen, as well as in Timothy Morton's reflections on 'dark ecology'.[38] These post-green ecocritics all emphasize the misleading discourses of a green environmental imagination that insists on keeping out of sight and refuses to account for material agencies that do not match prefabricated ideas of what the natural world should be like. This way of thinking, predominant in ECOALF, could easily be co-opted by the dominant imaginary of economic growth (think of the oxymoronic 'green growth'), because it neither challenges historical and shifting constructions of human/nature nor problematizes existing asymmetrical power relations. This superficial environmentalism perpetuates the ideologies of disconnection ingrained in the hegemonic way of thinking. A cultural criticism more attentive to the political ecology of waste could better resist the temptations of green capitalism and ecomodernism while helping to unleash a radical economic imagination leading towards desirable postgrowth societies.

3.1. Politics and Aesthetics of Garbage in Post-2008 Spanish Culture

In the last two and a half decades, the generation of waste in Spain has increased by more than 90 percent as a consequence of urban growth, massive tourism, and a deficient regulatory legal frame. Only very recently, and as a consequence of pressure from the European Union, has Spain adopted comprehensive, but still insufficient, laws for waste management and reduction. Still, a sustained attention to waste as a serious socioecological problem was excluded from the Culture of Transition because of the Spanish transition's superficial and unproblematic treatment of consumerist cultural modes. After 2008, accumulating problems could no longer be hidden as the Culture of Crisis revealed the pathology of the dominant imaginary. For example, child malnutrition is peaking in the Spanish state while obscene quantities of edible food are wasted and discarded by supermarkets each day. A recent rise in Spanish cultural manifestations focusing on

---

38 Jeffrey Jerome Cohen, ed., *Prismatic Ecology: Ecotheory beyond Green* (Minneapolis: University of Minnesota Press, 2013); Timothy Morton, *Dark Ecology: For a Logic of Future Coexistence* (New York: Columbia University Press, 2016).

discarded materials, toxic pollutants, and degraded spaces mirrors the simultaneous waste management crisis affecting some Spanish cities.[39] These cultural expressions are exposing 'neoliberal fantasies', including human exceptionalism, individual hyper-autonomy, the assumption that humans can control and manage passive environments, and the belief that individual greed magically benefits the common good and deregulated capitalism optimizes resource allocation.

In his book *Malfeasance: Appropriation through Pollution?* Michel Serres makes a relevant distinction between hard and soft pollution. By 'hard pollution' he means the negative environmental disturbances of our economic activities and consumerist patterns, the toxic outputs of our growth-oriented economic metabolism. 'Soft pollution', instead, refers to corporate and capitalist semiotic pollution:

> tsunamis of writing, signs, images, and logos flooding rural, civic, public and natural spaces as well as landscapes with their advertising. Even though different in terms of energy, garbage and marks nevertheless result from the same soiling gesture, from the same intention to appropriate, and are of animal origin.[40]

While environmental studies tend to focus on hard pollution and ignore the mental toxicity that goes with it, Serres urges us to pay attention to the pervasiveness of semiotic pollution and not to forget the fact that:

> images, colors, music, and sounds are just as excremental and invading and pollute space just as much as the stifling stench of carbon dioxide and tar. Hard pollution appropriates the hard world. Just as dangerous if not even more harmful, soft pollution appropriates humans with often subtle links and discreet consciousness.[41]

The political ecology of waste I propose is a good antidote to the soft pollution disseminated by the dominant imaginary, because it calls

---

39 This chapter does not attempt to enumerate all the cultural manifestations foregrounding waste in Spain that have appeared since 2008. Other good examples that could not be studied here include, just to mention a few, the graphic novel *Los vagabundos de la chatarra* by Jorge Carrión and Sagar Fornies, the latest novels by Rosa Montero and Rafael Chirbes, and Obsoletos (obsoletos.org), a collective that repurposes electronic waste. For a study of photography and waste in Madrid, see Samuel Amago, 'Basura, cultura, democracia en el Madrid del siglo veintiuno', *Journal of Contemporary Spanish Literature and Film* 2 (2014–2015): 33–69.

40 Serres, *Malfeasance*, 41.

41 Serres, *Malfeasance*, 62.

attention to the hard pollution that accompanies toxic discourses (as Brieva's cartoon does). Two good examples of deploying the political ecology of waste in a playful but effective way are the collective Basurama and the website ConsumeHastaMorir. Both subvert the dominant imaginary by expanding creativity in unexpected ways through an intentional and critical repurposing of waste materials and toxic discourses. Rather than ignoring the massive circulation of soft and hard pollution, the interventions of these two artistic and political projects engage them in innovative ways and disrupt the commonplace patterns of thinking ingrained in the dominant imaginary.

Basurama is a multidisciplinary collective headquartered in Madrid and dedicated to research, creation, and cultural production. Its main focus is the dominant growth-oriented model of production and consumption, and its massive generation of waste. Basurama intends to foster fresh perspectives regarding the vast amounts of virtual and real waste resulting from consumerist societies through a number of creative interventions among discarded materials and spaces. While the dominant imaginary ignores the material reality that supports it and the downsides of its economic activities, Basurama, on the other hand, thinks through that materiality and explores the creative and critical potential of repurposing industrial and consumerist waste. Waste is explored from different complementary physical and symbolic angles (including design, architecture, performance, and the visual arts, as well as multiple aesthetic, social, ecological, political, and cultural possibilities) and on different continents.

Some of Basurama's most interesting installations are part of a project named 'urban solid waste'. This project develops different activities that gravitate around three principles: repurposing waste, using public space, and working with local communities to enhance existing projects. Similarly, the Autobarrios Sancristobal project in Madrid mobilizes local resources and the skills of local people to enhance the socioecological situation of degraded spaces in the low-income neighborhood of San Cristóbal de los Ángeles. Repurposing discarded materials, always with the collaboration of locals, these interventions transform disinvested public spaces into vibrant and inclusive places for communitarian education, entertainment, encounter, and cohesion (places to think and play together). Many of these projects clearly question the supposed benefits of neoliberal dynamics: attracting massive investment, fostering growth at all costs, encouraging privatization and corporatization of space, developing top-down macro-projects with huge socioecological downsides, and so on. Basurama demonstrates that by using local and discarded resources and channeling the synergy of local knowledge and cultures, communities themselves can create a socially desirable, aesthetically pleasant, and ecologically sound public space in which people can thrive and enjoy themselves.

The publications developed by Basurama are open access and can be downloaded from the collective's website (www.basurama.org). For example, *6.000 Km. Paisajes después de la batalla* (6,000 km: Landscapes after the Battle) is a multimedia reflection on the enormously destructive consequences of the urban metabolism of Spanish cities that is currently damaging vast parts of the landscape as a result of the construction boom. Another publication is *Enciclomierda* (Encyclopedia of Shit), an ironic glossary of concepts that directs readers' attention to the soft pollution ingrained in our common use of language, where neoliberal ways of expressing reality are normalized. By redefining common terms and coining new ones, the *Enciclomierda*'s entries challenge such normalizations and make the reader think about material and linguistic realities often ignored by consumerist and growth-oriented discourses. Basurama also offers practical guides for constructing several 'convivial tools' (to use Ivan Illich's term), from public couches to children's playgrounds, out of used tires. The problematic materiality flowing from excessive consumerism becomes not only the vehicle for a new functional and critical postgrowth aesthetics, but also the material with which to create a renewed public space. Unlike ECOALF, Basurama does not recycle, but reuses; it does not celebrate waste for its potential to become a new market commodity, but repurposes it in socially meaningful ways unmediated by monetary transactions and therefore enjoyable by all; it does not perpetuate the logic of unlimited growth by encouraging endless consumerism, but criticizes the dominant imaginary by embracing alternative ways to relate to community, materiality, and space.

Similarly, the website ConsumeHastaMorir (consumehastamorir.org) introduces itself with the statement: 'ConsumeHastaMorir es una reflexión sobre la sociedad de consumo en la que vivimos, utilizando uno de sus propios instrumentos, la publicidad, para mostrar hasta qué punto se puede morir consumiendo' [ConsumeHastaMorir is a reflection on the consumerist society in which we live, using one of its own tools, advertising, to show how it is possible to die of consumption].[42] If corporate advertising campaigns are a pervasive and ubiquitous semiotic waste that aggressively appropriates public space, ConsumeHastaMorir undermines their effectiveness by creating counter-narratives that oppose or subvert their marketing strategies. The members of ConsumeHastaMorir generate counter-advertisements in different media. They also organize workshops and a variety of pedagogical activities focused on processes of collective creation. The site includes tabs

42 'Quiénes somos', http://consumehastamorir.com.

such as *contrapublicidad, contranuncios* (counter-advertising), *artículos* (articles), and *educación* (education). These tabs are subdivided into sections dealing with specific topics, such as food, environment, globalization, and so on. Most of the articles and counter-advertising pieces satirize and expose the contradictions of a consumerist society that needs to create nonexistent necessities to continue selling useless things that deplete the planet, exploit humans, and keep consumers dissatisfied. They also point out the neurotic and misleading aspects of a society that promotes an unsustainable over-consumption that compromises consumers' health, happiness, and self-esteem (promoting unhealthy industrial foods and beverages or impossible beauty standards, for instance) while offering false solutions to these manufactured problems by supplying other commodities produced by the same polluting chemical, agro-industrial, and pharmaceutical mega-industries that generated the problems.

The site reveals the devastating social and ecological consequences of mass consumption and how advertising not only tends to hide such problems, but also contributes to them. Highly harmful corporations sometimes celebrate their products' social and ecological friendliness. The counter-advertising pieces use irony, photo montages, and wordplay to subvert the logos deployed by popular advertising campaigns and to expose the systemic contradictions of the growth society. Most of the materials and publications produced by ConsumeHastaMorir are available online thanks to a Creative Commons license. On the site, it is possible to download several books, such as a guide to making graphic counter-advertising or a compilation of the best *contrapublicidad* created by the members of ConsumeHastaMorir. These interventions direct attention to the environmental and social effects of consumerism by combining a shocking dark humor with quotations from academic reports or other authorized sources that explicitly reveal consumerism's impact. Under the *videos* tab, the site presents an enlightening documentary about advertising strategies and consumerism titled *Gran superficie*. Advertising not only triggers unsustainable consumerist behavior, but the marketing industry itself directly depletes huge amounts of energy and materials in order to run an operation that is not only superfluous and unnecessary but also socially harmful. Advertising in a postgrowth society would not make any sense. In a context of climate change and energy crisis, why spend limited and vital resources to convince people to buy things that are not needed and whose production depletes more resources? Is this obscene waste of mental and physical resources what mainstream economists mean when they refer to the 'efficient allocation of resources' of capitalist markets? If ECOALF uses marketing strategies to create a greenwashed image of a company that perpetuates a depoliticized rationality of individual consumerism,

ConsumeHastaMorir repoliticizes and problematizes the culture of wasteful consumerism. In short, ConsumeHastaMorir subverts icons of soft pollution to direct attention to their adverse rhetorical and material consequences, while Basurama artistically repurposes and foregrounds solid waste to encourage public debate that exposes soft pollution. Both are a fine example of a powerful political ecology of waste. Rendering visible the transformative, uncontrollable, and subversive agency of discarded things makes waste thinkable and visible as a contested political issue.

From the vantage point of the political ecology of waste that I propose, the Anthropocene cannot be interpreted as a geological periodization that recentralizes human agency. Rather, it highlights nonhuman agency. During most of capitalist modernity, a main concern has been to make waste disappear from the urban space of industrial cities, but in the current time of planetary urbanization, overpopulation, climate change, and agroindustry, all possible sinks on the planet have become congested. Thus, waste management in the context of globalizing consumerist cultures and growth-oriented policies cannot provide a solution—it is only a futile attempt to cut off the hydra's heads. Addressing the root of the problem demands a rapid reduction of waste production, which entails a massive reduction of material and energy throughput (a downsizing of the global economy), a strategy that mainstream politicians and economists are ill-equipped to imagine, let alone pursue. The global success of the dominant imaginary is ironically making more visible what it can neither see nor imagine: the ecological limits of the Earth and its incapacity to absorb capitalist waste.

The oceans present a paradigmatic example of this lack of imagination. Oceans are vast planetary ecologies being used as pollution sinks that are often overlooked by our terrestrial-centric dominant thinking. Only recently has ecocriticism begun to pay attention. Stacy Alaimo's essay 'Oceanic Origins, Plastic Activism, and New Materialism at Sea' opens with an alarming list of problems:

> Climate change. Ocean acidification. Dead zones. Oil 'spills'. Industrial fishing, overfishing, trawling, long lines, shark finning. Bycatch, bykill. Ghost nets. Deep-sea mining. Habitat destruction. Dumping. Radioactive, plastic, and microplastic pollution. Ecosystem collapse. Extinction. The state of the oceans is dire. The destruction of marine environments is painful to contemplate and tempting to ignore.[43]

---

43 Stacy Alaimo, 'Oceanic Origins, Plastic Activism, and New Materialism at Sea', in *Material Ecocriticism*, ed. Serenella Iovino and Serpil Oppermann (Bloomington: Indiana University Press, 2014), 186.

Basurama 'Tsunami'

Alaimo studies activist practices that expose the harmful consequences of plastic in ocean ecosystems and points out 'the disturbing ways in which the materials of everyday consumerism are the very stuff of destructive global networks'.[44] The political ecology of waste strives to make visible this network by tracking the connections between growth-oriented consumerism, socioecological issues, and the proliferation of waste. Basurama does precisely this in one of its most interesting projects, 'Tsunami de basura' (Tsunami of Waste), installed along a semi-abandoned and deteriorating seaside walkway in Santo Domingo in 2009.[45]

Basurama's intervention consisted of the installation of a huge wave made out of discarded plastic bottles that seemed to stretch up from the sea and threaten the walkway. The installation was enhanced by lighting and music, and all locals were invited and encouraged to participate in the event. According to Basurama's website, the goal was to revitalize the public space while calling attention to the deficient waste management situation in the Dominican Republic. The installation serves as a symbolic and material node connecting and making visible the natureculture entanglements implicated in the 'destructive global network' of 'everyday consumerism', as well as the massive agency of waste that refuses to disappear in the sea and, instead, returns violently as a wave. As playful as the installation may be, it represents a tsunami, a fearful disaster for humans that, at least according to the dominant imaginary, is allegedly natural and not

44 Alaimo, 'Oceanic Origins, Plastic Activism, and New Materialism at Sea', 200.
45 http://basurama.org/en/projects/rus-santo-domingo-tsunami-de-basura/.

the result of human activity. The installation, however, implies that the wave is, substantially and semiotically, quite anthropogenic: the wave itself is made out of industrially produced and discarded plastic bottles, and the current global increase in the frequency and intensity of tsunamis has been attributed to anthropogenically induced climate change.[46] The installation can be read as revealing that the water coming from the sea is actually composed of wa(s)te(r): waste (the discarded bottles) and water (the tsunami) are symbolically interchangeable.

The plastic tsunami calls attention to the vast amount of plastic pollution in the oceans: some areas of the ocean hold a mass of plastic particles six times greater than that of the plankton they contain, and virtually all the fish on the planet have plastic in their stomachs. The uncanny agency of waste embodied by an artificial tsunami made out of ordinary plastic junk, such as shampoo and soda bottles, highlights the dark reality that our current wasteful lifestyle is giving shape to catastrophic agencies that can kill us slowly as does cancer from petrochemical overexposure or, in the case of the tsunami, suddenly exterminate us in a massive disaster. This installation aligns with Alaimo's advocacy for a 'more potent marine trans-corporeality [that] would link humans to global networks of consumption, waste, and pollution, capturing the strange agencies of the ordinary stuff of our lives'.[47] The 'innocent' and 'familiar' plastic bags and receptacles made out of synthetic polymers and used to package our daily commodities can become terrifying and dangerous killers when operating on different scales and temporalities.

Today there are five giant Garbage Patches growing in the oceans, all of which serve as useful 'hyperobjects' to highlight the colossal scale of global waste production and its rhetorical invisibility. The Great Pacific Garbage Patch is a plastic soup estimated to be the size of Mexico, yet it has almost no presence in corporate media, political speeches, and daily conversation. It remains invisible as long as it does not disturb the fantasies of constant growth and the daily consumerist activities that spur the proliferation of such waste. As Alaimo points out, 'the Western conception of the ocean as "alien", or as so vast as to be utterly impervious to human harm, encourages a happy ignorance about the state of the seas'.[48] An effective political ecology of waste highlights the atrocious dimensions of such harm and its links to

---

46 See Bill McGuire, *Waking the Giant: How a Changing Climate Triggers Earthquakes, Tsunamis, and Volcanoes* (Oxford: Oxford University Press, 2012).

47 Alaimo, 'Oceanic Origins, Plastic Activism, and New Materialism at Sea', 188.

48 Stacy Alaimo, 'New Materialisms, Old Humanisms, or, Following the Submersible', *NORA—Nordic Journal of Feminist and Gender Research* 19, no. 4 (2011): 283.

economic growth, in order to mobilize its symbolic powers and question the material, political, and ethical implications of superfluous overconsumption and continual growth.

On his 2011 album *Presidente*, the Andalusian indie singer and composer Sr. Chinarro (Antonio Luque) included a song, 'Vacaciones en el mar', that explicitly talks about plastic in the sea.[49] Its ironic chorus promotes 'vacaciones en los plásticos del mar' (vacations in the sea's plastics) as an exciting and paradisiac experience. The second stanza suggests that the Great Pacific Garbage Patch is an appealing tourist destination: 'He visto en Google Earth un sexto continente: / botellas, trastos y presentes / flotan en un remolino, creo que es divino' (I have seen a sixth continent on Google Earth: / bottles, junk, and gifts / float in a whirlpool, I think it is delightful). The excerpt emphasizes both the technological mediation that allows us to visualize such vast, unintended accumulations of waste, and the superfluous mainstream response to such disturbing reality. The final part of the song continues the joyful tone, which sharply contrasts with the alarming reality of plastic pollution. This extreme disparity between the playful treatment of the topic and its gravity replicates the divergence between the optimistic and celebratory discourse typical of the dominant imaginary and the dire socioecological situation that the globalization of that imaginary actually produces.

Sr. Chinarro not only foregrounds the global problem of plastic pollution in the oceans, but also shows the potential and perturbing dominant response to such an issue: transforming the problem into a business opportunity for further growth by convincing consumers that the Garbage Patch is not a problem, but an ideal tourist destination.[50] We can assume that those tourists in the sea of plastics will further contribute through their unnecessary activities to the plastic pollution they are 'enjoying'. Considered in the context of the international branding of Spain during the last few decades (la marca España)—where tourism has been often celebrated as an economic engine while its role as one of the world's greatest polluters is ignored—the song's combination of the ridiculous rhetoric used to market vacation destinations, the vast scale of plastic pollution, and the childish public response to a huge socioecological issue effectively reveals the senseless inertia of the dominant imaginary. The lyrics of the

49 Sr. Chinarro, 'Vacaciones en el mar', *Presidente*, Mushroom Pillow MP114, 2011, compact disc.

50 For a real example see 'Melting Ice Allows Northwest Passage Cruise—But at What Cost?' (interview with Michael Byers conducted by Robin Young), WBUR, September 12, 2016, http://www.wbur.org/hereandnow/2016/09/12/northwest-passage-cruise?utm_medium=RSS&utm_campaign=storiesfromnpr.

song suggest that the plastic sea is the result of a culture of ownership, competition, greed, induced desires, and commodification:

> yo tendré un velero y llegaré primero ...
> un gran bazar todo a 100 ...
> Descorcharé el champán, me dejaré besar,
> diré que es mío cuanto me rodea.

> [I will own a sailing boat and will get there first ...
> a big store where everything costs a dollar ...
> I will uncork the champagne, I will be kissed,
> I will say that everything around me is mine]

Sr. Chinarro depicts a culture of cognitive and emotional capitalism that constantly falls in love with novel commodified experiences, no matter what kind. From the vantage point of the dominant imaginary it is easier to accept that trash can be beautiful, consumable, and seductive than to admit the necessity of slowing down growth and the consumerist machine. 'Vacaciones en el mar' notes, as Alaimo did with regard to a video of environmental activism titled *Plastic Seduction*, 'the power of plastic to seduce us all into a collective consumerist state of blissful ignorance'.[51] Developing a romantic relationship with garbage and appreciating its beauty may be the last distorted twist given to the dominant imaginary once the scale and agency of planetary waste becomes impossible to ignore, as José Luis Pardo supposed in his essay and the rhetoric of ECOALF has confirmed. If we fall in love with the toxic outcomes of economic growth, the 'necro-politics'[52] of capitalism is suddenly transmogrified into a romantic passion to be consummated and to die for: it becomes an individualized erotic desire, not a political issue! Thus do we become pathologically trapped in an abusive emotional relationship with capitalism. An effect similar to the one created by Sr. Chinarro's song is achieved by the movie discussed in the previous chapter, *Gente en sitios*, in the sequence where a socially marginalized character strives to find a gift in a scrapyard to express his love for the person he has been dating. And several of Miguel Brieva's cartoons in *Memorias de la tierra* do the same using pictorial art. All of these cultural productions expose the absurdity of the neoliberal 'trash is beautiful' rhetoric by depicting characters who quite literally fall in love with or show their love through waste.

---

51 Alaimo, 'Oceanic Origins, Plastic Activism, and New Materialism at Sea', 197.
52 Achille Mbembe, 'Necropolitics', in *Biopolitics: A Reader*, ed. Timothy Campbell and Adam Sitze (Durham, NC: Duke University Press, 2013), 161–192.

Another good example of a cultural manifestation that deploys the political ecology of waste in an effective way is the documentary *Comprar, tirar, comprar: la historia secreta de la obsolescencia programada*.[53] Prior to 2011, the term 'planned obsolescence' was almost unknown to the average Spaniard, but that changed dramatically after the public Spanish channel RTVE broadcast the documentary in January of that year. *Comprar, tirar, comprar* investigates the historical formation of planned obsolescence, that is, the designing of products to have a short useful life cycle so that consumers need to replace them over and over again. This practice, although obviously unsustainable and overly wasteful, is widespread in consumerist cultures and emerges in the context of a society addicted to constant economic growth. The film emphasizes the disturbing amount of waste and the rapid environmental depletion that results from this practice. *Comprar, tirar, comprar* provides historical examples of products that were originally made to last indefinitely (light bulbs, nylon pantyhose, cars) and whose lifespans were purposely reduced to increase sales. These historical accounts are complemented by several voices critical of planned obsolescence, as well as by the personal experience of one of its victims. The first sequence of the film focuses on Marcos, a local computer expert from Barcelona who has a technical problem with his printer. After several IT stores tell him that it is cheaper to replace his printer than to repair it, Marcos decides to look for do-it-yourself solutions online. Eventually, using information volunteered by internet users around the world, he discovers that most printers are programmed to fail after a specific number of pages, and he learns how to deactivate this perverse program. The last scene of the documentary is a close-up of Marco's printer working properly again. The film ends with the repair of the malfunctioning electronic device introduced in its opening minutes, symbolizing the overcoming of planned obsolescence and the triumph of the circular economy demanded by a desirable, non-wasteful, postgrowth society on a limited planet. The film's circularity contrasts sharply with the linear metabolism of economic growth and its unsustainable tendency to accelerate entropy.

Comprar, tirar, comprar puts materiality in the spotlight and links it to the capitalist discourses, social injustices, and ecological processes in which it is embedded. It does so very effectively by paying attention to the massive electronic waste that results from a combination of digital culture, consumerism, and planned obsolescence. One of its featured narratives is the story of an iPod produced by Apple whose battery could not be replaced

53 Cosima Dannoritzer, dir., *Comprar, tirar, comprar: la historia secreta de la obsolescencia programada* (Pozuelo de Alarcón, Spain: RTVE, 2010).

when it failed, so that consumers had to replace the entire device. The irony is that Apple presents itself as a socially responsible corporation, a sort of model for green capitalistic innovation and creativity, while cheating its customers and seriously adding to the environmental challenge posed by e-waste. This situation provoked numerous consumer reactions, including a collective suit.

Another narrative line features Mike Anane, a journalist and activist committed to reporting the social and environmental consequences of e-waste in Ghana. The scenes devoted to this narrative are very effective in their deployment of the political ecology of waste, because of their combination of informative, emotional, and visual nuances related to e-waste's socioecological imbrications. Mike clearly explains that rich countries and corporations, in order to navigate the laws that prohibit sending e-waste to Ghana, deliver their electronic garbage under the guise of donating secondhand devices to help narrow the digital gap between the global North and South. The fact is that, according to Mike, 80 percent of the devices that arrive in Ghana do not work and end up polluting the waterways and making people sick. Mike laments how the hellish environment and toxic river shown by the camera was once a nice place where he used to play as a child. This personal and emotional account is reinforced by the combination of close and long shots framing the socioecological degradation Mike witnesses with shots from his perspective and the perspective of poor young men and children burning e-waste to earn an income on the side by harvesting the metals it contains. Staring into the camera with red eyes and haggard faces, they explain that they are getting sick from breathing toxic fumes. A couple of slow panning shots reveal the larger panorama in which the characters are embedded—a devastated landscape full of e-waste. The audience is left to connect the dots between the two stories, imagining how the Apple devices identified as cool and innovative rapidly become obsolete and end up contributing to the cancer of a poor child in Ghana by poisoning the country's rivers.

The film explicitly introduces a radical degrowth critique of the present order of things by featuring Serge Latouche. He explains that a growth society is not only unsustainable on a finite planet, it is also socially undesirable because the economy grows for the sake of growing and not to satisfy needs. According to Latouche, this economic model creates artificial and harmful needs while undermining the conditions necessary for meeting genuine needs. Advertising, planned obsolescence, and debt-driven credit are some of the dead-end strategies that maintain the high level of human dissatisfaction that leads to the consumption of unnecessary commodities. While other critiques of the current economic model featured in the film suggest that most problems can be avoided by modifying aspects of the existing system (implementing laws, insisting on corporate responsibility, introducing techno-fixes, and embracing industrial ecology and environmental economics), the degrowth movement advocates a radical change of paradigm.

Whereas the dominant imaginary hides the materiality of new media and its disturbing agency, the political ecology of waste moves it into the spotlight and situates it in the larger context of a pathological growth paradigm. *Comprar, tirar, comprar* focuses on how the abbreviated life cycles of electronic commodities will negatively affect the environment for centuries to come. The waste, energy pollution, and human exploitation involved in the creation of media technology can be traced back through time, as Jussi Parikka suggests when he speaks of the geology of media:

> minerals [were] sedimented for millions of years before being mined by cheap labor in developing countries for use in information technology factories. After that short use-period of some years, they become part of the materiality of e-waste leaking toxins into nature after river-dumping or incineration, making them into toxic vapors that attach to the nervous systems of cheap labor in China, India, Ghana, etc.[54]

The political ecology of waste need not limit itself to highlighting the aftermath of the consumer products churned out by the growth economy, but could also track all kinds of toxic material and energy outflows enmeshed in capitalist productive processes throughout a variety of historical periods with their different materialities and intensities. The political ecology of waste can examine all energy and materials degraded and mobilized through extractive activities, processing and assembling, chemical transformations, advertising, transportation and logistics operations, storage and retailing infrastructure, and so on. These processes often remain aesthetically separated from the final commodity as their social and ecological consequences are obliterated by the dominant imaginary and by mainstream economic calculations. The ecological and social costs are externalized, so that capitalists benefit from the operation but are not held accountable for its massive socioecological consequences.

---

54 Jussi Parikka, 'New Materialism as Media Theory: Medianatures and Dirty Matter', *Communication and Critical/Cultural Studies* 9, no. 1 (2012): 98.

3.2. Soft Pollution, Social Metabolism, and Surplus Population

In Spanish cultural studies much has been said in recent years about immigration and multiculturalism in relation to the demographic and cultural changes experienced in the Iberian Peninsula from the 1980s to the present. Very little, however, has been said about the root causes of these migratory movements. The connection between transnational movements of human bodies and other global flows of material, energy, and discourses has not been consistently made. Immigration flows follow in the wake of energy and materials that have often been extracted from migrants' territories. There is a clear correlation between global economic growth spurred by the planetary expansion of capitalist modernity and the massive proliferation of both unmanageable waste production and surplus population. Immigration may be understood as people displaced by (or escaping the toxicity generated by) the flows of material, labor, and energy mobilized by economic modernization to facilitate its consumerist, predatory, and wasteful practices. Ironically, in a perverse rhetorical turn, people escaping from toxicity are often represented by anti-immigration discourses as 'toxic people'. It never occurs to opponents of immigration that their lifestyles produced the toxicity that triggered the immigration they resist.[55]

According to Srnicek and Williams, the three principal capitalist mechanisms that produce 'larger and larger surplus population' are the following: automation of industrial activities, primitive accumulation, and the exclusion of necessary activities of social reproduction from wage labor.[56] The second and third of these destroy traditional livelihoods by exterminating subsistence economies and forcing people into market economies. As a result, their survival becomes dependent on wage labor and market dynamics. It has long been a capitalist strategy to appropriate other ecological spaces previously devoted to subsistent and communal activities outside the market and, in doing so, to create the abundant surplus population needed to perform industrial jobs cheaply. However, under contemporary conditions, the amount of surplus population in relation to available capitalist jobs—including even the most precarious forms of employment—is vastly disproportionate. The solution offered by orthodox economics for creating more capitalist jobs for the rapidly increasing global displaced population is, unsurprisingly, to grow further and expand the market economy as much as possible, hoping that such growth will translate

---

55 Thanks to Kata Beilin for reminding me of this important point.
56 Srnicek and Williams, *Inventing the Future*, 88–90.

into job creation (paradoxically, capitalist economic expansion itself created the problem it is now trying to solve with additional expansion).

The truth, however, is that the relationship between economic growth and job creation is not guaranteed under economic financialization. During the last few decades of global neoliberal hegemony, the mechanisms for producing surplus population have rapidly intensified with the appearance of new forms of 'accumulation by dispossession', while jobless growth and financial speculation have gained ground. Needless to say, under the slow-growth or no-growth scenarios faced by some Southern European regions after 2008, the perversity of this order of things becomes more visible (it has always been obvious for the impoverished regions of colonized lands). Moreover, efforts to recover the rate of economic growth that preceded the crisis may not be an option for these countries, given the ecological situation and current global geopolitics. The logical solution to the problem of surplus population (regulating global financial speculation and harmful economic activities, expanding and recovering local and traditional economies, transitioning from agroindustry to agroecology and from petromodernity to postcarbon cultures, introducing a universal income, reducing working hours, and so on) is never discussed in hegemonic discourses. From the perspective of the degrowth movement, it is obvious that the best way to stop population displacement is to reverse the ongoing processes of primitive accumulation, privatization of commons, and land dispossession in impoverished regions, while simultaneously reducing working hours and overconsumption in overgrowth countries. In other words, rich countries need to stop appropriating and monopolizing the Earth's carrying capacity with their disproportionate economic metabolisms and start liberating ecological space for other regions to thrive. Again, moving beyond capitalism is a condition *sine qua non*. Here is the ongoing capitalist conundrum:

> capital requires a particular *type* of surplus population: cheap, docile, and pliable. Without these characteristics, this excess of humanity becomes a problem for capital. Not content to lie down and accept its disposability, it makes itself heard through riots, mass migration, criminality, and all sort of actions that disrupt the existing order. Capitalism therefore has to simultaneously produce a disciplined surplus and deploy violence and coercion against those who resist.[57]

Most of the surplus population currently being produced has little chance of being incorporated into the urban proletariat, a fate that used to be

57 Srnicek and Williams, *Inventing the Future*, 98.

the norm throughout the history of industrial capitalism. Contemporary surplus population that serves no function in the dominant mode of economic and social organization accumulates in refugee camps, detention centers, prisons, slums, and shantytowns all over the globe.[58] Under neoliberal hegemony, the surplus population has been transmogrified from potential urban proletariats to human waste, as Zygmunt Bauman brilliantly highlights in *Wasted Lives: Modernity and its Outcasts*. Bauman notes that modern economic processes produce increasing quantities of unsustainable and unmanageable amounts of waste (human and nonhuman) in their constant expansion.[59] During the historical period in which capitalist modernization was limited to a few regions, it was possible, and relatively easy, for such privileged societies to appropriate and colonize other ecological spaces and use 'global outlets for local excesses'. Once the process of economic modernization had extended globally, however, both waste-producing sites and surplus population mushroomed, and the ecological sinks available to contain such excesses rapidly overflowed. As a consequence, more socioecological conflicts arise not only on the commodity frontiers, but also elsewhere as surplus populations rise and planetary boundaries are rapidly transgressed. One among many possible examples of this dynamic is the disturbing rise in foreign corporate acquisitions of land for toxic agro-industrial or extractive activities that expel people from their ancestral lands and condemn them to migration and poverty.[60]

The colonial and neocolonial tendency towards waste externalization and (mis)management cannot be universalized, for if all regions in the planet were to embrace wasteful consumerism, there would be nowhere to put the garbage produced by excessive material and energy usage (which is already the case). Economic growth always needs colonial/neocolonial ecologies and peripheral societies to absorb, suffer for, or pay for its externalities. That is why such a system cannot be sustained given its global aspirations. Rather than finding '*global* solutions to *locally* produced' problems, as colonial powers used to do (and still do under their neocolonial economic and epistemological structures), newcomers to the project of modernization and development are left to seek biophysically impossible '*local* solutions to *globally* produced problems'.[61] Once modern economic processes expand

58 See Mike Davis, *Planet of Slums* (London: Verso, 2006).

59 Bauman, *Wasted Lives*, 4–5.

60 Saskia Sassen, 'Migration Is Expulsion by Another Name in World of Foreign Land Deals', *The Guardian*, May 29, 2013, https://www.theguardian.com/global-development/poverty-matters/2013/may/29/migration-expulsion-foreign-land-deals.

61 Bauman, *Wasted Lives*, 6.

everywhere, it becomes more challenging and geopolitically frictional for each advanced economy to use 'the rest of the planet as a dumping site'.[62] Thus, economic growth becomes more socioecologically costly as toxic waste disturbs planetary ecological boundaries and 'wasted humans' disrupt social and political stability worldwide.[63]

Waste production, neocolonial eradication of traditional subsystem economies, and surplus population are therefore the signature outcomes of economic growth. Such a socially and ecologically parasitic process can only be managed and sustained as long as it is not globalized. Paradoxically, it is the nature of capitalism to expand by appropriating and depleting more and more ecological space, and so global capitalism creates the conditions of its own demise. The faster it expands, the more biophysically impossible and socially unbearable its project becomes: the sustaining capacity of the planet is transgressed, there are no more societies living outside of market economies to be dispossessed, and there is no 'empty' place to put waste and surplus populations. The scale of the problem becomes impossible to ignore, even for previously privileged regions (think of Southern Europe today). Unfortunately, this visibility does not necessarily destabilize the dominant imaginary and reconfigure the map of the sensible in politically meaningful ways. In a recent dangerous and perverse discursive turn, victims of economic globalization are being blamed for the insecurities and precarious conditions that neoliberal policies entail. Immigrants and refugees, rather than the inequities that produce them, are held responsible for the economic and socially insecure climate manufactured by neoliberal institutions. Neoliberal states, actively contributing to economic vulnerability and irresponsive to its social consequences, seek their legitimacy in fighting abstract security threats: 'Unlike in the case of market-generated threats to livelihood and welfare, the extent of dangers to personal safety must be intensely advertised'.[64] Such is the case in post-2008 Spain, where we see the simultaneous implementation of policies aimed at deregulating labor, cutting social services, and criminalizing poverty, immigration, and protest (a recent law, Ley Orgánica de Seguridad Ciudadana, explicitly claims to promote the personal security of citizens).[65] This toxic securitization discourse, the subject of Brieva's cartoon, has dire social and ecological consequences.

---

62 Bauman, *Wasted Lives*, 69.

63 Bauman, *Wasted Lives*, 70.

64 Bauman, *Wasted Lives*, 52.

65 'Ley Orgánica de Seguridad Ciudadana', Documento BOE-A-2015-3442, *Boletín Oficial del Estado*, no. 77, March 31, 2015, pp. 27216–27243, https://www.boe.es/boe/dias/2015/03/31/pdfs/BOE-A-2015-3442.pdf.

In this last part of the chapter, I want to show how cultural manifestations inspiring postgrowth imaginaries through a 'political ecology of waste' are well suited to effectively link the displacement of human bodies with toxic materiality and the discourses instigated by the paradigm of economic growth. As Bauman points out, paraphrasing Paul and Ann Ehrlich, rich consumerist societies are '"high entropy" centers, drawing resources, most notably the sources of energy, from the rest of the world, and returning in exchange the polluting, often toxic waste of industrial processes that uses up, annihilates and destroys a large part of the worldwide supplies of energy'.[66] Surplus populations are composed of people who lose their livelihoods in this process and are forced to relocate in order to survive. Environmental refugees and migrants are the logical consequence of the asymmetrical flow of energy and material mobilized to feed the voracious high-entropy centers. In order to cease creating surplus population, rich countries must stop being insatiable high-entropy centers and reduce their disproportionate economic metabolisms. Promoting walls and xenophobic discourses while encouraging overconsumption and economic growth is counterproductive, to say the least. Instead, the challenge is to promote postgrowth economies and radical empathy to create a society that produces neither human nor nonhuman waste.

In Europe this point is vital today, for as I write (early 2016), the so-called crisis of refugees (the largest since the Second World War) traveling to Europe mainly from Syria is generating enormous social and political tension. So far the European response has been not only divisive and inadequate, but shameful. Xenophobic discourses are gaining traction and most European nations are either washing their hands of the problem or, worse, making plans to seal their borders. In the meantime, refugees are abandoned in improvised and inadequate camps springing up in Greece, Jordan, and other regions; thousands of unaccompanied children are disappearing; and countless people are losing their lives either to malnutrition and illness or to the seas they must cross. Most European governments are not even honoring the flimsy terms agreed to in their communitarian agreements. Spain, for example, had initially committed to provide asylum to more than 17,000 refugees, but as of March 2016 had accommodated fewer than 50.[67] A recent agreement between the European Union and Turkey—ignoring international law

---

66 Bauman, *Wasted Lives*, 43.

67 Ernest Urtasun, 'Europa encierra los refugiados en Grecia y se lava las manos', Euroblog, *eldiario.es*, March 3, 2016, http://www.eldiario.es/euroblog/Europa-encierra-refugiados-Grecia-manos_6_490710954.html.

and human rights—allows all refugees who enter the former illegally to be sent to the latter.

Climate change is also tied to current patterns of mass migration.[68] The Syrian refugee crisis is a good example: changes in the hydrologic cycle due to global warming provoked an extreme drought that ruined over 60 percent of crop production in Syria and played a crucial role in the destabilization of the country that triggered the civil war. According to many reports, environmental refugees are going to increase dramatically during the next few decades as a consequence of climate change.[69] Targeting the root causes and not manipulating the symptoms for political gain is paramount in order to avoid not only catastrophic ecological collapse, but the opportunistic emergence of right-wing populism, neofascism, and eco-totalitarian regimes that would benefit from such chaos. The risk of embracing simplistic explanations that promote an ideology of disconnection would be catastrophic in every sense.

On November 15, 2015, Manel Fontdevila, a regular contributor of satirical political cartoons to *eldiario.es*, published a drawing titled 'Llueven refugiados'.[70]

Two figures holding umbrellas converse while a literal rain of human bodies is falling from the sky. One character states the obvious: 'It is starting to rain refugees'. The other, a tall white man wearing an elegant suit who represents the European Union establishment (he holds a blue umbrella with yellow stars) replies, 'It is because of the water cycle! This is not our fault either!' Fontdevila's cartoon captures the relationship between the forced and traumatic mobility of bodies (surplus population), the manipulative 'naturalization' and 'depoliticization' of ecological cycles that human economic activity is disrupting, and the dominant discourse in European nations that pretends that there is no connection between their international politics, their financial activities, their overconsumption, their irresponsibility, and the ongoing traumatic disruption of ecological and social phenomena. The dialogue in the cartoon calls attention to the dominant ideology of disconnection as well as to the dire material and human consequences of both its economic policies and semiotic pollution. By transforming the rain into refugees, the cartoon creates a

68 Ellie Mae O'Hagan, 'Mass Migration Is No "Crisis": It's the New Normal as the Climate Changes', *The Guardian*, August 18, 2015, https://www.theguardian.com/commentisfree/2015/aug/18/mass-migration-crisis-refugees-climate-change.

69 Jessica Hellmann and David Ackerly, 'We Are Entering a New Era of Migration—and Not Just for People', *The Conversation*, October 15, 2015, https://theconversation.com/we-are-entering-a-new-era-of-migration-and-not-just-for-people-48650.

70 http://www.eldiario.es/opinion/Llueven-refugiados_10_448755126.html.

Manel 'Llueven refugiados'

visible socioecological network of human and material flows mobilized (and denied: 'this is not our fault either') by hegemonic economic practices and political discourses. In the Anthropocene, environmental issues and migration dynamics cannot be separated from the economic activities and political institutions that set them in motion.

Interferències [*Interferences*], an interesting and well-researched low-budget audiovisual experiment in Spanish and Catalan, is another example of a recent Iberian cultural manifestation that strives to connect the material and discursive dots concealed by the dominant imaginary of economic growth.[71] Released in May 2011, *Interferències* brings together the energy and immediacy allowed by minimalist theatrical techniques—such as abundant body language, improvisation, a limited number of actors who each play several roles, and sober but symbolic scenarios—with the disseminative and multimedia possibilities of audiovisual technologies. The film, blurring the limits between process and product, documentary and fiction, theater and film, diegesis and extradiegesis, and acting, directing, and writing, combines fragments of a play rehearsal with discussions among the crew (actors and director) about how to better express the complexity of the topic that the play engages, namely, the acceptance of the unacceptable in the exploitative relationship between the global North and South. The film suggests a meta-reflection on effective and original ways to make visible the historical continuity of North-South economic and epistemological

71 *Interferències*, http://www.interferencies.cc/proyecto.

domination through a complex network that connects irresponsible Western consumerism, illegitimate debt, perverse international financial mechanisms, neoliberal free-trade agreements, the systemic violence and corruption that perpetuate existing power asymmetries, environmental injustice, and neocolonial exploitation of humanity and the nonhuman.

In a discussion about the minimalist staging of a scene (black plastic bags and a photograph of a poor child playing with garbage), the actors ask themselves if that materiality is enough to express 'el consumo exagerado del norte que convierte al sur en un basurero' [the excessive consumerism of the North that transforms the South into a landfill]. The title of the film refers to the historically iterative interferences of colonial/neocolonial powers in the impoverished global South in order to exploit their ecologies and labor. As in *Tirar, comprar, tirar*, the connection between economic growth and global destruction is explicit, and the film clearly endorses the notion that the efforts of rich countries to help 'poor' regions develop are nothing but a fraud. The latter do not need help from the former. Rather, they need to be liberated from their compulsory subsidization of the wasteful consumption patterns of the wealthy.

One of the most interesting features of the film is a discussion about the limits of representation. The main challenge the characters face is how to effectively talk about, and modify, the distribution of the sensibility perpetuated and monopolized by the dominant imaginary. The difficulty of representing and thinking about the insidious material and semiotic networks that hegemonic discourses conceal leads the actors to conclude that they do not have a coherent topic to represent, and they decide to cancel the premiere of the play. At that moment, real images of the 15-M movement in the streets are incorporated into the film, replenishing the energy that the actors were losing. Afterward, the crew meets again and experiences an epiphany: 'Las alternativas, ése es el tema' [Alternatives, that is the topic]. Some alternatives to the dominant imaginary that are aligned with the degrowth movement are enumerated, and at the end of the film there is an homage to Ramón Fernández Durán (a recently deceased radical Spanish thinker and one of the most sophisticated critics of the growth society). The homage to Fernández Durán reinforces the film's alignment with postgrowth imaginaries.

Jason Moore recently argued that 'flows of nutrients, flows of humans, and flows of capital make a historical totality, in which each flow implies the other'.[72] *Interferències* intends to render this totality perceptible and thinkable, so it can re-enter the arena of the politically and ethically

72 Moore, 'Nature in the Limits of Capital', 15.

relevant. Along these same lines, one of the most effective films in presenting the aforementioned web of flows in a way that aligns with what I call the political ecology of waste is the Spanish and Mexican film *La jaula de oro* (Golden Cage, 2013), written and directed by Diego Quemada-Díez.[73] The majority of the movie follows three teenagers, later joined by a fourth (an indigenous boy from the Chiapas region who does not speak Spanish), as they try to emigrate from a shantytown near a landfill in Guatemala to the United States. The freight trains crossing Mexico, over whose packed roofs the characters move, provide the recurring motif that dominates the movie. The metallic, rusty solidity of the trains is contrasted with the vulnerable bodies of the main characters. A few panoramic shots capture the Mexican landscapes through which the train passes, but during most of the film the camera leisurely frames the body movements and facial expressions of the characters as they interact with each other, using an abundance of close and medium shots. The film generates a sense of intimacy, but also points to the fragile materiality of the human bodies, which sweat and experience fatigue, pain, distress, hunger, and fear. The main characters remain vulnerable throughout the trip and all become victims of aggression and mistreatment. The harsh realities of migrants' lives are not overlooked, as one character dies, another gives up, and yet another is kidnapped by a criminal gang dedicated to sexual trafficking. Nevertheless, they also experience some enjoyable moments. Interestingly, while most of the traumatic events are triggered by monetarized and exploitative activities, the happy moments are not tied to commodified goods but are the result of human interactions with no direct link to goods produced by the market economy (dancing, singing, laughing, and playing).

The aforementioned web of the flows of nutrients, humans, and capital that the film reveals, as well as their connections with the production of both industrial waste and surplus population, are at the heart of the film. The setting of the first sequence, the shantytown where the three teenagers live is constructed of discarded materials and recovered waste. The scene features Juan, the leading character, walking through the informal and marginal human settlement made out of discarded objects where discarded people (surplus population) struggle to survive. The significance of this disposable materiality is reinforced in a subsequent scene, when Juan looks for his friend in an adjacent landfill. His friend is searching with others through the garbage to find elements with which to make a life. Industrial commodities that have reached the end of their life cycle pile up in the landfill, out of sight of the original consumers. This endgame of the consumerist process

73 Diego Quemada-Díez, dir., *La jaula de oro* (Barcelona: Cameo, 2013), DVD.

becomes the symbolic beginning of the film and the trip. Waste materials and surplus population converge in the shantytown, acquiring agency and refusing to accept the disposable, passive, and invisible place assigned to them by the economic system that produced them.

Similarly, at the end of the movie, there is a relatively long and slow scene without dialogue (93:02–96:19) featuring the meat factory where Juan works, presumably illegally, after entering the United States. The shots are unified by the white (workers' uniforms) and red (meat and blood) colors that predominate in the factory, and by peaceful but melancholic offscreen music. The camera slowly moves along the mechanized lines where meat is cut and packed by the factory workers. Juan's task is to clean up the leftover tissue (a sticky amalgam of blood and nerves) that adheres to the factory floor and equipment. What is most relevant in this scene is not the obvious irony of Juan risking his life to escape the landfill of Guatemala only to end up collecting waste at a different stage of the industrial chain, but the fact that waste is produced throughout the process and, no matter where he goes, he will always be located on the side of visible waste production, not the side of consumption.

The choice of a meat factory is significant for several reasons. Industrial meat production and the globalization of its overconsumption is ecologically devastating. According to the United Nations, raising animals for food 'is one of the top two or three most significant contributors to the most serious environmental problems, at every point on the scale from local to global'.[74] The high-density animal populations on industrial farms produce enormous amounts of methane (a potent greenhouse gas) and a highly toxic runoff. Another problem is that according to many environmental organizations, we are literally 'destroying the Amazon to make burgers for the North'. The need for forage to feed the animals triggers the clearance of forests and the replacement of traditionally diverse agricultural practices that sustained the local populations with extensive monocrops engineered to support industrial animal farming. The globalizing, unhealthy meat-based diet of the North is not only deforesting the South, but also contributing to climate change, water depletion, chemical pollution, eradication of food sovereignty and security, land grabbing and human displacement, and many other socioecological problems. It is important to note, in order to reinforce this connection between asymmetrically distributed flows of commodities and human bodies, that Juan only achieves his goal of physically crossing the Mexico-US border by carrying drugs for a criminal organization.

---

74 Henning Steinfeld et al., *Livestock's Long Shadow: Environmental Issues and Options* (Rome: Food and Agriculture Organization of the United Nations, 2006), xx.

La jaula de oro is a film about the correlation between overconsumption and waste production in the North (represented by the meat factory at the end of the movie) and waste accumulation in the South (seen in the landfill at the beginning of the movie), along with the flows of humans and other materials between sites of waste production and waste accumulation. The trains travel from south to north as they simultaneously transport both raw materials to be consumed in the high-entropy centers of the North and people who have been displaced and disposed of as a consequence of the appropriation of such materials by the global market economy. Most of the film focuses on these simultaneous flows of surplus population and commodities as they are juxtaposed on the trains. The surplus population follows the flows of energy and materials mobilized by economic globalization. Interestingly, the materials that are destined to feed the overconsumption of the North travel undisturbed, while all significant diegetic action is triggered by the different obstacles, official or not (police, army, criminal organizations), that prevent human flows from following the commodity flux. Commodities circulate legally, surplus population illegally. The surplus population is hardly able to follow the material flows put into motion by the entropic dynamics of neoliberal globalization.

The toxic securitization discourse discussed earlier in this chapter is central to the film, which depicts the persistent intervention of police and military forces that discourage the movement of surplus population. A similar dynamic governs one of the final scenes after Juan and Chauk have finally crossed the border. They are wandering through US territory when suddenly a sniper shoots and kills Chauk. Because the sniper does not wear an official uniform, he is presumably a member of one of the informally organized racist groups who patrol the borders to stop illegal immigrants. The disturbing proliferation of xenophobic aggressions, securitization policies, and toxic discourses proves lethal, just as it did at Tarajal Beach in February 2014. Fifteen migrants attempting the short swim from the northeastern border of Morocco to the neighboring city of Ceuta, a Spanish territory located on the North African coast, died in Spanish waters while Spanish security forces fired rubber ammunition to prevent them from reaching the shore instead of assisting them.[75]

Even when official institutions can no longer ignore the effects of climate change on mass migration, corporate mass media outlets, research funding, and irresponsible political statements favor a 'threatening narrative' whose effect 'has been a progressive shift of the environmental immigration

---

75 *Tarajal*, a recent documentary, investigates the facts and makes visible these perverse dynamics.

studies towards security studies'.[76] This tendency towards a securitization discourse grossly ignores the root causes of the problem by focusing on its symptoms: the attempts at relocation made by the most vulnerable victims of neoliberal globalization. Migrants are identified as the main problem, to be addressed with severity, while the true causes remain unchecked and concealed. This securitization is a challenge to democracy itself and does not recognize the nexus between capitalism, inequality, and climate change.[77] Today, the environmental problems and social instability caused by economic expansion are used as excuses to reinforce and secure the military power and economic neocolonial domination that created them in the first place.

Paisajes de desolación is a collection of photographs that clearly captures the connections between surplus population, securitization, and the disproportionate social metabolism (including appropriation of ecological space and massive waste production) of the overdeveloped regions.[78] José Palazón Osma's series won the 2015 Ortega y Gasset Award in the category of graphic journalism. One photo shows the fence that separates Morocco from Melilla, another Spanish city on the North African coast, from the perspective of an adjacent golf course located on the Spanish side. While a couple in sportswear play golf on abundantly irrigated green grass, a group of 11 black migrants are trapped on top of the fence, waiting to be deported by a policeman ascending a ladder. Two dramatic contrasts are projected by the image: on the one hand, the leisurely recreation of the indifferent golfers juxtaposed with the migrants' plight and, on the other, the lush golf course separated by the fence from an arid and thirsty landscape. The indifference of the golfers is even more disturbing given the proximity of the migrants. The panoramic composition of the photograph resists the temptation to zoom in on the individual features of the trapped migrants, as is usually the case in graphic journalism that strives to create empathy and awareness. It focuses instead on the space produced and guarded by the fence, as well as the contrasts it hides and perpetuates. In other words, the image, rather than appealing to an audience's depoliticized empathy and compassion for individual stories and characters, encourages the viewer to question the global systemic and structural socioecological network in which both the

76 Marco Armiero, Richard Tucker, and Sergio Prieto Díaz, 'From the Apocalypse to the Possibilities. New Stories about Immigrants and the Environment', *Miradas en Movimiento* (January 2012): 8.

77 Carol C. Gould, 'Beyond the Dual Crisis: From Climate Change to Democratic Change', *Minded Nature* 9, no. 1 (2016): 15.

78 http://periodismohumano.com/migracion/el-video-de-la-foto-juegan-al-golf-mientras-varios-inmigrantes-intentar-saltar-la-valla-de-melilla.html.

Palazón 'Desolation Landscapes'

migrants and the privileged golfers are inextricably enmeshed. This image
disturbs the hegemonic distribution of the sensible by making visible and
thinkable the social and ecological interdependency that the dominant
imaginary keeps in its discursive blind spot.

The framing of the image displaces the dominant order of the perceptible
from the preferred subject of depoliticized individual misfortune onto the
structural injustice that creates such misfortunes. The golf course occupies
more than two-thirds of the image, crowding the migrants and the parched
landscape beyond the fence against the upper border of the photograph. The
relationship between human density and ecological conditions on both sides
of the fence is also asymmetrical. Only two people are using the golf course,
which consumes vast amounts of water, while 11 people are fleeing the arid
environment on the other side of the fence. The asymmetrical framing of
the image graphically depicts the relationship between the appropriation
of a disproportionate ecological space for superficial and wasteful activities
and the displacement of surplus population. The water, soil nutrients, and
energy mobilized by the golf course could have been utilized on the other
side of the fence to grow multiple crops to feed the local population. This
unfair order of things can be easily extrapolated to the global level, where
human bodies, as we saw in *La jaula de oro*, follow the asymmetric flows of

energy and material mobilized by the growth economy in order to survive. In this light, the indifferent golfers are transformed from innocent people trying to enjoy themselves into insensitive participants in the slow violence that creates the surplus population they refuse to see. Their superficial consumption of materials and energy causes real human suffering. The physical securitization that the fence achieves is effective at stopping the victimized bodies from entering the physical space of the golf course, but they disrupt the visual landscape for the players, as well as for people who encounter the photograph on social media. The deregulation of trade and financial activities to facilitate the global circulation of commodities and capital parallels the strict regulation of nonprivileged human bodies and the criminalization of their circulation. Ironically, the same neoliberal discourse that celebrates mobility and freedom severely represses it when it is not market-oriented, as is evidenced by the rapid proliferation of fences in Europe in the past couple of years and the global proliferation of border walls and border agents over the last 25 years.[79]

The dominant imaginary assumes that migrants move to 'developed' countries because such regions are desirable destinations due to their sociopolitical models and economic success. Accordingly, orthodox economists of different ideological colors recommend helping underdeveloped countries to develop in order to reduce migration (although they may disagree on the most effective ways of doing so). José Palazón makes visible and perceptible what these discourses both omit and conceal, namely that the economic growth of overdeveloped countries is what triggers the socioecological conditions that create surplus population. Development understood as constant economic growth is the problem, not the solution!

For Donna Haraway, the Anthropocene implies the massive disappearance of places of refuge that abounded during the Holocene and sustained biocultural diversity: 'Right now, the earth is full of refugees, human and not, without refuge'.[80] I agree with Haraway that the best we can do under contemporary circumstances is to 'join forces to reconstitute refuges, to make possible partial and robust biological-cultural-political-technological recuperation and recomposition, which must include mourning irreversible losses'.[81] Human walls, economic growth, and neoliberal fantasies are rapidly destroying the last planetary refuges by filling the Earth with their semiotic

79 Wayward Wandering, 'Las fronteras de la historia', *Diagonal*, January 5, 2016, https://www.diagonalperiodico.net/blogs/wayward-wandering/fronteras-la-historia.html. See the work by Reece Jones for a global evolution and proliferation of border walls.

80 Haraway, 'Anthropocene, Capitalocene, Plantationocene, Chthulucene', 160.

81 Haraway, 'Anthropocene, Capitalocene, Plantationocene, Chthulucene', 160.

and material pollution.[82] It is my hope that the cultural manifestations collected in this chapter under the auspices of the political ecology of waste might help to disrupt the dominant order of the perceptible, foster postgrowth imaginaries, and motivate radical economic cultures. A persistent cultural focus on nonhuman agency, socioecological interdependency, material flows, and waste visibility has the potential to expose the fallacies embraced by the toxic discourse of economic growth.

82 Haraway, 'Anthropocene, Capitalocene, Plantationocene, Chthulucene', 160.

CHAPTER FOUR

Disaster Fiction, the Pedagogy of Catastrophe, and the Dominant Imaginary

> Mankind, which in Homer's time was an object of contemplation
> for the Olympian gods, now is one for itself. Its self-alienation
> has reached such a degree that it can experience its own
> destruction as an aesthetic pleasure of the first order.
>
> —Walter Benjamin[1]

*B*uena crisis: hacia un mundo postmaterialista (2009) by Jordi Pigem and *La buena crisis* (2010) by Alex Rovira are two of the many examples of recent Iberian texts that understand the ongoing crisis as an opportunity to challenge the cultural hegemony and to abandon the dominant imaginary.[2] However, the notion of crisis is also co-opted by neoliberal reason as a business opportunity for those equipped with entrepreneurial adaptability and personal flexibility. A number of recent blog posts and op-eds with titles such as 'Bendita crisis' (Blessed crisis) and the like offer acritical celebrations of personal strength and private motivation as recipes for navigating the current crisis, leaving no room for a political or historical interpretation of its root causes.

Thinkers who openly criticize the neoliberal order of things disagree on whether financial crises and ecological catastrophes can serve as pedagogical opportunities. Naomi Klein, for instance, examines the mechanisms of 'disaster capitalism' that produce all sorts of crisis with profitable aftermaths for the capitalist elite, as well as new opportunities for appropriation

---

1 Walter Benjamin, 'The Work of Art in the Age of Mechanical Reproduction', in *Illuminations: Essays and Reflections*, trans. Harry Zohn (New York: Harcourt, 1968), 242.

2 Jordi Pigem, *Buena crisis: hacia un mundo postmaterialista* (Barcelona: Kairós, 2009); Alex Rovira, *La buena crisis* (Madrid: Santillana, 2010).

through dispossession.[3] Similarly, Rob Nixon's notion of 'slow violence' denounces the invisibility of the pervasive socioecological violence and massive environmental injustice unleashed by neoliberal global dynamics.[4] Conversely, Serge Latouche—an intellectual at the center of the degrowth movement—has articulated on several occasions the potential usefulness of a non-naive 'pedagogy of disaster' for challenging the 'blissful (and passive) optimism' ingrained in the dominant imaginary.[5] Along these same lines, Jean-Pierre Dupuy advocates an 'enlightened doomsaying' committed to actively countering 'the invisibility of harm' that is prevalent in capitalist modernity.[6] Dupuy claims that the main danger for humanity lies in techno-scientific optimism, and that an enlightened doomsaying can disrupt such destructive optimism.[7] Both positions are useful for viewing the neoliberal crisis in critical and fruitful ways. Unfortunately, the most popular recent cultural depictions of environmental catastrophe in post-2008 Spain are far from being pedagogical, as they perpetuate a neoliberal rationality oblivious to the harm it produces. Although catastrophe can be pedagogical under certain circumstances, the current hegemonic perception of disasters does not challenge the growth imaginary. Cultural critics are also to blame for the unchallenged perpetuation and reinforcement of an agenda that manufactures unprecedented risks and unleashes monumental catastrophe. Timothy Clark is right to suggest that 'received or mainstream modes of reading and criticism, even when socially "progressive" in some respects, are now, despite themselves, being changed into what are effectively implicit forms of denial as the world alters around them'.[8]

This chapter will focus on audiovisual disaster narratives that explore the disturbing ecological consequences of our current scientific hubris and socioeconomic dysfunction in both the recent past and the immediate future. The rapid anthropogenic changes in the Earth's ecological systems regularly unleash widespread catastrophes on a regional and global level. Sensationalizing these catastrophes has commonly been assumed to have pedagogical implications because it highlights the destructive practices

---

3 Naomi Klein, *The Shock Doctrine: The Rise of Disaster Capitalism* (New York: Metropolitan Books, 2007).

4 Nixon, *Slow Violence and the Environmentalism of the Poor.*

5 Serge Latouche, 'Disaster, Pedagogy of', in *Degrowth: A Vocabulary for a New Era*, ed. Giacomo D'Alisa, Federico Demaria, and Giorgos Kallis (New York: Routledge, 2015), 95; Latouche, *La apuesta por el decrecimiento*, 255–260.

6 Jean-Pierre Dupuy, *The Mark of the Sacred*, trans. M.B. Debevoise (Stanford, CA: Stanford University Press, 2013), 28, 36.

7 Dupuy, *The Mark of the Sacred*, 29–30.

8 Timothy Clark, *Ecocriticism on the Edge* (London: Bloomsbury, 2015), xi.

of humanity and promotes an activist lifestyle in order to correct them. I hope to demonstrate, by studying two of the most popular catastrophe fictions of post-2008 Spain—the TV series *El barco* and the movie *The Impossible*—that the utility of pedagogical interpretations of catastrophe should be re-evaluated. First of all, many studies in social and behavioral science indicate that promoting fear is not a good basis for mobilizing activism.[9] Second, disaster fiction—at least in visual media—tends to focus on sensationalist and spectacular effects and individual heroism, ignoring the root causes of catastrophic events involving drastic anthropogenic change and pervasive environmental injustice. Fictional catastrophe does not necessarily constitute a good pedagogy for shaping an effective political ecology in the Anthropocene because it often perpetuates the current post-political and managerial mainstream culture rather than challenging it. Catastrophe-oriented fiction also tends to ignore or, in the worst cases, conceal the pervasive structural violence against humans and nonhumans resulting from global neoliberal policies. Third, even in cases when pedagogical readings might be derived from disaster fiction, cultural scholars may not be trained to engage in (or perceive the possibility of) such criticism. In order to encourage an effective political ecology, other kinds of narratives might be much more effective and more resistant to co-optation by the dominant imaginary—namely, stories and projects that either expose the toxic fantasies of the growth imaginary (e.g., the political ecology of waste articulated in Chapter 3) or envision and depict *desirable* postgrowth imaginaries (e.g., the narratives of transition towns studied at the end of Chapter 2).

In the concluding chapter of the edited volume *Culture, Catastrophe, and Rhetoric*, Ralph Cintron considers the notion that 'the trope of revolution has been superseded by the trope of catastrophe as a primary means for imagining social change'.[10] As Robert Hariman points out in the introduction to the same book, the twenty-first-century popularity of post-apocalyptic narratives in all media implies a

9 George Marshall, *Don't Even Think About it: Why Our Brains Are Wired to Ignore Climate Change* (New York: Bloomsbury, 2014); Per Espen Stoknes, *What We Think About When We Try Not to Think About Global Warming: Toward a New Psychology of Climate Action* (White River Junction, VT: Chelsea Green, 2015); Eddie Yuen, 'The Politics of Failure Have Failed: The Environmental Movement and Catastrophism', in *Catastrophism: The Apocalyptic Politics of Collapse and Rebirth*, ed. Sasha Lilley et al. (Oakland, CA: PM Press, 2012), 15–43.

10 Ralph Cintron, 'What Is Next? Modernity, Revolution, and the "Turn" to Catastrophe', in *Culture, Catastrophe, and Rhetoric: The Texture of Political Action*, ed. Robert Harriman and Ralph Cintron (New York: Berghahn, 2015), 231–255.

reconfiguration of the era's central myth of progress ... The catastrophic model comes without that [capitalist] teleology: progress can occur, but the processes of modernization can also lead to disaster and decline. Thus, catastrophe ... expose[s] the fragility and teleological vacuity of modern economic, technological, and political systems.[11]

Obviously, from the critical postgrowth perspective I propose, challenges to the hubristic and linear hegemonic conception of progress are welcome. Nevertheless, it is vital to acknowledge that the catastrophe trope can easily lead to a dangerous securitization discourse that serves to justify the implementation of a constant state of emergency and extreme forms of neoliberal biopolitics. Along these lines, Robert Marzec's recent book *Militarizing the Environment* studies with historical depth the way in which this disturbing discourse (which the author calls 'environmentality') has become a significant part of today's dominant reformist environmental (not ecological) thought.[12] Marzec explains how accepting climate change as inevitable and preparing for worst-case scenarios of environmental catastrophe through market and military adaptation is already being used as an excuse to further militarize, privatize, and enclose ecological commons. This dominant 'environmentality' frames the problem in terms of national security, technical and military management, and energy geopolitics, completely ignoring the historical root causes of ecological depletion. As a result, the environment is depicted as something separated from humans and as a threat which must be feared and managed with the same technological, economic, and utilitarian logic that alienated humans from their ecological context and created the ecological crisis in the first place. Obviously, the rapid acceptance of environmentality by the elites shows not only that catastrophe is neither pedagogical nor politically disruptive *per se*, but may actually reinforce neoliberal cultural hegemony and growth-oriented framings. Environmentality, similar to eco-modernist approaches, is a depoliticized environmentalism. It implies that there is nothing we can do to change the ongoing disaster trajectory of rapacious capitalism, other than preparing to weather the storm. As such, this discourse is 'politically disempowering and demobilizing'.[13] It is true, as shown in the previous chapter, that catastrophic socioecological events

---

11 Robert Hariman, 'Introduction', in *Culture, Catastrophe, and Rhetoric: The Texture of Political Action*, ed. Robert Hariman and Ralph Cintron (New York: Berghahn, 2015), 12.

12 Robert P. Marzec, *Militarizing the Environment: Climate Change and the Security State* (Minneapolis: Minnesota University Press, 2015).

13 Kallis, *In Defense of Degrowth*, 198.

could move to the forefront the powerful agency of nonhuman forces that tend to be conceived of either as mere background or passive resources. But if this agency is simply perceived as a threat to be managed and countered by a separate human agency, rather than being understood as an inextricable part of the ecological totality in which humans are inscribed, the core logic of the dominant imaginary is not challenged at all and, worse, dangerous geoengineering projects could be encouraged.

4.1. *El barco*

In the following paragraphs, I will show how the television series *El barco* (The Boat, 2011–2013) aligns much better with the cultural logic of 'environmentality' than with the pedagogy of 'enlightened doomsaying'. For several reasons, *El barco* (produced by Globomedia for Antena 3) is a paradigmatic example useful to test dominant Spanish cultural sensibilities: it is one of the most successful and profitable TV series ever produced in Spain, setting records for viewership. It is also one of the first TV shows in Spain to successfully incorporate transmedia storytelling to enrich and extend the narrative through different digital platforms (Twittersodes, Facebook, a videogame, a blog, an official website), as well as the first to deploy a 360-degree market strategy to integrate all media.[14] The series's aggressive pre-broadcast publicity paid off as it enjoyed an average audience of five million viewers. *El barco* narrates the adventures of 42 people, most of them very young, on a training ship. After a global catastrophe, presumably caused by a particle accelerator like the Large Hadron Collider in Geneva, the ship's crew are among the last surviving humans on the planet, whose land is now mostly underwater. The main plot of *El barco* could function as the ultimate Anthropocene narrative, given that the unintended consequences of human large-scale technological intervention are a massive ecocide claiming many terrestrial species. Extradiegetically, the Large Hadron Collider is 'the largest machine in the world', as proudly noted on its official web page,[15] and the first experiments performed there were conducted from 2010 to 2013 (paralleling the broadcast of *El barco*).

El barco, in which most of the diegetic action takes place on the reduced space of a ship with limited resources, can be read as an allegory of an

14 Luis Deltell Escolar, Florencia Claes, and José Miguel Ostero López, 'Audiencias televisivas y líderes de opinión en Twitter. Caso de estudio: El Barco', *Estudios sobre el Mensaje Periodístico* 19, no. 1 (2013): 350; Francesc Mayor Mayor, 'Transmedia Storytelling desde la ficción televisiva serial española: el caso de Antena 3', *CIC Cuadernos de Información y Comunicación* 19 (2014): 77–79.

15 http://home.cern/topics/large-hadron-collider.

overstressed and overpopulated finite Earth that cannot sustain the economy of growth much longer. Such an interpretation would entail an invitation to humbly acknowledge ecological restrictions on capitalist activity and rethink humans' function and place as earthlings who need to learn how to live and thrive on a finite planet. However, the camera arrangements and the plots of the episodes push the ecological catastrophe into the background until it serves as a mere excuse for developing the mainly romantic (and competitive) social relationships among the human—mostly white and heterosexual—characters. The redeeming power of romantic love is a repeated motif, replicating the neoliberal insistency on erasing the visibility of political and historical structural problems by focusing on the personal and subjective level. The Western- and human-centric frames and narratological strategies of the series either exclude nonhumans or construct them as a threat to humans, rather than depicting nonhuman agency and presence as a *sine qua non* for human existence.

The ecophobia and biophobia of *El barco* do not extend ethics to nonhuman living beings but, far from it, almost completely erase or separate their agency in order to embrace the fantasy of human self-sufficiency and autonomy. The ship, the main setting of the story, is depicted as a human-made ecology without nonhuman ecologies (a biophysical impossibility). When nonhumans infiltrate the ship, they must be quickly expelled to keep the human environment safe. As Bruno Latour would put it, the desperate and futile modern attempt to separate the social and the natural is, ironically, radically marked and obsessively maintained in *El barco*, even after most humans have been wiped out as a consequence of the most dramatic naturecultural event in history.[16] The catastrophe is both historical and geological, blurring the boundaries between natural history and human history. There is, as Timothy Morton points out regarding the Anthropocene, a 'horrifying coincidence of human history and terrestrial geology'.[17] At this geo-historical crossroads it is impossible to distinguish whether the cataclysm is due to the agency of humans or that of nonhumans (it is actually due to the entanglement of both). Paradoxically, the world without us produced by the catastrophe is filmed by the camera as claustrophobically human. The density of human (mainly white) flesh framed by the camera is overwhelming, especially considering that most of the planet has no humans. Nonhuman agency is mostly foregrounded as a threat to be managed with paternalistic, hierarchical, martial, and secretive plans formulated by the boat-owning elites, usually combining the mediation

16 Latour, *We Have Never Been Modern.*
17 Morton, *Hyperobjects*, 9.

of scientific authority and the heroic actions of some individuals. The rest of their problems are triggered by conflicts between characters as well as the lack of communication and trust among the crew. After the end of the world, caused by technocratic capitalism, the last humans seem incapable of generating a more functional participatory and inclusive system of decision-making to enhance their collective intelligence.

Interestingly, on a couple of occasions the crew's dominant environmentality—which seeks to solve self-generated threats with the managerial, aggressive, and technocratic authority that created them—fails miserably and the problem is resolved without violence by Burbuja, one of two characters who show deep empathy towards nonhuman living beings and try to understand their feelings and motivations (the other empathetic character is the only child on board).[18] Considering that Burbuja has brain damage, these two sequences call for an interesting ecocritical interpretation that combines posthumanism and disability studies. Burbuja's condition, however, is of recent origin, and before his accident he was a brilliant Harvard-educated scientist involved in the experiment that set the catastrophe in motion. The sequences featuring Burbuja may suggest that a radical change of logic which moves towards a posthuman ethics, combined with current techno-scientific capabilities, might be desirable. However, these sequences are the exception to the rule; most of the episodes promote the environmentality approach.

El barco, where food and energy scarcity due to the inaccessibility of biomass becomes the norm, could have provided an opportunity to challenge consumer capitalism and its unsustainable exploitation and depletion of planetary ecosystems. In this dystopic setting, however, there is an endless supply of Coca-Cola, a brand that symbolizes capitalist global omnipresence and is also an industrial product infamous for using enormous amounts of fresh water and other vital limited resources to make a very unhealthy beverage. A study of product placement in the first season of *El barco* shows that Coca-Cola was mentioned 31 times and appeared in ten of its 13 episodes.[19] Ironically, the show implies that even if most humans do not survive a global cataclysm, capitalist ideology certainly will. As Timothy Morton points out, 'Ideology is not just in your head. It's in the shape of a Coke bottle. It's in the way some things appear natural ... A profound political act would be to choose another aesthetic construct'.[20]

18 See two episodes in the first season: episode 5, 'El graznido' (Cawing), broadcast on February 14, 2011, and episode 8, 'Pesca mayor' (Sport fishing), broadcast on March 7, 2011.

19 Erika Fernández Gómez, 'La presencia de las grandes marcas en la ficción española: el caso de Coca-cola en El Barco de Antena 3', *REMARKA UIMA* 9 (2012): 74.

20 Morton, *Hyperobjects*, 106.

El barco is incapable of imagining a disruptive postgrowth, posthumanist, non-Eurocentric aesthetic even after a near-human-extinction event has occurred. This is another indication that, from the standpoint of cultural hegemony, 'it is easier to imagine the end of the world than to imagine the end of capitalism'.[21] Interestingly, this excessive Coca-Cola marketing campaign has ended up being unintentionally pedagogical for some segments of the show's audience. A number of Facebook groups were created to mock the ridiculously overwhelming presence of this brand in a diegetic context of supposed scarcity and rationing. The ironic names chosen by these groups speak for themselves, for example: 'Se acabará el mundo pero seguiré teniendo Coca-cola' [The world will end but I will still have Coca-Cola], 'El Barco, el único lugar donde sólo Coca-cola perdura' [El Barco, the only place where Coca-Cola remains], and 'Yo también creo que en El Barco está la fábrica de Coca-cola' [I too believe that there is a Coca-Cola factory on El Barco].[22]

Paul Julian Smith, one of the few cultural scholars to discuss *El barco* (interestingly, most of the academic publications dealing with *El barco* appear in journals devoted to marketing, journalism, or communication studies and focus on topics such as audience response, transmedia strategies, and applied marketing), interprets the TV show as 'an allegory of a Spain adrift in the grip of unprecedented circumstances'.[23] Although his reading of *El barco* as a Spanish audiovisual text 'emblematic of the long running [economic] crisis' is perfectly valid, the complete absence of the ecological global crisis in his analytic frame is revealing—especially when we consider that *El barco* depicts a global ecological catastrophe, not a national economic collapse.[24] Smith's interpretation of *El barco* as a fiction of the economic crisis focuses on the identification of individual lines of desire frustrated by the economic crisis. Again, it is the critical interpretation of the culture of crisis as a personal, subjective, and private navigation of a social or economic situation independent from the ecological context in which it is embedded that prevents cultural critics from reading the crisis as a socioecological issue. The invisibility of nonhuman agency in a series in which major diegetic action—as well as most of the episodes' overall dramatic tension—is motivated by drastic anthropogenic changes of global

21 Fredrick Jameson, 'Future City', *New Left Review* 21 (2003): 76.

22 Erika Fernández Gómez, 'La presencia de las grandes marcas en la ficción española', 85.

23 Paul Julian Smith, 'Notes on the Future (and Past) of Spanish and Latin-American Media Studies', *Bulletin of Spanish Studies* 92, no. 3 (2015): 338.

24 Smith, 'Notes on the Future (and Past) of Spanish and Latin-American Media Studies', 338.

ecosystems indicates that we urgently need, as Ursula Heise suggests, to develop 'a holistic understanding of ecological connectedness, as well as of the risks that have emerged from human manipulations of such connected systems'.[25]

It is worrisome to witness how, in the current age of social inequality and ecological collapse, most cultural critics and popular media audiences routinely disregard the relevance of nonhuman matters in all human affairs—even in fictions such as *El barco*, where anthropogenic intervention unleashes an unintended nonhuman agency with massive consequences. It is more urgent than ever to question this human-centric neocolonial cultural hegemony that directs both our theoretical radars and our focus of attention to our navels while our common (human and nonhuman) boat sinks. Put otherwise, 'the climate crisis is upon us because we are intoxicated by our subjectivity'.[26] This human-centric (or, to be fair, Western-centric) 'regime of the visible' cannot see what it is not trained to see, no matter how obvious and dangerous it becomes. In this regard, Jane Bennett's posthumanist reading of Rancière is enlightening. According to Bennett, we urgently need to make an effort to think of the political act as a human and nonhuman assemblage if we are to become capable of imagining a disruptive political ecology that can really modify the dominant partition of the perceptible.[27] I believe that a cultural criticism helpful to overcome the Capitalocene would pay due attention to material culture and nonhuman agency in order to recognize our unavoidable *naturecultural* interdependency and to challenge the dominant ideology of human-nonhuman disconnection. From this posthumanist critical perspective, *El barco* fails to be pedagogical because it foregrounds and privileges the visibility of human agency and personal desire over the collective and unequally distributed agency of human-nonhuman connections, as well as differential power relations. This failure perpetuates the illusion of human autonomy and independency: 'there was never a time when human agency was anything other than an interfolding network of humanity and nonhumanity; today this mingling has become harder to ignore'.[28] In this regard, *El barco* can be interpreted as a postapocalyptic audiovisual narrative of ecological denialism: even after a global cataclysm has exposed the fragile ecological interdependency of the human species, the show's narrative focus desperately strives to

25 Heise, *Sense of Place and Sense of Planet*, 22.

26 Clive Hamilton, 'Why We Resist the Truth About Climate Change', paper presented at the 'Climate Controversies: Science and Politics' conference, Museum of Natural Sciences, Brussels, October 28, 2010, 15.

27 Bennett, *Vibrant Matter*, 104–109.

28 Bennett, *Vibrant Matter*, 31.

're-impose the Enlightenment's allocation of humans and Nature to two distinct realms'.[29]

The most disturbing aspect of *El barco*, other than its ecological denialism, is its depiction of the post-political environmentality that the fictional 'Proyecto Alejandría' (the Alexandria Project) promotes and which is represented by the pathological social Darwinism of the antagonist Gamboa. This project was a top-down backup plan intended to ensure the survival of the human species in the event that the particle collider should generate a global cataclysm. It is unclear whether this plotline is intended as a critique of the current global neoliberal biopolitics that massively destroys and administers life, or whether it is merely a way to maintain diegetic tension and dramatic intensity. I am inclined to believe the latter because an intentional critique of neoliberal biopolitics would be inconsistent with the show's ecological denialism as well as its massive mobilization of intradiegetic and extradiegetic corporate marketing. In any case, the secret project that led to the disaster in which the ship's crew find themselves uses the manufactured crisis as a justification for assassinating, torturing, and manipulating any person who represents an obstacle to the project's plan. The environmentality of the technocratic and militarized characters implicated in the Alexandria Project—the ones who know the real reasons for the disaster and are following a prearranged plan for its aftermath—perpetuate and amplify the logic of neoliberal biopolitics after the catastrophe without questioning the role of such technocratic, hierarchical, anthropocentric, and militarized logic in the activation of the disaster. The vast majority of people are part of the plan without knowing it. This remaining assemblage of human life was selected in advance, and each person has a specific function in the technocratic plan. Their humanity is reduced to bare life and denied political agency, as Agamben would put it, and consequently it is strictly regulated by technocratic and hierarchical interventions.[30] The minds administering the Alexandria Project decide who lives and who dies at every moment. They cure de la Cuadra's cancer without his consent or knowledge, but assassinate several other characters who might compromise their plan.

Another problematic aspect of *El barco* is the lack of attention to environmental justice in the context of the Anthropocene, namely the uneven distribution of risks and the inverse correlation between agents' degree of responsibility for the environmental crisis and their

29 Hamilton, 'Why We Resist the Truth about Climate Change', 15.
30 Giorgio Agamben, *Homo Sacer: Sovereign Power and Bare Life*, trans. Daniel Heller-Roazen (Stanford, CA: Stanford University Press, 1998).

degree of exposure to its deleterious consequences. Dispossessed and underprivileged populations not responsible for climate change are those most vulnerable to its resultant environmental risks, but they are not even considered worth mentioning in *El barco*. The series, as Rob Nixon notes in relation to the dominant ways of narrating the Anthropocene, depicts the consequences of collective human agency without considering 'the question of unequal human agency, unequal human impacts, and unequal human vulnerability'.[31] As I will show shortly, to understand the importance of this systemic neocolonial erasure for the maintenance of the hegemonic politics of representation, a convergence of ecocritical and postcolonial criticism is vital.

4.2. *The Impossible*

On December 26, 2004, the Indian Ocean tsunami, one of the deadliest 'natural' disasters ever recorded, claimed over three hundred thousand lives and devastated entire regions in countries including India, Bangladesh, Indonesia, Thailand, and Sri Lanka. The catastrophe affected more than two million people. This destructive event generated a lot of media attention as well as an intense mobilization of humanitarian aid from the international community. Subsequently, a number of audiovisual cultural manifestations depicted the tsunami and its aftermath. *The Impossible* (2012), an English-language movie by Spanish director Juan Antonio Bayona, was arguably the most popular.[32] *The Impossible* was a great success, nationally and internationally, in terms of both box office numbers and the quantity of awards it received. Based on the true story of a Spanish family who survived the tsunami, the film focuses on a white, well-off, British family of five who are enjoying a vacation at a luxury tourist resort in Thailand. Their vacation is interrupted by the tsunami and, from that point on, the dispersed members of the family struggle to find each other and eventually reunite and fly back to their homeland in a private jet provided by their high-end insurance policy.

Most of the reviews in magazines such as *Film Journal International*, *Rolling Stone*, *Film Comment*, and *Variety* were overly celebratory, highlighting the director's gift, the film's technical accomplishments, and the actors' talents. A few commentators, however, noted the banality of the story of the separated and reunited family (David Denby, *New Yorker*),[33] the

---

31 Nixon, 'The Great Acceleration and the Great Divergence'.
32 Juan Antonio Bayona, dir., *The Impossible* (Summit, 2012), DVD.
33 David Denby, 'Stiff Upper Lips', *New Yorker*, January 28, 2013, 80.

worrisome whitewashing narrative (David Cox, *The Guardian*),[34] and the sensationalist treatment of the disaster (Erik Kohn, *Indiewire*).[35] Beyond reviews, blog comments, and feature articles in the cultural sections of newspapers and magazines, the movie has not yet been studied in depth by cultural scholars in order to understand its politics of representation. I believe that a postcolonial ecocritical reading of *The Impossible* is well suited to illuminate the film's disturbing politics of invisibility—the enormous blind spots afflicting the film's narrative and visuals. Using this approach, the hegemonic order of the visible and the ideology of disconnection which *The Impossible* espouses and perpetuates can be exposed and radically challenged.

This high-budget transnational production incorporates a number of technically sophisticated special effects to depict the sudden, unexpected violence unleashed by the tsunami in a specific location and how a family of European tourists deals with the disaster. It grossly ignores economically and socially different vulnerabilities to environmental events and culturally and racially different perceptions of environmental risk, as well as the slow violence that preceded the catastrophe and will continue to affect the local communities for many years to come. The film presents the tsunami as a 'natural disaster' (mainly ahistorical and apolitical) that suddenly threatens the taken-for-granted bodily safety of the wealthy European family—a family that succeeds in heroically overcoming this disruptive force of nature and thus ironically confirms not the unpredictability, power, omnipresence, and relevance of nonhuman agency, but rather the idea that 'Nothing is stronger than the human spirit', as one of the official trailers of the movie puts it. Not only is the movie not pedagogical, socioecologically speaking, but what is worse, it re-centers humans in a context where the obvious lesson should be that humans are not in control of an ontologically external nature, but rather interconnected, interdependent, ecological beings that are inextricably enmeshed in a web of ecological processes and differential power relations.

In the Anthropocene, a geo-historical crossroads where the distinction between nature and culture can no longer be sustained, *The Impossible* uses the disaster trope not to erase such a distinction but, paradoxically, to reinforce

34 David Cox, 'Attempting the Impossible: Why Does Western Cinema Whitewash Asian Stories?', *The Guardian*, January 2, 2013.

35 Eric Kohn, 'Toronto Review: Juan Antonio Bayona's "The Impossible" Is an Intense Realization of the 2004 Tsunami at Odds With Overstated Sentimentalism', *IndieWire*, September 9, 2012, http://www.indiewire.com/2012/09/toronto-review-juan-antonio-bayonas-the-impossible-is-an-intense-realization-of-the-2004-tsunami-at-odds-with-overstated-sentimentalism-241703/.

it. Moreover, the movie privileges—and tries to universalize—a single cultural response to the disaster (a white, heterosexual, European, wealthy one), ignoring two facts: first, the vast majority of victims of the tsunami were neither white nor European, and second, 'not all cultural responses are equal ... and disasters result in fierce competition over which interpretations hold sway over the collective imagination and, more to the point, the political establishment'.[36] Interestingly, given the fact that the movie interprets the destructive disaster (its unequally distributed consequences are not even suggested) as something disconnected from economic, social, and political issues, the neocolonial legacy implicated in neoliberal global tourism and in the ecologically disruptive consumerist lifestyle of rich countries is not even suggested. Far from it, in a perverse turn, the members of the European family—the unconscious perpetuators of the global structure of privilege—are depicted in the film as universal victims with whom a global audience must fully empathize. Most of the special effects of the movie are intended to submerge the audience in the main character's experience. This simplistic treatment of the tsunami's symptoms, from the locus of perception and enunciation of wealthy Western European tourists, serves to avoid systemic thinking and, as a result, socioecological problems are viewed as a matter of personal misfortune rather than understood as the semiotic and material consequence of neocolonial historic processes of unequal economic relations and pathological socioecological metabolisms that need to be radically confronted. Reading the film from a postgrowth critical perspective and focusing on the socioecological aspects it conceals can help to unmask the movie's acceptance and perpetuation of the harmful dominant growth imaginary.

The destruction brought on by the tsunami, viewed through a postcolonial ecocritical lens, will be interpreted here as a symptom of a long, multiscale, socioecological process rather than as a sudden natural event without ties to social, political, cultural, and economic hegemonic structures. I will emphasize how the interaction of human and nonhuman agency plays out in the material and semiotic network from which the tsunami emerges as a naturecultural disaster. In other words, the destructive force that *The Impossible* depicts as an expression of sudden, spectacular, natural violence with no political or historical ties will be reread as part of a long process of slow violence that can be traced historically on different temporal and geographical scales. My intention is to disrupt, in Rancière's sense, 'the distribution of the sensible' prearranged by the disaster narrative of

---

36 Mark D. Anderson, *Disaster Writing: The Cultural Politics of Catastrophe in Latin America* (Charlottesville: University of Virginia Press, 2011), 2.

The Impossible and its symbolic order that determines what can and what cannot be visible and thinkable.[37] To significantly 'reconfigure the map of the sensible' in politically meaningful ways, I will call attention to the long-term slow violence that the visual aesthetics of *The Impossible* hides and disguises. As a reminder, Rob Nixon defines slow violence as

> violence that occurs gradually and out of sight, a violence of delayed destruction that is dispersed across time and space, an attritional violence that is typically not viewed as violence at all. Violence is customarily conceived as an event or action that is immediate in time, explosive and spectacular in space, and as erupting into instant sensational visibility. We need, I believe, to engage a different kind of violence, a violence that is neither spectacular nor instantaneous, but rather incremental and accretive, its calamitous repercussions playing out across a range of temporal scales. In so doing, we also need to engage the representational, narrative, and strategic challenges posed by the relative invisibility of slow violence.[38]

The Impossible is a paradigmatic example of how the framing of violence as an 'explosive and spectacular' event of 'instant sensational visibility' results in the perverse obliteration of the slow violence implicated in that event and, consequently, the erasure of all political, historical, and ethical alternative interpretations of the destructive consequences of the tsunami.

There are obvious links between anthropogenic climate change and the increase in the number and intensity of tsunamis.[39] Arguably, the carbon-intense lifestyle of the wealthy European tourist family is more responsible for greenhouse emissions than that of most of the locals affected by the tsunami. Surprisingly, although the film is about a family of tourists affected by a disaster, it does not even suggest that 'there are many ties between tourism and disaster' and that a neocolonial pattern of 'tourism-related dispossession' exists.[40] The setting of the movie is a luxury coastal resort where the main characters are staying along with many other white tourists. From a postcolonial ecocritical perspective, it is obvious that a luxury coastal resort is a significant locus that could be related

---

37 Rancière, *The Politics of Aesthetics*.

38 Nixon, *Slow Violence and the Environmentalism of the Poor*, 2.

39 McGuire, *Waking the Giant*.

40 Anthony Carrigan, '"Out of This Great Tragedy Will Come a World Class Tourism Destination": Disaster, Ecology, and Post-Tsunami Tourism Development in Sri Lanka', in *Postcolonial Ecologies: Literatures of the Environment*, ed. Elizabeth DeLoughrey and George B. Handley (Oxford: Oxford University Press, 2011), 274, 287.

to a neocolonial and neoliberal history of rapid and dire socioecological transformations of postcolonial regions. The resort should be understood in context, as one of multiple examples of how the coastlines of many regions in the global South have been ecologically transformed beyond recognition in past decades by massive foreign tourism, not to mention the industrial production of commodities to feed global markets.

These top-down technocratic adjustments transformed functional local economies into transnational industrial operations that displaced local inhabitants from their ancestral land and dispossessed them of their traditional livelihoods while radically altering and depleting regional ecosystems. As Indian ecofeminist Vandana Shiva explains, 'The effects of the wave that struck the coasts were mainly the fault of the human race. The coasts, bereft of their natural defenses because of the construction of tourist villages and the destruction of the mangrove forests for agro-industrial purposes, have been left completely exposed'.[41] According to Carlo Petrini, 'the presence of mangroves is extremely important in these areas because they protect the coast against the force of the sea (significantly, the tsunami did less damage along those parts of the coast that were still protected by the mangroves)'.[42] Thus, from a historical perspective of neocolonial dynamics and changing ecologies, intense neoliberal slow violence preceded and conditioned the tsunami's socioecological destruction significantly. The growth-oriented policies imposed in these regions made their population extremely vulnerable to the deleterious environmental effects which such policies exacerbated.[43] Many of the locals in the affected areas were already developmental refugees, 'those forced into flight by development and barred from once-accessible commonage',[44] long before the tsunami turned them into environmental refugees.

Without a historical postcolonial environmental perspective, the movie's representation of wealthy tourists as universal victims seems to be unproblematic, because the implication of tourism's neoliberal dynamics in the socioecological transformations that exacerbated the disaster are ignored. The movie is not pedagogical, because it reinforces the dominant ideology of disconnection by refraining from making any relevant

---

41 Cited in Petrini, *Slow Food Nation*, 111.

42 Petrini, *Slow Food Nation*, 112.

43 For a really insightful and rhetorically powerful explanation of these issues in relation to Haiti's 2010 earthquake, see the brilliant article by Junot Díaz, 'Apocalypse: What Disasters Reveal', *Boston Review*, May 1, 2011, http://bostonreview.net/junot-diaz-apocalypse-haiti-earthquake.

44 Rob Nixon, 'Neoliberalism, Genre, and "The Tragedy of the Commons"', *PMLA* 127 (2012): 596 (paraphrasing Thayer Scudder).

socioecological connections. Instead, the movie focuses on the symptoms of the tsunami from a Eurocentric perspective, ignoring its root causes. The result is the perpetuation of the dominant interpretation of the tsunami and the victimization and celebration of those who benefit more from the neoliberal/neocolonial status quo and whose lifestyles are more responsible for the slow violence of which the tsunami is only a part. The movie does not help to find systemic solutions to socioecological issues—quite the opposite, because 'if the key actors responsible for ecological destruction are systematically erased from environmental discourse then the danger is that solutions are sought at the wrong level'.[45]

The end of the movie is immensely revealing. It coincides with the moment when the white tourists leave on a private plane provided by their insurance company. Once they stop being affected by the problem (a problem to which their carbon-intensive lifestyle contributed), the problem disappears and becomes irrelevant because everything returns to what the dominant imaginary conceives as 'normal': namely, white, wealthy Europeans return to their privileged spaces while underprivileged and disenfranchised people fade into invisibility. The destructive lifestyle of the well-off can continue undisturbed without anyone recognizing its negative effects elsewhere. The long-term continuity of slow violence after the tsunami seems irrelevant and not worth considering from the Eurocentric perspective of the film. The family members board a private jet—which could have been put to good use to help many of the locals affected by the disaster—and return to their intact homes as heroes. The space of the airplane is exclusively reserved for the family, a disturbing (and unethical) waste of resources and fossil fuel in the context of an emergency situation. The spacious and quiet interior of the plane contrasts with the hectic and dense post-disaster environment that the tourists leave behind. The end of the movie is by no means the end of the socioecological violence; the long-term, attritional, slow violence suffered by the locals and regional ecosystems due to capitalist growth dynamics (including global tourism) orchestrated from above will continue long after the Europeans have flown off into the sunset.

The politics of representation in the movie actually contribute to reinforcing the dominant interpretation of the tsunami, which permits the implementation and justification of neoliberal slow violence after the tsunami. By prioritizing a white tourist family as the camera's main interest, as well as focusing on individuals helping individuals and on the emotional and physical strengths of specific characters, the film conceals the systemic sociopolitical and economic structures of power and domination

45 Stibbe, *Ecolinguistics*, 148 (paraphrasing Mary Schleppegrell).

intertwined in the disaster, as well as the need to radically challenge, politically and collectively, those dynamics and, more importantly, the imaginaries that legitimate them. In other words, the film privileges the dominant interpretation of the disaster and serves as effective global publicity for such an interpretation, as the box office numbers attest. This publicity might be unintended, but it nonetheless has significant political consequences. According to Mark Anderson, 'Political power is at a premium during the recovery process':

> The process of narrating the disaster mobilizes existing social and political power relations at the same time that it negotiates them ... Disaster narratives serve to legitimize and to delegitimize political discourse, always in competition with rival versions ... In the end, the triumphant version of events ... achieves canonical status as the basis for political action.[46]

For this reason, cultural scholars should analyze 'the politics of interpretation' deployed by a given disaster narrative to understand the nuances in its negotiation of meaning.[47]

The Impossible, despite its pretense of political neutrality (the director insisted in several interviews that the movie is not about class, race, and so on because, according to him, all that was wiped away by the tsunami), perpetuates the dominant interpretation of the disaster, an interpretation that is not going to prevent (quite the opposite) growth-oriented politics from controlling the reconstruction process and displacing the remaining locals—using the disaster as an excuse—to make room for the next generation of tourist development. Actually, 'for many doubly disenfranchised locals, reconstruction came to be viewed as "the second tsunami"'.[48] In fact, in most of the regions affected by the tsunami, neoliberal global institutions (the World Bank, IMF, and WTO) working in tandem with regional technocrats and elites have been using reconstruction funds and international aid to expand, implement, and reinforce the same infrastructures (tourist resorts, industrial prawn farms, and so on) that deplete the environment, compromise food sovereignty, and displace local communities.[49] Not surprisingly, the slow violence which is perpetuated by post-tsunami developmental politics

46 Anderson, *Disaster Writing*, 2, 7.

47 Anderson, *Disaster Writing*, 7.

48 Carrigan, 'Out of This Great Tragedy Will Come a World Class Tourism Destination', 274.

49 Petrini, *Slow Food Nation*, 110–113; Carrigan, 'Out of This Great Tragedy Will Come a World Class Tourism Destination', 273–275.

is completely disregarded by *The Impossible*, a movie where the main heroes are foreign tourists who benefit from neoliberal developmental violence prior to the tsunami and will continue to do so in the post-tsunami context. Under disaster capitalism, manufactured catastrophe opens up further growth opportunities for capitalists who will generate subsequent dispossession and disaster.

From a postcolonial ecocritical perspective, the title of the film is also highly problematic and intriguing. What is *The Impossible* referring to? Is it really referring to the survival of the white tourists with intensive carbon lifestyles supported by a global structure of privilege and fully covered by private insurance policies? To me, it seems much more 'impossible' to oppose and end the structure of neocolonial privilege in which the lives of white, rich tourists are considered more worthy of preserving (and representing) than the lives of more vulnerable populations. What really seems impossible (although the movie does not even register it as a problem) is to prevent the global growth dynamics (from which the white tourists benefit) from manufacturing environmental and developmental refugees and then making them irrelevant and invisible (as the movie does). What seems impossible, thanks to movies like this, is the possibility of challenging the dominant politics of representation and conceiving alternative interpretations of the disaster that look for systemic causes without perpetuating the cultural hegemony. And what seems truly impossible is for the film to imagine the end of a disaster capitalism (because it is impossible to imagine the end of something that it is not even perceived and recognized) that makes room for luxury tourist resorts by transforming regional ecologies at the price of displacing, dispossessing, and impeding the continuation of traditional, low-carbon livelihoods.

What the movie does not mention is that the traditional ecological knowledge that is disappearing thanks to the proliferating tourist-intrusive infrastructures was, in part, what saved the lives of some of the tourists. In many regions, locals fled to the mountains to save themselves and, after the wave hit, returned to the coast to help the tourists. The end of the movie indicates that nothing was learned, as it embraces a cruel optimism that celebrates a return to the hegemonic normality in which privileged people remain blind to the dire social and ecological consequences of their lifestyle. Is that ending really the materialization of an impossible or unlikely event, or is it just the logical outcome of a neocolonial, growth-oriented inertia? *The Impossible* imagines no avenues for collective political engagement as a response to neoliberal disaster, because the systemic dimensions of such a disaster do not exist from the film's privileged perspective. Privilege, hegemony, and colonial/neocolonial dynamics are invisible to such a degree that their negative socioecological consequences are completely obliterated and their positive influence on the privileged characters is confused with an unlikely, almost miraculous (the impossible!) combination of their individual strength and personal luck.

Jane Bennett is right in affirming that 'the locus of political responsibility is a human-nonhuman assemblage'.[50] The post-political narrative of *The Impossible* actively avoids the visibility of such an assemblage, making it difficult to think of the tsunami politically in any meaningful way. It is disturbing to witness the absence of socioecological issues even in movies that represent socioecological disasters. The two audiovisual narratives studied in this chapter focus on personal consequences and not the systemic causes of the disasters. In such narratives, the catastrophe functions as an entertainment-driven spectacle for consumption, rather than a denunciation of the cultural consumerism and dominant economic ideology that exacerbate and manufacture such socioecological disasters. Both narratives are overwhelmingly human-centered—a paradoxical irony, given that the main cause of diegetic action is the unexpected intrusion of nonhuman agency. Neither is pedagogical, for their depictions of catastrophe do not encourage a radical rethinking of our disaster-producing socioecological metabolism. Neither *El barco* nor *The Impossible* is useful to 'counter those maladaptive forms of reason that radically distance us from the non-human sphere'. They both fail to 'situate humans ecologically and nonhumans ethically', as Val Plumwood recommends if we are to successfully navigate the current ecological crisis.[51] Both cultural manifestations actively avoid the issue of environmental justice and frame the disaster mostly from the locus of enunciation of white Europeans. They ignore the most vulnerable populations, the ones most affected by environmental degradation although they are the least responsible for it. Both narratives are examples of the epistemological limitations self-imposed by the dominant imaginary: 'Amid generalized historical amnesia concerning the past, and impoverished abilities to imagine the future except in fantasy sci-fi mode, human existence on the planet is increasingly "poor on future" to adapt Heidegger's phrase'.[52]

To conclude, I concur with Jason Moore:

We are frequently warned of the alleged dangers of civilizational 'collapse'. But is the 'collapse' of capitalism—a civilization that plunges

---

50 Bennett, *Vibrant Matter*, 36.
51 Plumwood, *Environmental Culture*, 239.
52 Srinivas Aravamudan, 'The Catachronism of Climate Change', *Diacritics* 41, no. 3 (2013): 17.

a third of its population into malnutrition—really something to fear? ... The most pessimistic view is one that hopes for the survival of modernity in something like its present form. But this is impossible, because capitalism's metabolism is inherently an open-flow system that continually exhausts its source of nourishment.[53]

Most mainstream disaster fictions depict the collapse of the dominant system as something that should be avoided at all costs, perpetuating the cruel optimism that it is better to tolerate a perverse status quo that constantly becomes more socially and ecologically costly than to actively transition to something else. At best, these fictions force audiences to think about the unsustainability of the current system, but they never encourage them to develop alternatives to it. Steve Mentz writes that 'The great weakness of our industrial fossil-fuel economy is its exclusion of other forms of production, so that when systemic catastrophes come—wars, oil spills, financial crises—we have few alternatives. We need options, not sustainability'.[54] We need desirable postgrowth imaginaries.

In order to truly challenge the dominant imaginary, I suggest that we abandon the apocalyptic frame and move from the ineffective—usually counterproductive—pedagogy of catastrophe to a more assertive 'pedagogy of degrowth'.[55] Alternatives can emerge only if we think beyond the self-imposed epistemological limitations of the cultural hegemony, and in order to mobilize activism and collective politics, it is much more effective to depict and perform socially desirable and ecologically sound alternative ways to be in the world. I believe we need more narratives that represent a society that happily degrows and learns how to live better with less, embraces more fulfilling and less intensive material and energy lifestyles, and seeks meaningful and just prosperity without growth (*decrescita felice* or *décroissance conviviale*, as the Italians and French like to call it). As Del Río, coordinator of the Transition Town movement in Spain, laments:

> Dónde están las películas que hablan de una sociedad que, siendo capaz de prever una crisis inminente y evitable, responde ante ella de forma imaginativa, empleando la creatividad y la reflexión participativa para conseguir, finalmente, alterar el curso de la historia?[56]

---

53 Moore, 'Nature in the Limits to Capital (and Vice Versa)', 19.

54 Steve Mentz, 'After Sustainability', *PMLA* 127, no. 3 (2012): 591.

55 Luis I. Prádanos, 'The Pedagogy of Degrowth: Teaching Hispanic Studies in the Age of Social Inequality and Ecological Collapse', *Arizona Journal of Hispanic Cultural Studies* 19 (2015): 81–96.

56 Del Río, *Guía del movimiento de transición*, 10.

[Where are the movies that talk about a society that, being able to anticipate an imminent and evitable crisis, responds to it imaginatively, using creativity and participatory reflection to succeed, eventually, in altering the course of history?]

The lack of such postgrowth stories in mainstream media is an indication of the crisis of imagination that the hegemonic culture perpetuates and that a postcolonial ecocriticism can help to correct. However, as demonstrated in the preceding chapters, there has already been a significant emergence of counterhegemonic postgrowth imaginaries in post-2008 Spain.

Jeffrey Cohen describes 'Apocalypse' as 'a failure of the imagination, a giving up on the future instead of a commitment to the difficult work of composing a better present'.[57] I hope this book encourages us to commit ourselves, as cultural critics, to this difficult task of imagining and materializing a better present, one that dares to imagine life beyond economic growth and capital accumulation. I hope our field embraces 'ethics that produce more than just an apocalyptic sentiment ... an ethics that does not center on the human—or its non-existence—as the only axis that is of significance ... A proper ethics moves on multiple ecological scales'.[58] We need not inevitably be trapped between Scylla and Charybdis, as the dominant imaginary insists. And we do not have to grow at all costs, limiting our politics to a pre-framed choice between a suicidal, fearful, and conservative 'business as usual' model and a risky, more or less progressive, techno-optimist version of the same logic. Both offer only the illusion of democratic choice while excluding the possibility of a historically informed, meaningful politics that will enable us to collectively build the present we want. Fortunately, as this book has demonstrated, there *is* an emerging and hopeful cultural resistance to the growth imaginary in the Iberian Peninsula. The time has come to dare to imagine prosperity without growth for all!

57 Cohen, *Prismatic Ecology*, 285.
58 Parikka and Richterich, 'A Geology of Media and a New Materialism', 223.

Conclusion:
The Global Rise of Postgrowth Imaginaries

The great secret and the great accomplishment of capitalist civilization have been to not pay its bills. Frontiers made that possible. The closure is the end of Cheap Nature—and with it the end of capitalism's free ride.
—Jason W. Moore[1]

Cultural hegemony is being contested and challenged in post-2008 Spain by a significant number of cultural manifestations. *Postgrowth Imaginaries* has explored how many of these emerging cultural sensibilities in Spain are actively detaching themselves from the dominant imaginary of economic growth. The first part of the book, 'Spanish Culture and Postgrowth Economics', combines cultural studies and postgrowth economics to articulate a degrowth-inspired Iberian ecocriticism able to expose the contradictions of mainstream Euro-American environmentalism. This ecocritical approach reveals that the main obstacles to articulating a political ecology able to deal effectively with the most pressing social and ecological issues arise not only from right-wing denialism but also, and more disturbingly, from progressive techno-optimism. The second part, 'Urban Ecologies', invites scholars of urban culture to think of modern cities in terms of socionatural metabolisms embedded in unsustainable energy regimes and growth imaginaries. Such a framework enables a critical review of cultural representations of urbanity as well as an assessment of their effectiveness in challenging the dominant imaginary. The last part of the book, 'Waste, Disaster, Refugees, and Nonhuman Agency', advocates considering the socioecological significance of nonhuman agency and embracing a political ecology of waste to productively disrupt the dominant imaginary. I also urged cultural activists and scholars to move from a reactive

1 Moore, 'Nature in the Limits to Capital (and Vice Versa)', 19.

fear-infused pedagogy of catastrophe to a more empowering, playful, and proactive pedagogy of degrowth. Moving into the future, the combination of a decolonial ecocriticism and a critical politics of hope may be able to overcome mainstream apolitical techno-optimism. For a critique of the growth imaginary is necessary but not sufficient; imagining and enacting desirable postgrowth societies is also vital.[2]

This book demonstrates that a postgrowth imaginary is emerging on the Iberian Peninsula today and offers several ways of reading its cultural implications from a degrowth-inspired environmental humanities perspective. The complex interrelations among cultural practices, economic paradigms, and ecological processes are vastly under-theorized. I have tried my best in this book to provide an innovative and functional frame, articulated around the notion of postgrowth imaginaries, that can illuminate these important connections. My hope is that this intervention will foster a more systemic, posthumanist, and ecological understanding of culture that helps Iberian cultural studies to effectively mobilize its emancipatory political potential.

I also believe that beyond Iberian studies, the notion of *postgrowth imaginaries* will prove fruitful for the field of cultural studies in general and make a valuable contribution to transnational debates within the environmental humanities. The radical cultural change I identify in my book is by no means limited to this region of Southern Europe, but rather represents a global pattern expressed around the world in different cultural fashions based on distinct historical conjunctions. I hope that the interpretative frame developed in *Postgrowth Imaginaries* will be enriched by incorporating insights from other regions to better understand the unfolding global challenges to the dominant growth paradigm and their diverse articulations of alternative economic cultures. The notion of postgrowth imaginaries might even serve as a conceptual anchor for a coalition of socioecological movements united by their radical critique of neoliberal reason as they mobilize their collective intelligence and effort in order to envision and materialize desirable and sustainable economic cultures beyond growth.[3] The goal of such a coalition would be to articulate a cohesive critique of the

2 A new collaborative project was initiated in Spain in 2016 with the goal of exploring this affirmative politics of representation: *Environmental humanities: Strategies for ecological empathy and the transition towards sustainable societies*. Hopefully, we will see many more projects like this proliferating in the near future. See http://ecohumanidades.webs.upv.es/.

3 Arturo Escobar, 'Development, Critiques of', in *Degrowth: A Vocabulary for a New Era*, ed. Giacomo D'Alisa, Federico Demaria, and Giorgos Kallis (New York: Routledge, 2015), 31; Martínez-Alier, 'Environmental Justice and Economic Degrowth', 66.

Printed and bound by CPI Group (UK) Ltd, Croydon, CR0 4YY

16/04/2025

14658573-0004

growth imaginary while carrying out diverse, decentralized experiments with alternative postcapitalist models. In other words, I envision a united global critique of the cultural hegemony combined with a synergetic network of alternatives: an ecology of knowledges, beyond Northern epistemologies, bringing about diverse postgrowth imaginaries and practices.[4]

The systemic crisis of growth calls for a collective effort to overcome the dominant ideology of disconnection through the creation of decolonizing practices, postgrowth narratives, and aesthetics of interdependence. To change the dominant imaginary is not an easy task. It requires us to imagine and create assertive visions of the future,[5] new vocabularies and different uses of language,[6] counter-narratives of recovery able to displace mainstream toxic discourses,[7] and 'realizable forms of politics that reject human exceptionality'.[8] It also demands patience during the cultivation of alternative models of social reproduction and the constant preparation of spaces for testing post-capitalist paradigms, as well as the creation and promotion of specific strategies and policy proposals.

As I was writing this book many things happened that provided further justification for its arguments, most of them under the radar of corporate media. When I started writing *Postgrowth Imaginaries*, 85 people owned more wealth than 50 percent of the human population; by the time I was writing this conclusion the figure had shrunk to eight people.[9] The year 2016 was the warmest on record and atmospheric carbon dioxide levels surpassed the critical 400 ppm threshold.[10] Some of the worst ecological disasters ever recorded took place: Indonesia was ravaged by forest fire, monster hurricanes devastated entire regions, and Brazil experienced a

---

4 Santos, *Another Knowledge Is Possible*. The think tank Foro Transiciones (http://forotransiciones.org/) in Spain, Unitierra in Oaxaca, and the international Great Transition Initiative (http://greattransition.org/) are among the many existing spaces already cultivating much-needed seeds for a postgrowth socioecological transition.

5 Srnicek and Williams, *Inventing the Future*, 74–75.

6 Stibbe, *Ecolinguistics*, 42.

7 LeMenager, *Living Oil*, 192–193.

8 Smith, *Against Ecological Sovereignty*, 134.

9 Oxfam International. 'Just 8 Men Own Same Wealth as Half the World Population', 16 January, 2017, https://www.oxfam.org/en/pressroom/pressreleases/2017-01-16/just-8-men-own-same-wealth-half-world.

10 James Hansen et al., 'Global Temperature in 2016', January 18, 2017, http://www.columbia.edu/˜jeh1/mailings/2017/20170118_Temperature2016.pdf; Earth System Research Laboratory, Global Monitoring Division, 'Trends in Atmospheric Carbon Dioxide', U.S. National Oceanic & Atmospheric Administration, https://www.esrl.noaa.gov/gmd/ccgg/trends/index.html.

massive ecological disaster due to the rupture of a reservoir for storing toxic mining waste, just to mention a few examples. Meanwhile, the Paris 2015 Climate Summit confirmed the global persistence and hegemony of the growth imaginary and its delusional effects on our political leaders (many of the same leaders were simultaneously promoting and discussing new transoceanic neoliberal trade agreements). The Paris Agreement tries once more to solve the climate problem without questioning the growth ideology at its roots. It actually perpetuates a managerial and techno-fix—ecomodernist—approach, and is unable to imagine a desirable world without growth. The Paris Agreement bears an underlying assumption: future global economic growth and massive international trade is taken for granted and must go on no matter what, even in a collapsing biosphere full of environmental and developmental refugees. In the meantime, global inequality rises, the subsidization of fossil fuels is between four and six times greater than that of renewable energy, and xenophobic discourses proliferate in Europe and North America.

The lack of significant media attention to vital events—or its fragmentation, decontextualization, and disconnection—is nothing new. However, corporate media (let alone 'fake news') does not only conceal the root causes of our socioecological problems, it also ignores or undermines the massive resistance to the growth imaginary and the creative alternatives that are emerging everywhere. Many hopeful things also happened while I was writing this book: 2015 was both the International Year of Soils (let me state the obvious: our well-being and survival depend much more on the health of the topsoil than on the continuous growth of the economic dynamics that erode it) and the year in which the pope of the Roman Catholic Church released an encyclical letter identifying the dominant economic system as the root of most ongoing environmental degradation and human suffering. It seems that the abstractions and fantasies of orthodox economics are soon exposed once we pay due attention to the material ('soiled') ground level of our social and ecological reality. Recently, a few prestigious global media outlets have started covering the suicidal growth inertia of capitalism. Even *Forbes*, a venue that overtly celebrates and perpetuates the growth imaginary, published an op-ed in 2016 titled 'Unless it Changes, Capitalism Will Starve Humanity by 2050'.[11] Since 2008, academic conferences and publications exploring degrowth have been rapidly increasing in number, and over the last couple of years I was pleased to see that several nonacademic books critical of the socioecological disaster-producing machine of capitalism

---

11 Drew Hansen, 'Unless it Changes, Capitalism Will Starve Humanity by 2050', *Forbes*, February 9, 2016.

and its associated techno-optimism became international bestsellers—for instance, Naomi Klein's *This Changes Everything: Capitalism vs. the Climate* (2014), Paul Mason's *Postcapitalism: A Guide to Our Future* (2015), and Andrew Keen's *The Internet Is Not the Answer* (2015).[12]

Massive protests in Brazil opposing the growth-driven construction of pharaonic and socioecologically harmful infrastructures for the 2016 Olympic Games contrast dramatically with the celebratory rhetoric of progress and modernization trumpeted during Spanish media's presentation of the 1992 Barcelona Olympic Games. Back in 1992 nobody in Southern Europe was talking about degrowth, while now the degrowth movement is gaining momentum in 'overdeveloped' countries and discussions about postdevelopment, postextractivism, and decolonial redefinitions of what living well entails are proliferating in Latin America and everywhere else. In the last few years, climate justice movements have mushroomed, indigenous environmental networks and movements are gaining visibility and popularity, food security and food sovereignty movements are rising, and a number of municipalities, both large and small, are experimenting with postcarbon and participatory urban models. In postindustrial cities, an increasing number of people are interested in permaculture, biomimicry, and agroecology, and pro-common initiatives are demonstrating that collective intelligence can collaboratively repurpose nonconvivial capitalist technologies and neoliberal spaces, transforming them into decentralized tools and communitarian places able to enhance social and ecological well-being. Locally owned, decentralized renewable energy, care, and food cooperatives are thriving. As John Holloway warns, to crack capitalism there is no right recipe, 'just millions of experiments'.[13]

People everywhere are not only resisting the growth imaginary materially and semiotically, but generating (or regenerating) postgrowth narratives and postcapitalist ways of relating to others (humans and nonhumans) in order to guarantee their social reproduction. Plural economic theories and practices—from feminist to common good economics—are gaining visibility. Nonacademic and non-Western pedagogies are claiming their space. New independent media outlets are challenging corporate media accounts (good Spanish examples include *eldiario.es* and *Saltamos*). Artists are striving to make visible the slow violence that neoliberalism manufactures and hides. Students are demanding not only a public education, but one that

12 Klein, *This Changes Everything*; Paul Mason, *Postcapitalism: A Guide to Our Future* (New York: Farrar, Straus and Giroux, 2015); Andrew Keen, *The Internet Is Not the Answer* (New York: Atlantic Monthly Press, 2015).
13 John Holloway, *Crack Capitalism* (London: Pluto Press, 2010), 256.

is transformational and decolonial as well. Medical staff and patients are turning to counterhegemonic medicine and mindfulness in order to detach their physical and mental health from growth-driven, disempowering, energy-intensive, and technocratically managed mainstream corporate medicine. Transition towns, slow cities, ecovillages, urban community gardens, and repair cafes are thriving.

Given that the ecological regime of capitalism is coming to an end because it created a global economic metabolism that could not be sustained by the ecological systems of the Earth, constant economic growth is not an option, biophysically speaking, going into the near future. A degrowing economic future should be expected, whether we want it or not. The question we face is how we can transition to a desirable society with very limited or no economic growth. If we go on with business as usual and maintain our dominant imaginary of economic growth, applying its pathological logic in a context of extreme social corrosion and increased ecological restrictions, the future prospects of humanity are not very appealing. Probably, under that scenario, the technocratic and managerial tendencies of neoliberal biopolitics will translate into some kind of extreme eco-totalitarianism in which the anthropological machine will work in an accelerated mode to produce the many less-than-humans and infra-humans to be sacrificed for the sake of the survival of a few privileged humans (this is already happening!). The other option is to unleash our collective intelligence and abilities and start a collaborative dialogue to envision and activate postgrowth imaginaries and postcapitalist practices. Through them we may be able to imagine and enact desirable societies with circular metabolisms that enhance the environment rather than depleting it. These emerging postgrowth socioecological initiatives will direct the focus on facilitating the communitarian reproduction of a life worthy of being lived, not the private accumulation of capital.

The question of what constitutes a good life will have to be discussed by all members of any community, intentionally formed or not, but two criteria must be agreed upon as preconditions for any acceptable notion of the good life, as Amaia Pérez Orozco recommends: universality and respect of singularities.[14] The first premise entails that the conditions of possibility for our own good life should not undermine the conditions of possibility for other communities to live well; in other words, a consumerist lifestyle that depletes the Earth and depends on labor exploitation is not acceptable. The second condition counters the tendency of historically distinct, but persistent and perverse, social mechanisms to transform difference into

14 Pérez Orozco, *Subversión feminista de la economía*, 23.

inferiority and inequality through structural violence and oppression. As I interpret these self-imposed preconditions for defining collectively what a good life entails, the first point focuses on the need to voluntarily limit the social metabolism within which we reproduce the conditions for our postgrowth society, in order to make it socially and ecologically just. This includes avoiding exploiting humans and nonhumans within or without the borders of that society. The second point, it seems to me, is a preventive strategy, learned by paying attention to the lessons of colonial and neocolonial history in relation to iterative mechanisms of structural oppression. To put it another way, while capitalism and colonialism go hand in hand, nothing guarantees that moving beyond capitalism and growth will automatically bring about decolonization and justice. Thus, we have to make sure that we construct not only postgrowth imaginaries, but also decolonial imaginaries.

It is important to prevent the anthropological machine from articulating its hierarchical inclusive/exclusive distinctions. A historical perspective on oppressive practices teaches us that once distinctions are made, they soon become fossilized justifications for the structural oppression and exploitation of all humans and nonhumans that fall on the wrong side of the line. The main problem is that the distinctions are eventually translated through social imaginaries into institutional normativity (constituting a dominant imaginary). They become naturalized (invisibilized) and self-reproducing in a way that makes it more and more difficult both to track their historicity and to challenge them in the political arena that those very institutions monopolize and deactivate. That is why any emancipatory project needs to remain vigilant against the temptation to turn to the kind of dichotomous reasoning—human-nonhuman, society-nature—that can easily fire up the anthropological machine. If we fail to monitor our evolving postgrowth politics in the Anthropocene, we risk provoking unintended consequences that could trigger new versions of the oppressive mechanisms we wanted to fight in the first place—ecological sovereignty, ecofascism, extreme neoliberal biopolitics, environmentality, risky geoengineering, and so on. Thus, we should envision not only decolonial postgrowth imaginaries, but also posthumanist imaginaries.

To create the conditions of possibility for a desirable postgrowth society, it is crucial that we collectively repoliticize, in Jacques Rancière's sense. This entails challenging 'the distribution of the sensible' involved in the dominant imaginary of economic growth and its symbolic order that determines and prearranges what can be visible, sayable, audible, or thinkable. The dominant imaginary has constricted our aesthetico-political possibilities, confining us in an epistemological trap where we reduce our creativity to the iterative task of arranging different ways of growing the economy. To be able to 'reconfigure the map of the sensible' we need to persistently disrupt and disturb the dominant imaginary with postgrowth stories, narratives, and practices that redefine what can be said and seen. Rancière writes that 'Politics and art, like forms of knowledge, construct "fictions", that is to say *material* rearrangements of signs and images, relationships between what is seen and what is said, between what is done and what can be done'.[15] If we accept that the 'real must be fictionalized in order to be thought',[16] we had better start constructing affirmative and desirable postgrowth stories and practices, as well as creating coherent narratives about both the nowtopias that are materializing everywhere and the postgrowth living laboratories that are already transforming the world. They are real phenomena, but they need to influence meaning-making beyond their performative spaces if they are to become culturally relevant and politically significant.

Postgrowth Imaginaries pushes to enlarge the space of what is visible, thinkable, intelligible, perceptible, sayable, and, more importantly, desirable. I hope that if we persist in the construction of postgrowth imaginaries, we may eventually be able to displace the dogmatic neoliberal sequestration of reality and its monologic motto, 'there is no alternative'. Politics, as Rancière insists, 'replaces the dogmatism of truth with the search for conditions of possibility'.[17] We desperately need to envision postgrowth imaginaries in which to invest our affects, identities, energy, and creativity. Our (good) life quite literally depends on it. Our lack of political imagination (or, more accurately, our obduracy in maintaining our attachment to the harmful growth imaginary) is undermining such conditions of possibility. My hope is that this book does its humble part in contributing to our communitarian and collaborative search for the conditions of possibility for socially desirable and ecologically viable postgrowth societies to emerge.

15 Rancière, *The Politics of Aesthetics*, 39.
16 Rancière, *The Politics of Aesthetics*, 38.
17 Rancière, *The Politics of Aesthetics*, 50.

Selected Bibliography

Agamben, Giorgio. *Homo Sacer: Sovereign Power and Bare Life*. Translated by Daniel Heller-Roazen. Stanford, CA: Stanford University Press, 1998.

Agyeman, Julian. *Introducing Just Sustainabilities: Policy, Planning, and Practice*. London: Zed Books, 2013.

Alaimo, Stacy. *Bodily Natures: Science, Environment, and the Material Self*. Bloomington: Indiana University Press, 2010.

Alexander, Samuel. 'A Critique to Techno-Optimism: Efficiency without Sufficiency Is Lost'. Postcarbon Pathways Working Paper Series, Melbourne Sustainable Society Institute, Melbourne, 2014.

Badmington, Neil. 'Cultural Studies and the Posthumanities', in *New Cultural Studies: Adventures in Theory*, edited by Gary Hall and Clare Birchall. Edinburgh: Edinburgh University Press, 2016, 260–273.

Bauman, Zygmunt. *Wasted Lives: Modernity and its Outcasts*. Cambridge: Polity Press, 2004.

Beilin, Katarzyna. *In Search of an Alternative Biopolitics: Anti-Bullfighting, Animality, and the Environment in Contemporary Spain*. Columbus: Ohio State University Press, 2015.

Beilin, Katarzyna, and William Viestenz, eds. *Ethics of Life: Contemporary Iberian Debates*. Nashville, TN: Vanderbilt University Press, 2016.

Bennett, Jane. *Vibrant Matter: A Political Ecology of Things*. Durham, NC: Duke University Press, 2010.

Berlant, Lauren. *Cruel Optimism*. Durham, NC: Duke University Press, 2011.

Brenner, Neil. *Critique of Urbanization: Selected Essays*. Basel: Birkhäuser, 2017.

Brown, Wendy. *Undoing the Demos: Neoliberalism's Stealth Revolution*. New York: Zone Books, 2015.

Carpintero, Óscar. *El metabolismo de la economía española. Recursos naturales y huella ecológica (1955–2000)*. Lanzarote: Fundación César Manrique, 2005.

Castells, Manuel, João Caraça, and Gustavo Cardoso, eds. *Aftermath: The Cultures of the Economic Crisis*. Oxford: Oxford University Press, 2012.

Castoriadis, Cornelius. *The Imaginary Institution of Society*. Translated by Kathleen Blamey. Cambridge, MA: MIT Press, 1998.

Chakrabarty, Dipesh. 'The Climate of History: Four Theses'. *Critical Inquiry* 35 (2009): 197–222.

Cohen, Jeffrey Jerome, ed. *Prismatic Ecology: Ecotheory beyond Green*. Minneapolis: University of Minnesota Press, 2013.

Connolly, William E. *The Fragility of Things: Self-Organizing Processes, Neoliberal Fantasies, and Democratic Activism*. Durham, NC: Duke University Press, 2013.

D'Alisa, Giacomo, Federico Demaria, and Giorgos Kallis, eds. *Degrowth: A Vocabulary for a New Era*. New York: Routledge, 2015.

Del Río, Juan. *Guía del movimiento de transición. Cómo transformar tu vida en la ciudad*. Madrid: Catarata, 2015.

Fernández Durán, Ramón. *El Antropoceno. La expansión del capitalismo global choca con la biosfera*. Barcelona: Virus editorial, 2011.

Foster, John Bellamy, Brett Clark, and Richard York. *The Ecological Rift: Capitalism's War on the Earth*. New York: Monthly Review Press, 2010.

Ghosh, Amitav. *The Great Derangement: Climate Change and the Unthinkable*. Chicago, IL: University of Chicago Press, 2016.

Girardet, Herbert. *Creating Regenerative Cities*. New York: Routledge, 2015.

Guha, Ramachandra, and Joan Martínez-Alier. *Varieties of Environmentalism: Essays North and South*. London: Earthscan, 1997.

Harvey, David. *Rebel Cities: From the Right to the City to the Urban Revolution*. London: Verso, 2012.

Illich, Ivan. *Tools of Conviviality*. Glasgow: Collins, 1975.

Jackson, Tim. *Prosperity without Growth: Economics for a Finite Planet*. New York: Routledge, 2010.

Kallis, Giorgos. *In Defense of Degrowth: Opinions and Minifestos*. Edited by Aaron Vansintjan. Brussels: Uneven Earth Press, 2017.

Labrador Méndez, Germán. *Culpables por la literatura. Imaginación política y contracultura en la transición española (1968–1986)*. Madrid: Akal, 2017.

LeMenager, Stephanie. *Living Oil: Petroleum Culture in the American Century*. Oxford: Oxford University Press, 2014.

Martínez, Guillem. 'El concepto CT', in *CT o la Cultura de la Transición. Crítica a 35 años de cultura española*. Edited by Guillem Martínez. Barcelona: Mondadori, 2012, 13–23.

Marzec, Robert P. *Militarizing the Environment: Climate Change and the Security State*. Minneapolis: University of Minnesota Press, 2015.

Moore, Jason W., ed. *Anthropocene or Capitalocene? Nature, History, and the Crisis of Capitalism*. Oakland, CA: PM Press, 2016.

Moreno-Caballud, Luis. *Cultures of Anyone: Studies on Cultural Democratization in the Spanish Neoliberal Crisis*. Translated by Linda Grabner. Liverpool: Liverpool University Press, 2015.

Nixon, Rob. *Slow Violence and the Environmentalism of the Poor*. Cambridge, MA: Harvard University Press, 2011.

Pérez Orozco, Amaia. *Subversión feminista de la economía. Aportes para un debate sobre el conflicto capital-vida*. Madrid: Traficantes de sueños, 2014.

Plumwood, Val. *Environmental Culture: The Ecological Crisis of Reason*. New York: Routledge, 2002.

Rancière, Jacques. *The Politics of Aesthetics: The Distribution of the Sensible*. Translated with an introduction by Gabriel Rockhill. London: Continuum, 2012.

Resina, Joan Ramon. *Iberian Cities*. New York: Routledge, 2001.

Rockström, Johan, et al. 'Planetary Boundaries: Exploring the Safe Operating Space for Humanity'. *Ecology and Society* 14, no. 2 (2009): 1–33.

Rose, Deborah Bird, et al. 'Thinking through the Environment, Unsettling the Humanities'. *Environmental Humanities* 1 (2012): 1–5.

Santos, Boaventura de Sousa, ed. *Another Knowledge Is Possible: Beyond Northern Epistemologies.* London: Verso, 2008.

Scranton, Roy. *Learning to Die in the Anthropocene: Reflections on the End of a Civilization.* San Francisco, CA: City Lights, 2015.

Smith, Mick. *Against Ecological Sovereignty: Ethics, Biopolitics, and Saving the Natural World.* Minneapolis: University of Minnesota Press, 2011.

Srnicek, Nick, and Alex Williams. *Inventing the Future: Postcapitalism and a World without Work.* London: Verso, 2015.

Steffen, Will, Paul J. Crutzen, and John R. McNeill. 'The Anthropocene: Are Humans Now Overwhelming the Great Forces of Nature?' *Ambio* 36, no. 8 (2007): 614–621.

Stibbe, Arran. *Ecolinguistics: Language, Ecology, and the Stories We Live By.* New York: Routledge, 2015.

Wilkinson, Richard, and Kate Pickett. *The Spirit Level: Why Greater Equality Makes Societies Stronger.* New York: Bloomsbury Press, 2010.

Wolfe, Cary. *What is Posthumanism?* Minneapolis: University of Minnesota Press, 2010.

Index